THE HISTORY OF
ARCHITECTURE

THE HISTORY OF
ARCHITECTURE

MICHAEL STEPHENSON

WORTH
WPRESS

First published 2019 by Worth Press Ltd.,
Bath, England
worthpress@btconnect.com

British Library Cataloguing in Publication Data
A catalogue record for this book is available from the
British Library

ISBN: 978-1-84931-144-1

10 9 8 7 6 5 4 3 2 1

Publisher's Note Every effort has been made to
ensure the accuracy of the information presented in
this book. The publisher will not assume liability for
damages caused by inaccuracies in the data and makes no
warranty whatsoever expressed or implied. The publisher
welcomes comments and corrections from readers,
emailed to worthpress@btconnect.com, which will be
considered for incorporation in future editions. Every
effort has been made to trace copyright holders and seek
permission to use illustrative and other material. The
publisher wishes to apologize for any inadvertent errors
or omissions and would be glad to rectify these in future.

Consultant Editor: Edward Hollis

Editor: Nirad Grover
Design: Malini Saigal, Utsav Bhattacharya
Assistant designer: Arun Aggarwal

Contributors: Indira Zuljevic, Sanjay Prakash,
Razia Grover, SK Das, Mohan Rao, Professor Sidney
Robinson (biographical profile of Frank Lloyd Wright);
Professor Stuart Cohen (biographical profile of Le
Corbusier and Those That Got Away: Visionary & Unbuilt
Architecture); Professor Louis I Rocah (biographical
profile of Mies van der Rohe).

Editorial & Picture Research: Ruth Kogan, Jennifer Gray
(Columbia University, New York); Laura Stephenson, Anne
de Verteuil, Allen C Klein, Ali Bothwell, Beena Kamlani,
Dr Indira Singh, Liz Allen & Chris Butler (Automobile
Association Library, UK); Robert Medina (Chicago
Historical Society); Michelle Clark (Polshek Partnership);
Tim Ciconne www.orientalarchitecture.com
Ipshita Bhattacharya, Manju Khanna.

Packaged by BookBuilder, India.

Printed and Bound in China.

Features section:
Features, independent of the timeline chronology
on the right, provide a host of interesting insights on
the many aspects of architecture through history.

Timeline section:
Entries on significant buildings of the world,
from prehistory to the present day, flow down
in a chronological order.

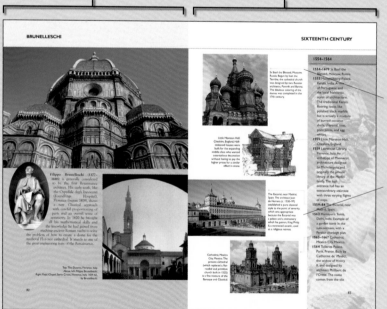

Images are
linked to
their entries
by leader
lines.

Descriptive
captions for
images.

CONTENTS

Introduction, 6

TIMELINE OF ARCHITECTURE, 11

Glossary of Architectural Terms, 234

Those That Got Away: Visionary & Unbuilt Architecture, 264

From Pyramids to Modern Architecture: A Snap-shot History of Architecture, 266

Index, 268

Opera House, Sydney, Australia.

A BUILDING IS NOT ONLY A STRUCTURE, IT IS SPIRIT MADE MANIFEST

History of Architecture is not meant to be a comprehensive history of human building; the limitations of space prohibit that. But it does set out to show representative types of building from different parts of the world at any given time in history. Many of the buildings included here are world famous while others are humbler, vernacular structures that serve to put the grander edifices in context. They also serve to underline the continuity of building traditions. For example, the Idlib mud huts of Iraq or the Mongolian yurt are still being constructed today pretty much as they were thousands of years ago.

By taking the comparative world view it is fascinating to put western European architecture in context. For example, the Temple of the Magician at Uxmal on the Yucatan peninsula of Mexico was constructed at about the same time as the great Byzantine church of Santa Sophia in Istanbul; the Iroqois longhouse of the Woodland Indians of eastern North America sits next in time to the Duomo in Florence; Machu Picchu in Peru stands alongside some of the great Loire châteaux like Chambord and Chenonceaux.

The objective of *History of Architecture* is to make us aware of the history of architecture throughout the world, and in so doing break the mold of many introductions to the history of architecture that are Euro-centric and focus only on 'great' buildings.

Solomon R Guggenheim Museum by Frank Lloyd Wright, 1959, New York, USA.

DATING

Sometimes we can discern from the records when a building was constructed but in many cases there is inadequate or confusing evidence. A building may be planned but not immediately executed. Or it may be planned but take centuries to complete, with many changes of personnel. The medieval cathedrals of western Europe are a good example. Let us look at the progression of just one of the greatest, Durham Cathedral, England:

1093–99	Choir
1099–1128	Nave
1128–33	Nave vault
1133–40	Chapter house
c. 1170	Galilee
c. 1220	West towers (upper stages)
1242–80	Chapel of Nine Altars
c. 1341	West window
1366–71	Kitchen
1375–80	Reredos (Neville screen)
1390–1418	Cloisters
1465–75	Central tower (lower stage)
c. 1483–90	Central tower (upper stage)

On the other hand, the great church of Hagia Sophia, Constantinople (modern Istanbul), was built for the emperor Justinian in an amazingly fast time between 532 and 537 CE.

In some cultures, notably Japan and China, ancient buildings were reconstructed on the same pattern over and over again down through the centuries. The culture was less interested in innovation than it was in continuity, and the building materials themselves, mainly wood, allowed for this kind of renovation.

Style is not always as clear a guide as one might imagine. The neat academic delineations between, say, Carolingian, Romanesque, and Gothic, turn out to be shifting boundaries. Different regions not only adopted styles at varying times but they also adapted them to their own needs and taste.

The dates we give here are either starting or completion (when noted) dates, and, where possible, the span of time from start to finish.

Above: Durham Cathedral, England.
Left: Hagia Sophia, Istanbul, Turkey, sixth century.

THE ARCHITECT

To construct is to collaborate. The complexity of buildings has to involve teams of specialists. Although we know the name of the architect of one of the earliest structures recorded here—the Step Pyramid of Zoser at Saqqara in Egypt, built by the pharaoh Zoser's chief minister and architect, Imhotep, in about 2778 BCE—many architects of Antiquity and the Middle Ages are, if not anonymous, known by different titles than we would recognize today. We know the names of medieval patrons like Abbot Suger of St Denis in France, for example, and we may know the names of many of the stonemasons and craftsmen of the great medieval European cathedrals but the 'architect', the central guiding hand, was most probably a master mason, like Villard de Honnecourt, whose 13th-century sketchbooks (now in the Bibliothèque Nationale, Paris) cover the wide range of subjects a medieval 'architect' was meant to master: mechanics, geometry, trigonometry, architectural design, plans, elevations, sections, designs for ornaments, figures, and furniture. He was head of all the workmen, priced the materials, and was responsible for the administrative duties of the Clerk of the Works, but his principal duties were to provide plans and elevations, which were often drawn on parchment documents which, because they were precious commodities, would be cleaned and reused for subsequent buildings—hence the great scarcity of medieval plans. In recognition of his skill he was paid three or four times as much as a skilled craftsman, and often even had his likeness carved on his buildings.

It was not until the Renaissance that the architect began to take on the modern sense of 'author' of a building. But even then, many 'architects' looked on their building work as an extension or addition to other accomplishments. Like Imhotep (who was a courtier, priest, and man of medicine), many architects prided themselves on their multi-faceted achievements. Raphael and Pietro da Cortona saw themselves primarily as painters; Michelangelo and Bernini as sculptors; Bramante a poet and sculptor; Wren and Guarini as mathematicians; Vanbrugh as a soldier and playwright.

Often great buildings had many architects involved over time. Take St Peter's in Rome as an example. In 1503 Pope Julius II decided to replace the ancient basilica of St Peter's and commissioned Bramante to design a new building. The Pope laid the first stone in 1506 but Bramante died in 1514. Between 1514 and 1547 (when Michelangelo took over and worked on it until his death in 1564) several other architects were involved: Peruzzi, Giuliano da Sangallo, Raphael, and Antonio da Sangallo. The dome was completed in 1587–90 by Giacomo della Porta and Domenico Fontana.

Above: Giovanni Lorenzo Bernini, 1598–1680.
Left: A medieval master mason, with square and rule, oversees his craftsmen.

FIRST SETTLEMENTS

Our prehistoric forebears were nomadic hunter-gatherers living in caves or temporary shelters made of hide-covered branches or transportable tent-like dwellings, perhaps similar to the yurt. The transition to organized agriculture took place in different regions across the world between *c.* 12000 and *c.* 500 BCE, and small farms and agricultural communities were established. No longer itinerant, the people now had a need for permanent buildings to live in, to store food, and to protect themselves from raiders.

Their main building material was sun-dried bricks made of mud or clay and the houses they built were square or rectangular, with either a flat or pitched wooden-beam roof covered with straw and sealed with clay. Mud bricks do not last long, and as houses were degraded by weather they were simply leveled and new ones built on the site, reusing as much of the original material as was salvageable.

Chirokitia Neolithic settlement, Cyprus, *c.* 6000 BCE.

The world's first monumental structures were built by the Sumerians of Mesopotamia around 3500 BCE. They were temples, usually perched on the top of ziggurats—stepped mounds built of dried mud brick reinforced with reeds and bitumen. It is fascinating to see from the earliest beginnings of monumental building an almost universal spiritual need to reach up to the heavens. The specific gods may change through history but the ambition remains constant.

Brick structures at the planned settlement of Harappa, Indus Valley Civilization, *c.* 2500 BCE.

Mesolithic hut, Europe. A tent design made of wood, turf, and branches.

Idlib house, Iraq. Mud-covered (adobe) houses like these may have been the first permanent settlements of agrarian communities.

Marsh Arab (*Ma'dan*) reed-constructed *mudhif* or guest house, Iraq.

The Step Pyramid of Zoser, Saqqara, Egypt. The first building with a named architect: Imhotep.

10,000–3000 BCE Mesolithic hut, Europe.

***c.* 6000 BCE** Neolithic village, Chirokitia, Cyprus. Circular, domed houses built of brick or mud blocks.

***c.* 6000 BCE** Painted building, Zaghe Tepe, Qazvin plain, Iran. This Neolithic building with highly ornamented walls was probably used as a tribal religious place or gathering center.

6000 BCE–present Idlib house, Iraq.

***c.* 5000 BCE** Lepenski Vir, Serbia. A Mesolithic site, it has houses laid out on the basis of a circle segment of exactly 60 degrees, constructed in the manner of an equilateral triangle.

***c.* 3000 BCE** Tholos, Arpachiyah, Iraq. A beehive-shaped house entered through an outer rectangular section.

3000 BCE–present Reed-constructed guest house, Iraq.

2778 BCE The Step Pyramid of Zoser, Saqqara, Egypt.

***c.* 2600 BCE** Mohenjodaro, Sind, present Pakistan. A large city-settlement of the Indus Valley Civilization, with a planned grid of streets, and buildings of sun-dried bricks of baked mud and burned wood.

PYRAMIDS AND TEMPLES

The founding of the First Dynasty in 3100 BCE marks the beginning of Egyptian civilization as we usually conceive it. In the Third Dynasty, about 2770 BCE, Pharaoh Zoser commissioned his first minister and chief engineer, Imhotep, to build a magnificent funerary step-pyramid at Saqqara. Imhotep is generally recognized as the first named architect in history, as well as being the first to build with cut stone.

Prior to this architectural watershed, royal tombs had been fairly modest affairs—low flat-topped brick boxes called *mastaba*. Imhotep superimposed one *mastaba*-type box on the other until he had six levels reaching up to 200 ft (61 m).

The Fourth Dynasty (2615–2494 BCE) was the great age of pyramid building. The three most significant pyramids are clustered on the Nile on the outskirts of what is now Cairo. The largest was built for Pharaoh Khufu (Cheops in Greek) by the architect / engineer Hemon. The base is 571,000 sq ft (63,000 sq m) rising to 500 ft (166 m) and constructed of 2.5 million blocks of dressed stone, each weighing 2.5 tons / tonnes. For nearly 5,000 years it was the tallest building in the world.

By 2000 BCE the political center of Egypt had moved up the Nile to Thebes, where vast temples were built. The most famous, the Temple of Amun at Karnak (completed *c.* 1300 BCE), has a hypostyle hall, a large room with a flat roof supported by multiple rows of columns.

Pyramid and Sphinx, Giza, Egypt, *c.* 2500 BCE.
Overleaf: The temple of Amon, Karnak, Egypt, *c.* 100 BCE.

The Great Pyramid of Cheops, Giza, Egypt. Originally covering 13 acres (5.26 ha), the Great Pyramid (center) was twice the size of St Peter's, Rome.

Newgrange burial mound, Ireland. Great care was taken by the builders to ensure a dry resting place for the dead—unlike the flimsy domestic buildings the living had to inhabit at the time.

The Great Ziggurat of Ur, Iraq. Temple to the moon-god Nanna, built of mud bricks.

Stonehenge, Wiltshire, England. Begun as early as 3000 BCE, the 80 Pembroke blue stone pillars in two concentric circles are early third millennium.

2575–2000 BCE

2575 BCE The Great Pyramid of Cheops, Giza, Egypt.

c. 2500 BCE Hypogeum of Hal-Saflieni, Paola, Malta. Originally a sanctuary, it became a necropolis, the only prehistoric underground temple in the world.

c. 2500 BCE Newgrange burial mound, Ireland.

c. 2450 BCE Acropolis Palace of Tel Beydar, Nabada, Syria. The presence of an acropolis is unusual for cities of this period. The palace was built in different phases; the earliest sections show walls of pale mud bricks.

2125 BCE The Great Ziggurat of Ur, Iraq.

2100 BCE Stonehenge, Wiltshire, England.

c. 2000 BCE–present Trullo, Alberolbella, Apulia, Itrea Valley, Italy. A prehistoric building technique still in use with whitewashed limestone in a dry-wall (mortarless) construction consisting of a cylinder or quadrangle capped by a conical roof, with an ornamental pinnacle formed by three overlaid rocks.

c. 2000 BCE Temple at Tarxien, Malta. Built of stone masonry in Neolithic style, it has the earliest known example of corbeled ceiling structures.

The Palace of Minos, Knossos, Crete. A construction of stone blocks, rubble filling, and mud bricks. Wood columns taper towards the base—the opposite of later Greek buildings.

Abu Simbel, Aswan, Egypt. The Abu Simbel temple, built during the reign of Pharaoh Ramesses II, was moved to its present site in the 1960s to avoid inundation by the Aswan High Dam.

Temple of Amun, Karnak, Egypt. A temple complex which, together with Luxor, is all that remains of Thebes, the capital of Ancient Egypt.

Jomon pit-post hut, Japan.

1600–800 BCE

c. 1600 BCE The Palace of Minos, Knossos, Crete.

c. 1400 BCE Choga Zambil Ziggurat, Susa, Egypt. A five-tiered temple with a labyrinth of internal chambers and stairways.

c. 1325 BCE Treasury of Atreus, Mycenae, Greece. A Tholos tomb with a beehive-shaped stone dome and a pyramidal door. The void triangle above the door lintel is characteristic of Mycenaean architecture.

c. 1304 Abu Simbel, Aswan, Egypt.

c. 1200 BCE Pillared house, Tel-el-Farah, ancient Tirzah, Israel. An example of domestic architecture in the Iron Age, this is a four-room house with a pillared courtyard and thick walls.

1153 BCE Mortuary Temple of Ramesses III, Medinet Habu, Egypt. The fortress-like temple complex was enclosed by a 35-ft (10.7-m) thick and 60-ft (21.4-m) high mud brick wall with a *migdol*, or a fortified gate house.

c. 1100 BCE Temple of Amun, Karnak, Egypt.

c. 1000 BCE Jomon pit-post hut, Japan.

c. 800 BCE An Dún Beag, or Dunbeag Promontory Fort, Ireland. Begun in the Bronze Age, the fort has four outer defensive banks, and an inner drystone rampart. Inside

THE MINOAN CITADEL

The Palace of Knossos, Crete, c. 1600 BCE.

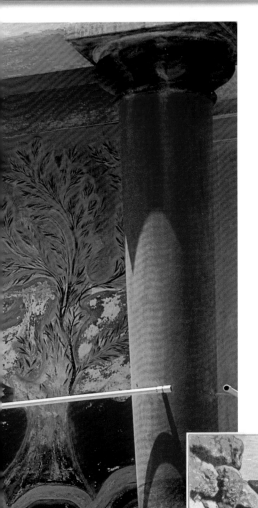

The second millennium BCE saw monumental building on the island of Crete, most spectacularly, the 'Palace of King Minos' at Knossos, which was destroyed about 1400 BCE and never rebuilt (what we see now is a rather crude reconstruction).

Minoan civilization spread to the Greek mainland and a new culture grew there centered on Mycenae on the Peloponnese. The citadel of Mycenae (close to the present-day port of Nauplia) was rebuilt about 1350 BCE, and the lion carving on the main gateway is the most ancient carved sculpture in Europe. About 1100 BCE the Mycenaen settlements were destroyed by invaders from the north but their legacy was inherited by the Hellenic Greeks several centuries later.

The Lion Gate, citadel of Mycenae, Greece, c. 1350 BCE.

THE CLASSICAL ORDERS

Greek architecture belongs to three main eras: the Archaic (c. 700–480 BCE); Early Classical (c. 480–200 BCE), and Later Hellenic (c. 200–146 BCE when Greece was absorbed by the Roman Empire).

The most important form was the temple, which was built to house an effigy of the deity rather than being a house of congregation as in the Christian, Jewish, and Islamic traditions. In this it performed a similar function to the temples of India and the Oriental East, where worshippers walked around the temple rather than gathered in it to worship.

All temples were raised on a platform (stylobate) with an entrance door placed in

The Parthenon, Athens, Greece, fifth century BCE.

the center of a wall behind a colonnaded porch (portico). Inside there was little natural light, and what there was was directed on to the statue of the deity. For example, the Parthenon of Athens (c. 447–432 BCE) housed a 40 ft (13 m) statue of the goddess Athena made of gold and ivory. The whole effect was designed to create a theatrical, dramatic atmosphere, a characteristically Greek interweaving of theater and religion.

The system of Orders that the Ancient Greeks devised had a profound effect on European architecture right up to our own time. Each Order (Doric, Ionic, Corinthian) consisted of a column with a base (optional) and a capital that supported a horizontal slab called the entablature. Each Order had its own specific relative proportions between the parts, which remained fixed no matter what the scale. The Greeks rarely used more than one Order on any single building. Simplicity and restraint were guiding principles. The Greek Doric Order, the most important of the Orders for the Hellenic Greeks, has something of Egyptian monumentality about it.

The Greeks were a maritime civilization and much influenced by their contacts with Egypt, Assyria, and Persia. Color was important to them and we tend to forget how richly painted were both their interiors and exteriors because most of it has been lost.

It is also difficult to get a sense of the living buildings from the ruins left to us, none of which is intact. The sculpture has been shipped to museums, the roofs are gone, the wood and metal elements destroyed by time. The Greeks (like the Japanese and Chinese) were not particularly interested in innovation for its own sake. Their concern was to work intensively on established forms, perfecting proportion and line to create an overwhelming harmony.

Left: Temple of Zeus, Olympia (reconstruction), Greece, c. 460 BCE.
Overleaf: Caryatids of the Erechteum at the Acropolis, Athens, Greece, c. 500 BCE.

Etruscan tumulus, Cerveteri, Italy. A burial chamber, which originally formed part of a large necropolis serving the Etruscan city of Caere.

The Ishtar Gate, Babylon (now in the National Museum, Berlin). Glazed brickwork decorated with heraldic beasts, the Ishtar Gate stood at the head of King Nebuchadnezzar's Processional Way.

The Parthenon, Athens, Greece. A temple dedicated to the goddess Athena, the Parthenon is the most beautiful example of the Doric Order, the simplest of the three Orders: Doric, Ionic, Corinthian.

The theater of the Sanctuary of Asklepios, Epidaurus, Greece. Theater designed by Polykleitos the Younger.

600–246 BCE

is a circular beehive hut with a square interior, known as a *clochan*.

c. 600 BCE Etruscan tumuli, Cerveteri, Italy.

c. 550 BCE The Ishtar Gate, Babylon (now in the National Museum, Berlin).

c. 485 BCE Treasury of the Athenians, Delphi, Greece. The first Doric building entirely in marble, it resembles a miniature temple with only two columns and a short central body (cella).

c. 447–38 BCE Parthenon, Athens, Greece.

c. 350 BCE The theater of the Sanctuary of Asklepios, Epidaurus, Greece.

c. 249 BCE (rebuilt c. 500) Dhamek Stupa, Sarnath, India. The oldest known stupa (Buddhist burial mound) is an elaborately carved solid cylinder of bricks and stone. The inscriptions are in the Brahmi script.

c. 246–210 BCE Mausoleum of Qin Shi Huang Di, Shensi, China. The four-sq mile (10-sq km) complex carved out of a low mountain top is laid out like an underground city. It contains Qin Shi Huangdi's pyramidal tomb (which remains unexcavated) and at a distance, the famous terracotta army—8,000

IMPERIAL STYLE: THE ARCH AND THE VAULT

The tribal settlement that was established on the Palatine Hill in Rome on the banks of the Tiber river in 753 BCE is traditionally accepted as the beginning of Roman civilization (as distinct from the earlier Etruscans). It remained a tribal organization until about 500 BCE, when Rome became a republic and began to absorb the surrounding tribes, eventually extending its empire from Britain and France in the north; Spain in the west; Sicily, Carthage (modern Tunisia), Egypt, and the eastern Mediterranean to the south; Greece and the Balkans to the east.

Architecturally, the golden age of Rome begins with the reign of Augustus (27 BCE–14 CE), who boasted that when he came to power Rome was a city of brick but that he left it a city of marble. And it is true that before his reign little marble was used in Rome. From the first century CE the quarries of Carrara were developed and marble was imported from Hymettus and Pentelicus (which had supplied the marble for the Parthenon) in Greece.

Ancient Rome was a restless entrepreneurial-imperial society. It loved engineering because it made things in the empire work and thus made conquests profitable, and it loved grandeur as the outward manifestation of its achievement. Rome's attitude to Greece was always ambiguous. On the one hand, the Romans despised the Greeks (because they were militarily and economically weak compared to Rome), but on the other, were also in awe of their civilization. If the Romans had might the Greeks had style. Roman architects used the Greek Orders but added to them and would often use more than one on a building: something the Greeks would have dismissed as vulgar excess. Where Greek buildings rarely exceeded two stories built on a simple post and lintel system, the Romans built up to four or five, using arches and vaults.

The Greeks used marble almost exclusively, but the Romans had access to a wide choice of materials: brick, marble, stone, tufa (a volcanic stone), and, most importantly, concrete, which

Pantheon interior and plan, Rome, Italy, c. 118–128 CE.

The Great Wall of China, 2,484 miles (825 km) of fortification. The present Wall belongs mainly to the Ming Dynasty (14th–16th centuries CE).

life-sized men and horses molded of three-inch thick clay.

c. 237–57 BCE Horus Temple, Edfu, Egypt. This Graeco-Roman temple has two pylons, in front of which is a large courtyard. The halls inside contain towering columns and the entrance pylon is covered with relief carvings.

c. 221 BCE The Great Wall of China.

c. 200 BCE House of the Vetii, Pompei, Italy.

c. 200 BCE Celtic stone and thatch hut, Galicia, Spain.

c. 200 BCE Karla Caves, Karli, Maharashtra, India. A complex of cave shrines built by Buddhist monks, it is among the earliest examples of Indian rock-cut architecture. These caves have arched entrances and vaulted interiors with intricately carved reliefs.

c. 200 BCE–present Yurt, Mongolia.

c. 200 BCE The Great Stupa, Sanchi, Madhya Pradesh, India.

c. 150 BCE Stoa of Attalus, Athens, Greece. A large double-storied building with limestone walls and a tiled roof. The ground floor is in the Doric style and the first floor in Ionic. The façade in Pentelic marble.

House of the Vetii, Pompei, Italy. An elegant Doric colonnade surrounds the garden of a wealthy Pompeian family.

Celtic stone and thatch hut, Galicia, Spain.

Yurt, Mongolia. A tent-like structure made of willow poles covered in oiled felt. Today almost two-thirds of the population of Mongolia still live in yurts which are now factory-made.

The Great Stupa, Sanchi, Madhya Pradesh, India. Originally a small unimposing burial mound (stupa), the Great Stupa grew in size as Indian Buddhism became wealthier.

Colosseum, Rome, Italy, c. 70 CE.

was crucially important in two of the greatest contributions Rome was to make to the history of architecture: the arch and the vault. During the years of the Republic (c. 500-44 BCE) the Romans adopted the Greek timber-and-tiled roof, but during the Imperial era (27 BCE-337 CE), when they needed great public buildings, like baths and basilicas, the roofs were often vaulted with brick and concrete, which lent a rigidity that made possible such stupendous expanses like the great dome of the Pantheon in Rome (118-129 CE).

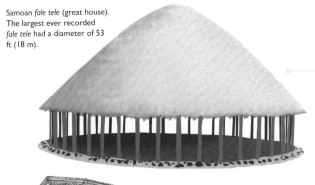

Samoan *fale tele* (great house). The largest ever recorded *fale tele* had a diameter of 53 ft (18 m).

Maison Carrée, Nîmes, France. One of the best preserved Roman temples, it was probably built by craftsmen sent to Nemausus (ancient Nîmes) from Rome.

Pont du Gard, Nîmes, France. Roman aqueduct built by Agrippa, it was originally 15 miles (24 km) long. The water channel on the top level is 180 ft (55 m) above the river.

The Colosseum, Rome, Italy. Designed to seat 50,000 people, the vast elliptical amphitheater measures 615 × 510 ft (188 × 156 m).

100 BCE–100 CE

c. 150 BCE Tiwanaku, present Bolivia. This site, laid out on a grid pattern to the south of Lake Titicaca, has civic and ceremonial structures, and elite residences (surrounded by a moat) in the center. The site contains many stone sculptures.

c. 100 BCE–present Samoan *fale tele* (great house).

c. 31 BCE Temple of Portunus, Rome, Italy. Eight steps lead to this circular structure with 20 Corinthian capitals.

c. 1 CE Maison Carrée, Nîmes, France.

c. 14 CE Pont du Gard, Nîmes, France.

65–68 CE Domus Aurea (Golden House), Rome, Italy. A large landscaped portico villa covered in gold-leaf.

70 CE The Colosseum, Rome, Italy.

80 CE Arch of Titus, Rome, Italy. A Pentelic marble triumphal arch with a single arched opening commemorating the capture of Jerusalem in 70 CE.

c. 100 CE The Pyramid of the Sun, Teotihuacán, present Mexico. The third largest pyramid in the world, it measures 738 ft (225 m) across and 246 ft (75 m) in height. A man-made tunnel leads to a cave,

THE EASTERN EMPIRE

The Roman emperor Constantine moved his capital to Constantinople (ancient Byzantium, modern Istanbul) in 330 CE and established the Christian Roman Empire of the East. Christianity was now the official religion of the Empire so it is not surprising that churches, the most durably built and important structures in Byzantine society, are mainly what survive today.

The Byzantine Empire was strongly affected by three factors: Christianity, Hellenism (from the predominantly Greek population of Constantinople who provided most of the craftsmen), and the stylistic influence of the countries to the immediate east.

One of its most distinctive characteristics was the dome. The Romans used domes, but were unable to develop their spatial possibilities because they did know how to counteract the massive thrust of such structures without building them on top of thick circular walls, as they did in the Pantheon. Byzantine builders broke out of these structural limitations by developing domes set on square spaces. At first they used brackets (squinches) to create an octagonal base, but later refined this with pendentives. This meant that huge domes could be built on buildings filled with light, the most famous being Santa Sophia in Constantinople (532–37 CE) built by Constantine's successor, Justinian (527–65 CE), who had reunited the Eastern and Western Roman Empires and embarked on a breathtaking program of building: whole cities, aqueducts, fortifications, bridges, theaters, as well as many churches.

In addition to the great building projects of the fifth and sixth centuries, Byzantine architecture had a second flowering in the 11th century, and one of the greatest buildings of that second period is undoubtedly St Mark's, Venice, a European city that had for centuries depended on trade with the east.

The influence of Byzantine architecture was widespread, particularly in Russia. The first great Byzantine church there was Santa Sophia, Kiev, in 1037, and the style flourished for many centuries. St Basil the Blessed in the Kremlin, Moscow, with its famous 'onion' domes is 16th / 17th century. Even as late as 1904, the Alexander Nevsky Cathedral, Sophia, Bulgaria, was built in full-blown Byzantine style.

Above: Interior of Hagia Sophia, 532–37 CE.
Left: Façade of St Mark's, Venice, Italy, c. 1040.
Overleaf: The Alexander Nevsky Cathedral, Sophia, Bulgaria, built in 1904 in full-blown Byzantine style.

The Pantheon, Rome, Italy. The most important temple of its day, the dome (142 ft [43.2 m]) in diameter) was the largest until Brunelleschi's dome for Florence Cathedral (1420–36).

Hadrian's Villa, Tivoli, Italy. The emperor Hadrian filled his palatial country retreat with a vast collection of statuary and artworks from Ancient Egypt and Classical Greece.

The Treasury, Petra, Jordan. Petra (from the Greek word for 'rock') was the capital of the Nabateans who controlled the caravan routes between Arabia and the Mediterranean.

Ruma gorga, Sumatera, Indonesia. Decorated house of the Toba Batak people of Lake Toba.

100–212 CE

perhaps a royal tomb, beneath the center of the structure.

c. 100 CE Arena, Pula, Croatia. The sixth largest surviving Roman amphitheater, with perfectly preserved four side towers.

c. 118–28 CE The Pantheon, Rome, Italy.

118–33 CE Hadrian's Villa, Tivoli, Italy.

120–35 CE Celsus Library, Ephesus, present Turkey. It had a two-tiered façade and the interior consisted of a single large hall, measuring 32 × 52 ft (10 × 16 m). The burial chamber under the floor contains the marble sarcophagus of Celsus.

c. 120 CE The Treasury, Petra, Jordan.

131 CE Hadrian's Arch, Athens, Greece. Pentelic marble triumphal arch with an Ionic architrave with an inscription at both ends, and an entablature with a triangular pediment in the middle.

c. 200 CE–present Ruma Gorga, Sumatra, Indonesia.

212–16 CE Thermae (Baths) of Caracalla, Rome, Italy. The main building contains a vaulted central hall, a circular domed *caldarium* (hot-room) and an open *natatio* (swimming pool), with bronze mirrors mounted overhead to

Interior of Santa Maria Maggiore, Rome, Italy. An early example of a basilica-type church (rectangular rather than round or octagonal like Santa Vitale, Ravenna).

The Pagoda of the Sung Yüeh Temple, Mount Sung, Honan, China. The oldest surviving brick temple in China.

San Vitale, Ravenna, Italy. The best preserved Byzantine church in the West. It was founded by Emperor Justinian.

Hagia Sophia, Istanbul, Turkey. Built by Emperor Justinian in only six years, Santa Sophia is the greatest of all Byzantine buildings.

305–532 CE

direct sunlight into the pool area. It is surrounded by an elaborate enclosure with an open-air gymnasium.

c. 305 CE Diocletian's Palace, Split, Croatia. Extremely well-preserved, the palace is an irregular rectangle with towers projecting from the western, northern, and eastern façades. Built of white limestone and marble it combines elements of a villa and a military camp, with huge gates and watchtowers.

432–40 CE Interior of Santa Maria Maggiore, Rome, Italy.

c. 500 CE Church of Dzveli-Gavazi, Georgia. An early example of a central-domed church in the 'tetraconch' configuration (a sixth-century variation of the cruciform as a square surrounded by a clover leaf).

523 CE The Pagoda of the Sung Yüeh Temple, Mount Sung, Honan, China.

526–48 CE San Vitale, Ravenna, Italy.

527–65 CE Church of the Nativity, Bethlehem. Built by Constantine, and rebuilt by Justinian on the traditional site of Christ's birth. The existing simple building has high columns with Corinthian marble capitals.

532–37 CE Hagia Sophia, Istanbul, Turkey.

Bourges Cathedral, France, begun 1190.

THE ROMANESQUE STYLE

The paramount authority throughout medieval Europe, the Church provided not only social and political stability but also intellectual and spiritual coherence. In the 11th and 12th centuries to build in granite, marble, or stone was an awesome undertaking, but with the Church's organizational abilities, financial authority, and spiritual motivation many vast buildings were undertaken throughout Europe.

Although there are strong regional variations, the Romanesque style has some shared characteristics. It was based on simple, strong geometric forms with widespread use of the semicircular-headed arch; the basilica form of church design; sturdy piers (often cylindrical) and thick walls; and vaulting, which tended to be semicircular and often barrel-vaulted. Capitals were derived from Roman and Byzantine models, though simplified.

The prime movers of the Romanesque world were the monasteries, and in particular, the Clunaic movement based at the Benedictine Abbey of Cluny

Above left: Pilgrimage church of San Martin de Frómista, Spain, 1066.
Left: Map of the medieval pilgrimage routes to Santiago de Compostella, Spain.

Rock-cut temple, Elephanta, Maharashtra, India. Hindu temple dedicated to Shiva, the god of destruction.

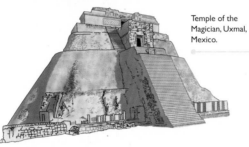

Temple of the Magician, Uxmal, Mexico.

Brixworth Church, England. A rare example of a wood-roofed Saxon church.

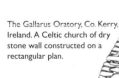

The Gallarus Oratory, Co. Kerry, Ireland. A Celtic church of dry stone wall constructed on a rectangular plan.

550–680 CE

c. 550 CE Rock-cut temple, Elephanta, Maharashtra, India.

569 CE Temple of the Magician, Uxmal, Mexico.

c. 597 CE St Martin's Church, Canterbury, England. The oldest church in England, with mixed Saxon and Roman features.

605–16 CE An-chi bridge, Chou-Hsien, Hopei, China. It has flat segmental arches, spandrel arches, and originally also had a fretted balustrade.

618 CE St Hripsime Church, Echmiadzin, Armenia. Among the oldest surviving classical churches in Armenia, with a remarkable inlaid mother-of-pearl altarpiece from 1741.

c. 650 CE Parashurameshwara Temple, Bhubaneshwar, India. An early example of temple architecture in Orissa, with the beehive-shaped tower or *deul* and pavilion or *jagamohan*.

674–82 CE Monkwearmouth, Jarrow Abbey, England. A twin-foundation stone structure. French architects and glassmakers worked on the abbey and reintroduced the art of glassmaking into England.

680 CE Brixworth Church, England.

c. 680 CE The Gallarus Oratory, Co Kerry, Ireland.

Notre-Dame La Grande, Poitiers, France,
11th and 12th centuries.

in Burgundy, France. Although the Abbey was largely destroyed in 1810, its massive scale bore witness to the belief that God was owed the finest buildings man could devise, not only in structural terms but also decoratively. Carving and wall painting were important elements in buildings designed to teach the Gospels to a largely illiterate congregation.

Religious relics attracted thousands of pilgrims from the length and breadth of Europe. The most famous destination was St James's church (begun 1077) at Santiago de Compostela in northwest Spain. Pilgrimage churches—often very sizable—are dotted all along the pilgrim routes of northern Spain, France, England, Germany, and Italy.

France is particularly rich in fine Romanesque churches. For example, St Etienne, Caen, has a magnificent exterior of grouped masses and towers; Notre-Dame La Grande, Poitiers; Autun Cathedral and St Madeleine, Vézelay, both in Burgundy; the Abbey of Fontevrault on the Loire; St Foy, Conques, as well as St Trophîme, Arles, are just a few of the more notable examples.

Romanesque architecture developed early in Germany and was at first much influenced by northern Italy due to the geo-political links between the two countries. Later, Germany developed its own Romanesque style: strongly dignified and austere. A characteristically German Romanesque feature was the church with an apse at each end: one for the abbot, the other for the bishop. Other German features were the dramatic towers, cupolas, and turrets. In the Rhineland the greatest examples are Worms, Mainz, and Speyer cathedrals. A little further north is the magnificently preserved Abbey Church of Maria Laach (begun 1093) with its six towers and four apses. Further south on the Mosel is Trier Cathedral and the Liebfrauenkirche, and in Bavaria, the Schottenkirche at Regensburg.

In Italy, Sicily has a particularly rich Romanesque legacy. During this period the island was under Norman rule, but their northern style was mixed with Saracen and Byzantine influences: the cathedral of Monreale near Palermo is a good example of these entwined styles. Perhaps the most

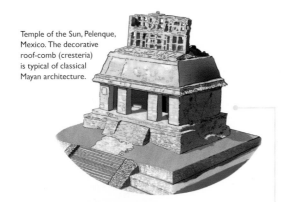

Temple of the Sun, Pelenque, Mexico. The decorative roof-comb (cresteria) is typical of classical Mayan architecture.

Dome of the Rock, Jerusalem, Israel. The gold-domed shrine is the third most sacred in Islam after the Ka'aba at Mecca and the Mosque of the Prophet, Medina.

The Shore Temple, Mamallapuram, Tamil Nadu, India. Built by Narasimhavarman II Rajasimha of finely dressed local granite and dedicated to the god Shiva.

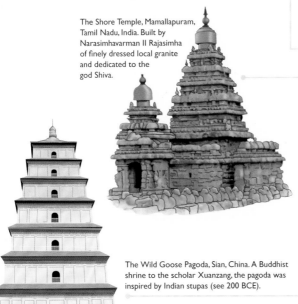

The Wild Goose Pagoda, Sian, China. A Buddhist shrine to the scholar Xuanzang, the pagoda was inspired by Indian stupas (see 200 BCE).

680–707 CE

c. 680 CE Escomb Saxon Church, Escomb, England. One of only three complete Anglo-Saxon churches, it is a tall building, tapering towards the top. Set within an oval walled enclosure, built largely of stone from a ruined Roman fort.

c. 680 CE Kondô (Golden Hall) Horyu-ji, Nara, Japan. Measuring 61 × 50 ft (18.52 × 15.20 m), which is two-thirds of its original floor area, it is the largest extant wooden structure in the world.

680–98 CE Yakushiji Temple, Nara, Japan. A symmetric, Chinese-style layout, with the main hall and lecture halls standing on a central axis, flanked by two pagodas.

c. 690 CE Temple of the Sun, Pelenque, Mexico.

690–92 CE Dome of the Rock, Jerusalem, Israel.

700–28 CE The Shore Temple, Mamallapuram, Tamil Nadu, India.

701–04 CE The Wild Goose Pagoda, Sian, China.

707 CE Great Mosque, Damascus, Syria. The oldest surviving congregational mosque, it has parts of altered Syrian and Greek temple buildings, with the corner towers converted into minarets, and a truss-beamed wooden roof.

famous Italian buildings of this period are those of the Piazza dei Miracoli in Pisa, consisting of the Baptistery, Cathedral, and, most famously, the Campanile (the 'Leaning Tower').

In Spain there are fine Romanesque churches (in addition to St James's at Santiago de Compostela): Meira Abbey Church, the Abbey Church of Santa Maria, Ripoll, and three in Segovia (San Martín, San Estéban, and San Millán). One of the most classic of the pilgrimage churches of the north is San Martín at Frómista. In the west, the most interesting examples are Zamora Cathedral, the Collegiate Church at Toro, the cathedral of Cuidad Rodrigo, and the Old Cathedral at Salamanca.

English Romanesque architecture is usually called 'Norman' after the dynasty founded in England by William I of Normandy in 1066. Norman building is found throughout the country, but undoubtedly the finest example is Durham Cathedral (begun 1093), particularly the interior, where its magnificent stone vaulting is a precursor of the Gothic. Other outstanding examples are the pilgrimage church of Southwell Minster (west front begun c. 1130), and the keep ('White Tower') of the Tower of London (1078).

'Gothic' was first used as a term of disapproval, even contempt, by the Italian Renaissance historian and architect Giorgio Vasari (1511–74). In comparison with what he saw as his own enlightened age, he looked back to medieval architecture as backward, a product of the Dark Ages of the barbaric Goths, hence the name.

The exact start-date of any new movement is difficult to pin down exactly. Gothic evolved from the Romanesque but its spirit is very different. Where the Romanesque is solid and rooted to the earth, Gothic is light and soaring, and is defined by three architectural elements: the pointed arch, the ribbed vault, and the flying buttress, all of which are to be found in pre-Gothic buildings, but when combined define the Gothic style.

The White Tower, the Tower of London, England, 1078.

Palace at Yaxchilán, Chiapas, Mexico.

Temple II, Tikal, Guatemala. Around 830 CE the population of Tikal declined and the city was abandoned in the 10th century.

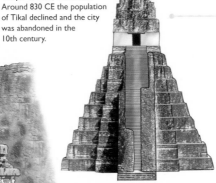

The tower of the Kailasa Temple, Ellora, India. Carved directly out of the mountainside, each story of the tower is decorated with miniature buildings to house the gods.

Façade of the Great Mosque, Cordoba, Spain. Founded by Abd ar-Rahman I, the mosque is one of the most magnificent buildings of the Islamic tradition.

720–785 CE

c. 720 CE Palace at Yaxchilán, Chiapas, Mexico.

734 CE Temple II, Tikal, Guatemala.

743–44 CE Palace of Mshatta, present Jordan. A desert winter residence from the Umayyad period, it contains an entrance hall, mosque, an audience hall, and residential quarters. Made of burnt bricks resting on a foundation of stone, unusual for the time. A large part of the ornately decorated façade is now in the Pergamon Museum in Berlin, Germany.

757–73 CE The tower of the Kailasa Temple, Ellora, India.

764 CE Lorsch Abbey, Lorsch, Germany. One of the most famous monasteries of the Carolingian empire. The Königshalle, (entrance hall) built in the ninth century by Emperor Louis III, is the oldest and among the most beautiful of Franconian Romanesque monuments.

785 CE Interior of the Great Mosque, Cordoba, Spain.

c. 800 CE Badrinath Temple, Uttarakhand, India. Around 50 ft (15 m) tall and made of stone covered with a gold gilt roof, this temple with its brightly painted façade resembles a Buddhist *vihara*.

35

France, and particularly the Ile-de-France around Paris, was the cradle of the Gothic. No other country, and no single area within a country, can boast of such extraordinary architectural treasures. One of the first Gothic buildings was the great Abbey of St Denis (started 1137), the life's work of the remarkable Abbé Suger. Born into a poor family in 1082 Suger was given as a child to the royal Abbey of St Denis, where he was educated with the king's son. In 1122 he became abbot and 15 years later was able to put into effect his long-cherished dream of rebuilding the abbey. Interestingly, Suger never made reference to the architecture of the new building or commented on what was a new style; nor did he mention the name of the master-mason. St Denis was soon followed by an astounding number of new cathedrals in the years between 1150 and 1300: Laon (1160–1225) whose west front was imitated throughout the 13th century at Chartres, Reims, Strasbourg, and Halberstadt; Notre Dame, Paris (1163–1330), with its triple west portal and magnificent flying buttresses; Bourges Cathedral (1190–1275) modeled on Notre Dame by Bishop Henry de Sully, brother of Bishop Eudes de Sully, who had built Notre Dame; Reims (begun 1211), perhaps the richest and most glorious, as would be expected from the Coronation Church of the kings of France;

Top: Notre Dame Cathedral, Paris, France, begun 1163.
Above left and left: A figure of a gargoyle, and detail of arched doorway and sculptures from Notre Dame.

The Temple of Borobudur, Java, Indonesia. One of the most massive Buddhist shrines ever built. Pilgrims must circuit it nine times to reach the summit and its depiction of nirvana.

The minaret of the Great Mosque of Kairouan, Tunisia. This type of minaret may have been based on ancient lighthouses like the one at Alexandria.

Santa Maria de Naranco, Oviedo, Spain. A unique Visigothic church with two rectangular halls, one above the other.

The Little Metropole Cathedral, Athens, Greece. Byzantine churches in Greece tended to be smaller and simpler than their counterparts in Constantinople (modern Istanbul).

The Great Mosque of Susah, Tunisia. The fortified mosque was built by the Aghlabids by remodeling an ancient kasbah that had originally been used to repel the invading Byzantines. The domed structure (technically known as a 'kiosk') dates from the 11th century.

800–879 CE

c. 800 CE The Temple of Borobudur, Java, Indonesia.

c. 800–1100 CE St Emilion, France. Carved out of a limestone cliff over a period of three centuries, this Romanesque church with catacombs is Europe's largest monolithic cathedral, measuring 125 ft (37.5 m) long, 66 ft (20 m) wide and 36 ft (11 m) high.

810 CE The Citadel, Cairo, Egypt. Built on the limestone Muqattam hill overlooking Cairo, it was fortified by Saladin between 1176–83.

836 CE The minaret of the Great Mosque of Kairouan, Tunisia.

842 CE Santa Maria de Naranco, Oviedo, Spain.

c. 850 CE Fo Kuang Temple, Mt Wu Tai, Shansi, China. The earliest wooden building in China, with beams supported by corbeled bracket ends.

c. 850 CE The Little Metropole Cathedral, Athens, Greece.

c. 851 CE The Great Mosque of Susah, Tunisia.

879 CE Preah Ko Temple, Hariharalaya, present Roluos, Cambodia. Six brick towers are arranged in two rows on a sandstone platform. The elaborate carving on the lintel depicts warriors mounted on three-headed *nagas*

Gothic arches in crypt of Canterbury Cathedral, England, 1175-84.

Amiens (1220-88), a classic of the Ile-de-France pattern and an inspiration for Gothic cathedrals throughout Europe; Chartres, with its non-matching towers, fabulous windows (130, including the famous Rose Window), and exterior sculpture (2,200 external figures), while Le Mans, further north, has 13 side chapels sprouting off the apse; Beauvais Cathedral in northern France, High Gothic (begun 1247) and designed on a vast scale (the choir finished 1272, has the highest vaulted nave roof in Europe—157 ft / 52 m—with a forest of flying buttresses as supports).

England developed its Gothic style early and clung to it much longer than any other European country. There were four phases. The first three—Transitional, Early English, and Decorated— followed developments in France, whereas the fourth, Perpendicular, was uniquely English and was to last from c. 1375 to c. 1560.

The outstanding example of Transitional is the choir of Canterbury Cathedral (1175-84). Early English is best represented by Salisbury Cathedral (1220-58, the tower and spire a little later). Two fine examples of Decorated Gothic are the west fronts of Exeter and York cathedrals. The nave, southwest and central towers, cloisters, transepts, and Lady Chapel of Canterbury Cathedral illustrate Perpendicular at its best. Other examples are King's College Chapel, Cambridge (1446-1515); Eton College Chapel (1441); and St George's Chapel, Windsor (1475-1509).

Lingaraja Temple, Bhubaneshwar, Orissa, India. The decoration here is strictly subordinate to structure.

(snakes or dragons) Decorations were carved into stucco applied on the brick, instead of in the brick itself.

943–67 CE St Arak'eloc Cathedral, Kars, Turkey. A central-domed tetraconch built of cut stone blocks facing a rubble concrete core.

c. 950–1200 CE Khajuraho, Madhya Pradesh, India. A temple town with 22 surviving temples built by the Chandela dynasty in rough granite or sandstone, with intricately carved erotic sculptures.

c. 1000 Lingaraja Temple, Bhubaneshwar, Orissa, India.

c. 1000 The Castillo, Chichén Itzá, Mexico.

c. 1000 Avantiswami Temple, Avantipur, Kashmir, India. This tall angular stone shrine with a stepped-stone roof derives from the style of wooden houses in the Kashmir valley.

c. 1000–1100 Lamayuru Gompa (monastery) Ladakh, India. Spectacularly hewn out of a cliff at a height of 11,513 ft (3510 m). Only one of the five original buildings still stands.

1019–47 Trier Cathedral, Germany.

c. 1020 Abbey Church of Mont-St-Michel, France.

The Castillo, Chichén Itzá, Mexico. Each stairway has 91 steps making 364 total, with the sanctuary threshold at the top making 365—the solar year.

Trier Cathedral, Germany. The present Romanesque building incorporates a Roman temple that preceded it.

Abbey Church of Mont-St-Michel, France. Although founded in the eighth century, the present Norman Romanesque buildings date from the early 11th century.

Above: Cologne Cathedral and plan, begun 1248, and finished 19th century.
Overleaf: Detail of sculptures on the façade.

Medieval Germany did not adopt the Gothic style as readily as France or England. Until the end of the 13th century most cathedral building was still in the Romanesque style. The earliest Gothic ecclesiastical building shows French influence, especially that of Amiens. A characteristic German feature was the twin- and single-towered west front. Cologne, begun 1248, and Regensburg, begun 1273, are examples of the twin-tower model, while the Minster of Ulm (begun 1377) is an outstanding example of the single-tower model.

The Hallenkirche, or hall church, was a specifically German Gothic tradition where the vaults of the nave, choir, and aisles are all of the same height. One of the best examples of the Hallenkirche is the Marienkirche-zur-Wiese, Soest (started c. 1340). The Hallenkirche style was influential in eastern Europe, particularly Poland, where there are a large number of brick examples (Church of the Assumption, Chelmno, the Collegiate Church of Our Lady, Poznan, and the Church of St John, Torun are among the finest).

The pre-eminent Gothic building in the Czech Republic is St Vitus Cathedral, Prague (begun by Matthieu of Arras in the 1340s in the French style, and finished by Peter Parler).

St Mark's, Venice, Italy. Venice owed more to the Byzantine world than to western Europe and St Mark's is one of the glories of Byzantine style. The present building is the third on this site and became the Cathedral of Venice in 1481.

'Enemy Observation Pagoda', K'ai Yuan Temple, Hopei, China. Built of solid brick but without floors or staircases it was purely decorative despite its war-like name.

Tournai Cathedral, Belgium. The nave (right) is Romanesque; the transepts (center) are Transitional; the Choir (left) is Gothic.

St-Etienne, Caen, France. One of the greatest examples of Northern Romanesque.

1023–1068

1023–31 Shen Mu Hall (Hall of the Sacred Mother) Shansi, China. A double-roofed hall with seven bays.

c. 1040–1250 St Mark's, Venice, Italy.

1053 Hōōdō (Phoenix Hall) of the Byōdō Temple, Uji, Japan. Dating from the Heian period, it has a bird-like shape, with a central hall, wing corridors on both sides, and a tail corridor. A gold-plated bronze phoenix is set on the central roof.

c. 1055 'Enemy Observation Pagoda', K'ai Yuan Temple, Hopei, China.

1066–1338 Tournai Cathedral, Belgium.

1066 Motte-and-bailey Castle, Dover, England. Built by William the Conqueror, supposedly in just eight days, it typically consists of a castle built on a 'motte' or raised earth mound, with an enclosed courtyard called the 'bailey'.

1067–93 Kharraqan towers, Qazvin, Iran. Persian-Seljuk medieval brick mausoleums 49 ft (15 m) tall and 13 ft (4 m) wide.

1068 St-Etienne, Caen, France.

1068 Warwick Castle, England. Originally a a wooden fortification

If the Gothic style is primarily a northern European phenomenon then it is not surprising that the outstanding example in Italy should appear either in the north of the country: Milan Cathedral (1387–1410) in Piedmont is the closest to northern Gothic and is covered with sculpture and pinnacles. Tuscany has some exceptional Gothic in the form of the cathedrals of Florence, Orvieto, and, perhaps the greatest of the three, Siena (1245–1380), decorated in dramatic strips of black and white marble. Sicily has always been a crossroads of cultures as represented by the Cathedral of Palermo (begun 1185), which is a mix of Norman and Moorish styles.

Medieval Italy also produced a wealth of municipal buildings at this time. The most notable are the Palazzo Pubblico, Siena (1288–1309); the Palazzo Vecchio, Florence (1298–1344); Palazzo dei Priori, Volterra (13th century); and the Doge's Palace, Venice (1343–1438).

In Spain most of the Gothic work is in the north and dates mainly from the 13th century: Léon Cathedral is based on the French Ile-de-France type; Toledo Cathedral (begun 1226), one of the finest Gothic monuments in Europe; Burgos Cathedral (begun 1221) with its later German-style traceried spires (1486); and Barcelona Cathedral (begun 1298 but completed by the 15th century). Late Gothic work is represented spectacularly by Seville Cathedral, the largest in Europe, which was built over a long period beginning in 1402 at the west end but not finished until c. 1520.

Burgos Cathedral, Spain, begun 1221.

Doge's Palace, Venice, Italy, begun 1343.

Rajarani Temple, Bhubaneshwar, India. The tower (rekha deul) is flanked by a lower ritual dance pavilion (jagmohan).

The White Tower, Tower of London, England. The original keep, built by Bishop Gundulf, is the oldest part of the Tower of London complex.

Masjid-i-Jami, Isfahan, Iran. The Seljuk Turks controlled most of Asia Minor by the 11th century. One of their innovations was the round minaret.

1075–1092

built by William the Conquerer, it was rebuilt in stone in the 17th century. The barbican and towers make it a fine example of military architecture.

c. 1075 Rajarani Temple, Bhubaneshwar, India.

1078 The White Tower, Tower of London, England.

1080 Masjid-i-Jami, Isfahan, Iran.

1080–1120 Basilique St Sernin, Toulouse, France. A large basilica with vaulted ceilings on a cruciform (cross-shaped) plan. An ambulatory walkway goes around the nave and side aisles to allow access to the radiating (side) chapels.

1087 Church of Christos Pantepoptes, Istanbul, Turkey. An Eastern Orthodox church converted into the Ottoman mosque, Eski Imaret. It uses the technique of recessed brick (alternate courses of brick plunged in a mortar bed), typical of middle Byzantine architecture.

1092 Bab Zuweila Cairo, Egypt. The last remaining southern gate from the wall built around Cairo by Badr al-Jamali, a vizier of the Fatimid caliphs. It has twin towers and a platform once used for executions.

THE ISLAMIC TRADITION

Above: Ceramic panel showing Medina.
Right: Dome of the Rock, Jerusalem, Israel.
This is the third most sacred shrine of Islam,
c. seventh century.

MOSQUES AND MINARETS

From the death of its founder Muhammad in 632 CE it was a remarkably short time before the Muslim Arab armies began their triumphal conquests. By 634 CE they had conquered Palestine and Syria, in 640 CE Egypt had been invaded, by 644 CE Persia subdued, in 714 CE Spain was subjugated and, in 827 CE, Sicily fell. The architectural traditions of the occupied areas—Graeco-Roman, Byzantine, Christian—were absorbed into Islamic building. Even the *mihrab*, the niche within a mosque which indicates the direction of Mecca, probably derives from the Jewish Torah-niche. The first great building of the Umayyad dynasty, the Dome of the Rock (Qubba al-Sakhra), Jerusalem (begun 688), is based on a Byzantine centrally-planned shrine which, in turn, derives from ancient Roman mausoleums.

The essential elements of the Islamic mosque were established by Muhammad's own very simple house in Medina: a courtyard containing the *qibla* wall facing in the direction of Mecca, and within this wall, the *mihrab*.

By 750 CE the Umayyads had been defeated by the Abbasids (who were to hold power until 950 CE) and the center of power moved to Baghdad in 762 CE under Caliph Al Mansur. Although no trace of Mansur's Baghdad survives, the great fortress-palace of Ukhaidar (780 CE) remains. Samarra, Iraq, was founded in 836 CE and its remaining buildings show the origins of the four-centered arch and the first domed tomb, both precedents of the rich tradition of Islamic architecture that followed.

The Great Mosque at Kairouan, Tunisia, ninth century.

Interior of the Dome of the Rock, Jerusalem, Israel, seventh century.

The Great Mosque of Samarra (848 CE), built by Caliph Al-Mutawakkil, was the largest ever built, and its enormous heliconical (shell-spiral) minaret is one of the most spectacular examples of Islamic architecture.

Egypt had been invaded in the seventh century and the Mosque of 'Amr at Fustat (642 CE), Cairo, is the first of many Islamic buildings that traced the Arab route westward along the coast of north Africa. Among the most notable are the Ribat of Susah (810–21 CE) in Tunisia and the Great Mosque of Kairouan (836 CE), Tunisia, with its square minaret (a shape much copied, for example in the Giralda tower at Seville) perhaps inspired by ancient Graeco-Roman lighthouses. The Great Mosque of Ibn Tulun in Cairo, dating from 876 CE, was modeled on the Samarra mosque and in its time was one of the largest structures in the Nile valley.

With the defeat of the Umayyads in 750 CE one member of their ruling family, Abd al-Rahman, escaped the slaughter and fled to Muslim Spain (al-Andalus) and founded his caliphate at Cordoba. In 785 CE he laid plans for the Great Mosque of Cordoba which, with changes and additions over the following 200 years, became one of the great glories of Islamic architecture. By the early 11th century al-Andalus, battered by Christian attacks, was shattered into small warring Muslim principalities

Mosque of Ibn Tulun, Cairo, Egypt, ninth century.

Durham Cathedral, England. Perched high above the River Wear, Durham is one of the greatest, perhaps the most magnificent, of all Romanesque cathedrals. Apart from the towers, it was completed in only 40 years, with every part vaulted in stone.

Palazzo Loredan, Venice, Italy. Venetian Romanesque shows the strong influence of Venice's close links with Byzantium and the East.

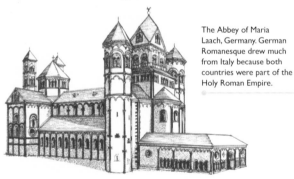

The Abbey of Maria Laach, Germany. German Romanesque drew much from Italy because both countries were part of the Holy Roman Empire.

Angkor Wat, Cambodia. Influenced by Indian temple architecture, Angkor Wat is the largest religious building complex in the world.

1093–1120

1093 Durham Cathedral, England.

c. 1100 Hall of Ambassadors, Alcazar, Seville, Spain. In Mudéjar style its columns support plain horseshoe arches. The interior has with polychrome tiles and decorative friezes, as well as a beautiful cedar wood stalactitic dome added in 1420.

c. 1100 Palazzo Loredan, Venice, Italy.

1100–20 Pagoda of Tianning Temple, Beijing, China. A 189-ft (57.8-m) tall, octagonal, 13-story brick and stone Chinese pagoda. It is entirely solid with no hollow space or staircase inside.

1108–1300 Southwell Minster, England. An example of Norman and Early English architecture, with its unique pyramidal spires of lead, locally known as 'Rhenish caps' or 'pepperpot' spires.

1112 The Abbey of Maria Laach, Germany.

1112–47 Basilica di San Frediano, Lucca, Italy. Romanesque basilica decorated with a huge Byzantine-style golden mosaic in the 13th century.

c. 1120 Angkor Wat, Cambodia.

1120–35 St Lazare Cathedral, Autun, France. Designed in the Romanesque style by

(Reinos de Taifas) which, despite civil wars, produced some wonderful architecture like the Aljaferiya, the palace fortress of Saragossa (1046–81) which, behind its formidable fortifications, contains exquisitely refined interiors; the Toledo Synagogue (Santa Maria la Blanca), 1075–85, a symbol of Jewish-Arab co-existence; and the *bañuelos* (baths) of Granada.

The 10th century saw the start of the rift in Islam between orthodox Sunnis and Shi'as, which remains to this day. The Shi'ite Fatimids, in opposition to the ruling Sunni caliphate in Baghdad, invaded Egypt in 969 CE and created their fortified capital at Cairo, where they built the al-Azhar Mosque, a prime center of Muslim learning and the first theological university in the world.

In 1061 the Almoravid dynasty of fundamentalist Muslims was founded in the Maghreb (modern Morocco, Algeria, Tunisia) and, in 1110, invaded Spain. In 1147 they were followed

Top: Cordoba Mosque, Spain, eighth century.
Above: Santa Maria la Blanca, Toledo, Spain, 11th century.

there by the Almohads, also Berbers from North Africa, whose capital was Rabat. Both groups favored a sober, severe art that rejected any motif other than the purely abstract. Sharply pointed arches, sometimes scalloped, sometimes in *muqarnas* (stalactite) style, and the fortress-like exteriors of mosques combined to define the Hispano-Moorish style that spread throughout the Maghreb and Andalusia. The Great Mosque of Seville (1171) has largely been lost under later Christian layers but the minaret, the Giralda Tower (so-called for the bronze angel that later topped its pinnacle), remains. One of the most impressive minarets of Almohad architecture towers 207 ft (69 m) over the Kutubiyya Mosque (1195) in Marrakesh, Morocco.

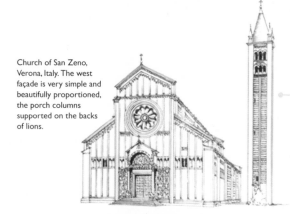

Church of San Zeno, Verona, Italy. The west façade is very simple and beautifully proportioned, the porch columns supported on the backs of lions.

Krak des Chevaliers, Syria. The 'chevaliers' (knights) in question were the Knights Hospitaller, a crusading military / religious order that took control of the site in 1144 and defended it successfully during 11 sieges. The castle finally fell to the Sultan of Egypt in 1271.

Borgund Stave Church, Norway. The mast or stave wooden churches of Norway are unique in Europe, although few have survived the ravages of time.

The Kutubiyya Minaret, Marrakesh, Morocco. Built by the Almohad dynasty, the minaret was originally faced with painted plaster.

1140–1152

Bishop Etienne de Bagé with spires, side chapels, and a new belfry in the 15th century.

1140 Church of San Zeno, Verona, Italy.

1140–42 The Church of St Mary and St David, Kilpeck, England. A Norman church famous for its beautifully detailed carvings in red sandstone.

1144 Krak des Chevaliers, Syria.

1150 Borgund Stave church, Norway.

c. 1150 The Kutubiyya Minaret, Marrakesh, Morocco.

1151–74 Zamora Cathedral, Spain. One of the finest examples of Spanish Romanesque architecture, with later Gothic features. A base with 16 double arches supports a dome with four corner turrets, the symbol of the city of Zamora.

1152–1363 Baptistry of St John, Pisa, Italy. Built by the architect Diotisalvi, the white marble Baptistry shows the transition from the Romanesque style to the Gothic: the lower registers with rounded arches are in the Romanesque style, while the upper registers with pointed arches are in the Gothic style.

Citadel at Cairo, Egypt, 10th century.

By 1078–79 the Turkish Seljuks had established themselves in Damascus and Jerusalem (triggering the First Crusade of 1095) and in intense warfare that ensued, the architectural emphasis shifted toward fortification. In 1176 the great Saladin began work on a huge citadel just south of Cairo, using materials from the pyramids of Giza, and his brother built a protective wall around the old city of Damascus. At Aleppo in Syria, Saladin's son constructed a formidable castle (completed 1209) on the site of a Roman-Byzantine fortress. Although later destroyed by the Mongols and then again by Tamurlane, it was rebuilt by the Ottomans in the 16th century to the original design.

The Seljuks were Sunni Muslims who were intent on spreading their version of Islam and to this end introduced a new type of architecture—madrassas, schools for the teaching of the Koran. The buildings combined two Persian forms: the *iwan* or covered area with one side opening through an arch to a courtyard, and the *muqarnas* decoration. One of the greatest examples is the Madrassa al-Firdaus in Aleppo (begun 1223).

Notre Dame, Paris, France. Pope Alexander III laid the first stone on a site of a Roman temple and started 170 years of intensive work by armies of Gothic architects and craftsmen. During the French Revolution much of its statuary was smashed and it was rededicated as the Temple of Reason, only to reopen as a cathedral in 1802.

The Campanile (Leaning Tower), Pisa, Italy. About 100 years after the start of construction the tower began to take on its famous tilt. It wasn't until 1350 that the topmost belfry was added.

The Giralda Tower, Seville Cathedral, Spain. Seville Cathedral is the largest Gothic building in Europe and was built on the site of a mosque, the minaret of which is the Giralda Tower.

Chartres Cathedral, France. Money to pay for the cathedral came from rich and poor alike. It is a city church, built for popular, rather than monastic or pilgrim worship.

1163–c.1330 Notre Dame, Paris, France.

1166 Church of the Intercession of the Virgin, on the Nerl, Russia. A three-apsed building, it has a single onion-shaped dome on a tall drum, typical of Russian churches.

1174 The Campanile (Leaning Tower), Pisa, Italy.

1175 Vordingborg Castle, Denmark. A defensive castle, with nine towers and a 2,624 ft (800 m) long wall of which little has survived. A golden goose perches on top of the Gåsetårnet or Goose Tower 85.3 ft (26 m) high, that was added in 1871.

1184 The Giralda Tower, Seville Cathedral, Spain.

1193–1386 Qutub Minar, Delhi, India. The world's tallest brick minaret and among the earliest Islamic buildings in India. Made of fluted red sandstone with tiered galleries, the minaret is 237.8 ft (72 m) high.

1194–1260 Chartres Cathedral, France.

1195 Hassan Tower, Rabat, Morocco. Part of an incomplete mosque, the 140 ft (44 m) red sandstone tower is only half of its intended height. It has ramps in place of stairs, which would have allowed the muezzin

Bourges Cathedral, France. Interior of the nave looking toward the choir. Bourges, begun by Bishop Henri de Sully, is one of the grandest of all medieval churches.

Torres Meliandi and Rognosa, San Gimignano, Italy. Look-out towers, defenses, drying towers for the town's famous saffron-dyed wool—or just one-upmanship between wealthy families?

Cliff Palace, Mesa Verde, Canyon de Chelly, Colorado, USA. The Pueblo Indians had occupied this site since c. 300 CE, but the present buildings date from the early 13th century. They exploited the natural caves and fissures in the cliff face by excavating the soft sandstone, then added more rooms and storage areas with sandstone blocks cemented together with mud-and-water (adobe) mortar.

San Millán, Segovia, Spain. The most unusual of the three Romanesque churches in Segovia, San Millán has a striking arcaded entrance.

1195–1205

to ride a horse to the top to make the call to prayer.

1195–1250 Bourges Cathedral, France.

c. **1200** Torres Meliandi and Rognosa, San Giminiano, Italy.

c. **1200** Aït Benhaddou, Ouarzazate, Morocco. A *ksar*, or fortified city of earthen buildings ringed by a defensive wall with corner towers. Situated along a former caravan route, it has some beautiful kasbahs (walled quarters with narrow maze-like streets.)

c. **1200** Cliff Palace, Mesa Verde, Canyon de Chelly, Colorado, USA.

c. **1200** San Millán, Segovia, Spain.

1202–1880 Rouen Cathedral, France. With its 495 ft (151 m) spire, it was the world's tallest building from 1876 to 1880. The 250 ft (76.2 m) steeple on the right is called the Tour de Beurre (Butter Tower), because it was built with funding by donations from rich citizens in return for the privilege of continuing to eat butter during Lent.

1205 Makaravank Monastery, Achajur, Tavush Marz, Armenia. The main church is built of dark-pink andesite and red tufa, with occasional greenish

Previous page: The Lion Court, Alhambra, Granada, Spain, 15th century. Above: Sultan Ahmed Mosque, Istanbul, Turkey, 1609–17.

By the late 13th century, Egypt, the last refuge of Islamic culture against the Mongol invaders, had been successfully defended by the Mamluks. The Mosque and Madrassa of Sultan Hussan (begun 1356) marks a high point of early Mamluk architecture and the height of Cairo's medieval prosperity. The city owed much of its finest building to Sultan Qaitbay, particularly his madrassa (1472–74), described as "the ultimate achievement of architectural development in Cairo."

By the second half of the 14th century Islamic Spain was crumbling in the face of Christian advances but the two cultures were still intimately entwined. For example, the Alcazar of Seville (begun 1364) was built for the

Beyazit Mosque, Istanbul, Turkey, 16th century.

Christian king Pedro I, but every detail, including the inscriptions, is Islamic. Only one minor Muslim dynasty, the Nasrids, survived in Spain until their expulsion in 1492, but their architectural legacy was extraordinary: the Alhambra, Granada (1338–90) is one of the most sumptuous of all Islamic palaces.

The Ottoman expansion of the 14th–16th centuries enveloped a huge area, from Hungary in the north, Basra on the Persian Gulf to the south, North Africa, and Greece. But it was in Europe that their particular style of architecture emerged most fully. Before the fall of Constantinople (modern Istanbul) to the Ottomans in 1453, their capital was at Adrianopolis (modern Edirne, Turkey), and the Uch Sherefeli Mosque (1438–47) is considered the first building in a truly Ottoman style: interlocking arches of alternating colors, *muqarnas* (decoration on capitals and door heads), and gently swelling lead-covered domes. Istanbul is full of major Ottoman buildings, some of the most outstanding being the Mosque of Beyazit (1501–08), the earliest surviving imperial mosque with its slim, multi-faceted minarets capped with tall steeples; Shezade Mosque (1544–48) built for Suleiman the Magnificent by the greatest Ottoman architect, Sinan, who also built the Süleymaniye Mosque (1551–58). It is in Edirne, however, that we find Sinan's masterpiece, the Selimiye Mosque (1569–74), with its eight huge piers carrying the largest dome in the Ottoman empire.

Salisbury Cathedral, England. A perfect example of the Early English style. The foundation stone was laid in 1220 and the Lady Chapel completed by 1225. The east transepts and choir were finished by 1237; the nave by 1284; and the tower and spire about 1380.

Burgos Cathedral, Spain. Like the cathedrals of León and Toledo, Burgos was based on French models and was built by French and English master-masons. The spires and pinnacles are 15th–16th century additions.

Toledo Cathedral, Spain. "Clothed in russet tones, the color of a browning roast or of a skin tanned like that of a pilgrim from Palestine."

Siena Cathedral, Italy. Clad all over in dramatic alternating stripes of black and white marble, it is also further embellished with mosaic, bronze sculpture, and marble veneer.

1220–1246

stones, giving the exterior an interesting array of hues.

1220–1380 Salisbury Cathedral, England.

c. 1221 Burgos Cathedral, Spain.

1223–24 Harihareshwara Temple, Harihar, Karnataka, India. A staggered square *mandapa* (hall) plan is typical of Hoysala dynasty temples. The soapstone structure has projections and recesses on the outer walls, and half pillars resting on the *mandapa's* parapet wall support the outer ends of the roof.

1227 Toledo Cathedral, Spain.

1228 Château d'Angers, Angers, France. Built on a site known since Roman times for its strategic defensive location. Almost 600 m (2,000 ft) in circumference, with 17 towers, the walls encompass 6.17 acres (2.5 ha).

1230–1472 York Minster, England. The second largest Gothic cathedral in northern Europe, it also has the largest expanse of medieval stained glass in the world.

1245 Siena Cathedral, Italy.

1246 La Sainte-Chapelle, Paris, France. A Gothic chapel in the *rayonnante*

HISTORY IN STONE

The architectural history of India begins with two great cities that flourished in the Indus valley about 3000–1600 BCE: Harappa and Mohenjodaro. Both were large and both planned on a grid system with buildings forming rectangular blocks. Both were constructed on a high platform surrounded by

The Great Stupa, Sanchi, India, c. 200 BCE.

a wall. By 1600 BCE both cities had been destroyed by Aryan invaders, who migrated from what is now Iran.

The earliest surviving architecture in India, mainly Buddhist (the religion was established in the sixth century BCE), are caves cut out of rock, of which there are two kinds: those made by

Carving at Kailashnatha Temple, Kanchipuram.

excavation into the rock, and those made by excavating around rock to make a freestanding structure. The sixth-century excavations at Ellora and Elephanta, both in Maharashtra, are good examples of the former; the temples of Mamallapuram, in Tamil Nadu, of the latter.

The Role of the Architect. A religious overseer, the *shthapaka* was responsible for the overall layout and prepared the site by carrying out certain rituals. The actual construction was supervised by the building-master or *sthapati*, aided by a master-mason, chief sculptor, and master painter-decorator. Their job was to turn the measurements and proportions laid down by the *shthapaka* into the solid reality of a building.

Mamallapuram. On the coast of eastern Tamil Nadu, south of Madras, the Hindu *rathas* (a temple structure based on a chariot used by the gods) of Mamallapuram were built under the Pallava dynasty who ruled southern India 566–894 CE. The grandest of all the buildings at Mamallapuram is the Shore Temple, built 700–728 CE and dedicated to Shiva. Unlike the other *rathas*, it is constructed out of dressed stone rather than carved from rock.

Cologne Cathedral, Germany. The largest Gothic cathedral in northern Europe—it remained unfinished until the 19th century.

Halles, Bruges, Belgium. An imposing statement of the city's wealth from cloth manufacture during the Middle Ages. The tower is 260 ft (80 m) high.

Caernavon Castle, Wales. The grandest of the 'golden age' of English castles built by king Edward I (reigned 1272–1307). There are 13 towers, none of them identical.

Palazzo Pubblico, Siena, Italy. Medieval Italy produced a wealth of town halls—the centers of government of the city-states. Siena's, with its imposing tower, castellated roofline, and Gothic windows, is typical.

1248–1295

(meaning 'to radiate') style, referring to its wonderful use of light, a lace-like delicate tracery on the exterior, and the Gothic rose-windows where the petals of the rose radiate from the center of the window.

1248 Cologne Cathedral, Germany.

1280 Halles, Bruges, Belgium.

1283 Harlech Castle, Gwynedd, Wales, England. Built on a cliff near the Irish Sea, it has a number of concentric defensive walls and a massive gatehouse. The outer walls are much shorter and thinner than the inner ones.

1283–1383 Caenarvon Castle, Wales.

1284–1304 Qalawun Complex, Cairo, Egypt. This is the first instance in Cairo when domed buildings (two mosques, two mausoleums, and a hospital) are built on a cruciform (cross-shaped) plan. Columns and capitals from nearby Roman ruins were used in the buildings.

1288–1309 Palazzo Pubblico, Siena, Italy.

1295 Beaumaris Castle, Anglesey, Wales. An incomplete, almost perfectly designed castle, by Master James of St George.

Elephanta. Just south of Bombay, on a small island in the Arabian Sea, sits one of the greatest achievements of rock-cut architecture. Dedicated to Shiva (the colossal three-headed representation of the god is one of the marvels of Indian sculpture), Elephanta is essentially a man-made cave created in the sixth century with a 20-pillared hall.

Ellora. About 180 miles (300 km) from Bombay a complex of caves show Buddhist, Hindu, and Jain work.

The three-headed Shiva, Elephanta, India, sixth century.

They span the sixth to ninth centuries but the most intensive period of building was under the Rashtrakuta dynasty (754–982). Cave 16, the Kailasa Temple, is the most important single structure of this remarkable group and was built between 757 and 773. Dedicated to Shiva, it is the largest monolithic structure in India.

Medieval Hindu Temples. The Chalukya dynasty began *c*. 450 CE and lasted until the 13th century. The three most significant cities of the era, Aihole, Badami, and Pattadakal, are clustered in what is now the state of Karnataka, in the southwest of India. Aihole's two main temples, the Ladh Khan (600–650 CE) and the Durga (675–725) are both freestanding dressed-stone buildings, the first with beautiful ornamental latticed windows, the second with its sturdy exterior portico around the whole building. At Pattadakal, the Mallikarjuna and Virupaksha temples were probably built by the same architect around 750 CE, and both have exterior carving and sculpture of the highest order. The Malegitti Shivalaya temple at Badami stands by its own lake (man-made during the sixth century) among a group of extraordinarily well-preserved structures dating from the seventh century.

Further to the south in the state of Tamil Nadu is the ancient city of Thanjavur, formerly the capital of the Chola Dynasty which, between 836–1267 CE, ruled most of southern India. The Brihadishvara Temple was founded about 1002 by the Chola king Rajaraja I. Set within a magnificent cloistered wall, the *gopuram* (ceremonial towers guarded by *dvarapalas*, frightening beasts) lead to the central sanctums. The crowning glory is the *shikhara*, a pyramidal building rising 120 ft (70 m) and topped with a domed stupa.

Kailasa Temple, Ellora, India, eighth century.

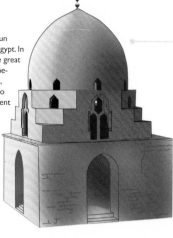

Fountain, Ibn Tulun Mosque, Cairo, Egypt. In the center of the great mosque is a dome-covered fountain, almost a shrine to that sacred element in Egypt—water.

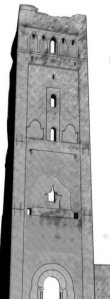

Timber house, Sør-Fron, Norway. Most buildings in Norway at this time were in timber as stone and brick were scarce and expensive. Cloth or moss was laid between the logs to make the walls air- and water-tight.

The Great Mosque of al-Mansura, Tlemcen, Algeria. When the Maranids besieged Tlemcen in the early 14th century they turned their camp into a city and built a great mosque. All that remains now is the huge tower-like minaret.

St Vitus, Prague, Czech Republic. The cathedral was designed by a Frenchman, Matthieu of Arras, who died in 1352 when the east end was almost complete. The building was actually finished by the great architect, Peter Parler.

1296–1350

1296 Fountain, Ibn Tulun Mosque, Cairo, Egypt.

1296 Basilica di Santa Croce, Florence, Italy. The largest Franciscan church with 16 chapels decorated with frescoes. The floor plan is an Egyptian or Tau cross, with a nave and two aisles separated by octagonal columns.

c. 1300 Timber house, Sør-Fron, Norway.

1309–1424 Doge's Palace, Venice, Italy. Made of masonry-cut marble in an Italian Gothic style, it has a strong planar façade with slender columns and arches.

c. 1320 The Great Mosque of al-Mansura, Tlemcen, Algeria.

1327 Djinguereber Mosque, Timbuktu, Mali. A famous learning center, the mosque is made entirely of earth, fiber, straw, and wood, except for a small part of the northern façade which is in limestone.

1344 St Vitus, Prague, Czech Republic.

c. 1350 Tschudi Complex, ChanChan, Peru. A former capital of the Chimú rulers. All Chimú buildings were red, white, and black. The walls of the complex are made of adobe bricks and have a smooth surface covered with carved images of fish and sea-birds.

Bhubaneshwar. Orissa, in the northeast, has, since the third century BCE been a wealthy center of commerce and architecture. The Nagara-style tower, with its strong vertical 'veins' (*pagas*), are superbly represented by the Mukteshvara temple (late 900s) and Brahmeshvara (*c.* 1074) complex. But the most striking building at Bhubaneshwar is the Rajarani Temple of the 11th century, with its ornate yet orderly tower (*rekha deul*) complemented by the rectangular dance-pavilion (*jagamohana*). The largest temple at Bhubaneshwar, the Lingaraja, dates from the mid-11th century and its *shikhara* (temple tower) rises 135 ft (45 m).

Khajuraho. The erotic sculptures that so shocked the West when the complex of 22 surviving temples was discovered in 1840 have been described as "the greatest masterpieces of medieval Hindu architecture." The earliest temple, Chaunsath Yogini, dates from before the 10th century, but one of the most complete, the Lakshmana, was founded in 954 CE by King Dhanga and was a turning point in temple planning. Instead of the arbitrary placement of buildings within a complex, Khajuraho reveals a unified vision, each part planned to relate to the other. One of the finest examples is the Kandariya Mahadeva Temple, which externally resembles a Gothic cathedral with its buttressing towers and multiple spires. Internally, however, it could not be more different with its dark and relatively small interior spaces.

Above: Kandariya Mahadeva Temple, Khajuraho, India, 10th century.
Left: Rajarani Temple, Bhubaneshwar, India, 11th century.

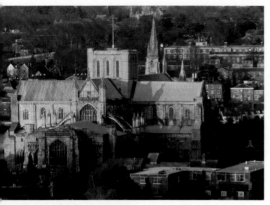

Winchester Cathedral, England. The west front (foreground) dates from 1360 although the transepts are much earlier (1079–93).

The Court of the Lions, Alhambra, Granada, Spain. The great palace complex was one of the last Moorish building enterprises in Spain (they were finally expelled in 1492). The lions surrounding the fountain are a rare example of freestanding sculpture in Islamic art.

Milan Cathedral, Italy. The greatest purely Gothic building in Italy (which is explained by Milan's proximity to northern Europe). Started under the Visconti dukes of Milan, the cathedral was not completed until the 19th century.

The Little Hall, Lavenham, Suffolk, England. A wood-framed house funded by the profits made from the local wool industry. A hall for eating and entertaining was at the right, while the sleeping quarters were on the upper floor on the left.

1360–1400

1360 Winchester Cathedral, England.

1360–86 Zhonghua Gate, Nanjing, China. Considered the greatest ancient city gate in China because of its complex structure, vast scale, and intricate design.

1362 The Court of the Lions, Alhambra, Granada, Spain.

1370 City walls, Pingyao, China. The walls with their six barbican gates form the shape of a turtle so Pingyao is also called 'Turtle City'.

1377–1890 Ulmer Münster, Ulm, Germany. A tall Lutheran church with a steeple measuring 530 ft (161.53 m). 768 steps lead to the top along a narrow spiral staircase.

1387–1410 Milan Cathedral, Italy.

1389 Mazar of Khoja Ahmed Yasawi, Türkistan, Kazakhstan. Though unfinished this Timurid mausoleum is well-preserved and has the largest double dome ever built in Central Asia 60 ft (18.3 m) in diameter and 92 ft (28 m) in height, decorated with green and golden tiles.

1390 The Little Hall, Lavenham, Suffolk, England.

c. 1400 Ancient House, Ipswich, England. Detailed wood carving and fine pargeting with

Tomb of Sheikh Salim Chisti, Fatehpur Sikri, India, 16th century.   Tomb of Akbar, Sikandra, India, 17th century.

Moghul. The earliest substantial Islamic buildings in India to survive are mosques and tombs at Ajmer and Delhi of the early 13th century, constructed by Indian craftsmen of local red stone. Early in the 16th century, the first Moghul emperor, Babur, used Ottoman architects who brought with them their extraordinary skill in dome construction. The third Moghul emperor, Akbar (1556–1605), rebuilt the Red Fort at Agra (1564–80) and within it the Jehangir Mahal, a palace for his son. The peak of Akbar's architectural achievements was the new city of Fatehpur Sikri (1569–c. 1580), which survives almost in its original state. Within the city are a series of remarkable buildings: the Panch Mahal; the Diwan-i-Khas (hall of private audience); the Diwan-i-Am (hall of public audience); the Great Mosque; the triumphal gate known as the Buland Darwaza; and the Tomb of Sheikh Salim Chisti (c. 1580, rebuilt by Jahangir, Akbar's grandson, in c. 1610); and the House of Raja Birbal (1572).

Although numerous mosques and palaces are of the highest quality it is the tombs of the Moghul rulers that have captured the popular imagination. Akbar himself lies in his great tomb (1604–12) at Sikandra near Agra. Other outstanding examples are the island tomb of the Afghan overlord Sher Shah at Sasaram, Bengal (begun 1545); the tomb of the Delhi Sultan Isa Khan (begun 1547); and the two most famous—the tomb of Humayun (Akbar's father, c. 1560); and Shah Jahan's mausoleum for his wife, the Taj Mahal (1630–53), Agra, which, according to an inscription, was built by a Turk to the design of an architect from Lahore, with calligraphy by a Persian. Shah Jahan went on to build the Red Fort and Palace, Delhi (1639–48), and the Jami Masjid (Great Mosque), both in Delhi (1644–58).

The Red Fort, Agra, India, 16th century.

The Castillo, Tulum, Mexico. Built on a headland overlooking the azure Caribbean Sea. Tulum represents the end of the great Mayan architectural tradition, with little of the sophisticated detailing found at Chichén Itzá or Uxmal.

The Forbidden City, Beijing, China. Most of the luxurious palaces of Chinese emperors were destroyed when their reigns ended. Only the Forbidden City, built during the Ming and Qing dynasties, survives.

Dogon house, Mali, Africa. The Dogon and Tellem peoples built their houses and granaries of stone and adobe. Sacred objects were placed in the niches on the façade.

Ospedale degli Innocenti, (Foundling Hospital) Florence, Italy. Filippo Brunelleschi's (1377–1446) façade is part in 'the ancient manner' and part Romanesque.

1400–1420

geometric, birds and foliage motifs, sometimes covering the entire wall.

c. 1400–08 Old Synagogue, Dubrovnik, Croatia. It remains the oldest Sefardic synagogue still in use in the world, built in the early 14th century.

c. 1400 The Castillo, Tulum, Mexico.

1403–28 Porcelain Tower, Nanjing, China. A 250-ft (75-m) high nine-storied tower on an octagonal base designed by the emperor Yung-lo. White porcelain bricks reflected the sunlight, with glazes and stoneware worked into the porcelain to create colored designs. Almost destroyed in the 19th century, it is under reconstruction.

1406–20 The Forbidden City, Beijing, China.

1400s–present Dogon house, Mali, Africa.

1416 Golden Hall, Wudang Mountains, China. A gilded bronze structure on a mountain peak, it is the largest of its kind in China and forms part of a palace complex.

1419 Ospedale degli Innocenti (Foundling Hospital), Florence, Italy.

c. 1420 Icomb Place, Gloucestershire, England. Built on the site of an earlier house, this medieval manor house

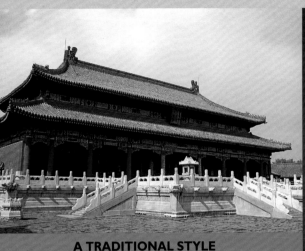

A TRADITIONAL STYLE

Dynasty Timeline	
206 BCE–220 CE	Han
265–420	Chin
581–618	Sui
618–907	T'ang
960–1279	Sung
1279–1368	Yüan
1368–1644	Ming
1644–1911	Qing

Being repeatedly rebuilt of perishable materials, rather than preserved in stone, ancient buildings survive in a different way in China than they do in the West, and few original structures remain in the original state from before the Ming Dynasty. Unlike Europe there was not an emphasis on innovation; buildings tended to be rebuilt or refurbished in traditional styles throughout Chinese history. It was a highly conservative tradition with only subtle changes of style across the centuries. Although masonry was used (the arch and vault were known early in Chinese history), it was employed mainly for fortifications, bridges, and engineering works. The primary material was wood, which, although allowing great flexibility, was also prone to decay.

It may seem odd to speak about common architectural principles that span 2,000 years but the basic uniformity and standardization of the Chinese tradition unites, both in structure and planning. The most striking is the reliance on timber for the frame construction common to Chinese buildings.

What are considered 'typical' Chinese architectural features appeared during the fourth–sixth centuries: overhanging eaves, curved roof line, bracket clusters, and columns spaced at intervals rather than walls. And it was during the Han dynasty that the characteristic ground plan was

Above left: Guardian Lion in stone at the Forbidden City, Beijing, China, built largely during the Ming and Qing dynasties, 15th and 16th century. Above: Roof detail of an imperial pagoda.

developed and remained stable through the centuries. The building complexes, temples, palaces, or other buildings were surrounded by protective walls (privacy was highly valued). The typical home was set within a walled enclosure around a courtyard, with the principal rooms oriented on a north-south axis. The east and west buildings were lower, and in one of these the servants would have been housed. Heating was from a portable charcoal brazier, although the Chinese preferred to dress more warmly during winter rather than rely on external heating. The kitchen was rarely an integral part of the building and was usually out in the open air in a veranda or outhouse.

The role of the architect was very different to the post-Renaissance European conception. Building techniques and designs were passed down in an oral tradition and rigidly limited by custom and convention. Sumptuary laws laid down what kind of building was suitable for different grades and distinctions of social class. A client 'ordered' a building like any other commodity, and the different types and construction and their suitability for different uses were so well known that the design was more or less a foregone conclusion. Architecture in China tended to be created collectively, fed by slow-moving traditions and less by the 'vision' of an individual.

China was largely a secular country and, unlike Hindu India, Christian Europe, or the Islamic world, not dominated by one overarching theology. Confucianism was more a socio-political doctrine, and Taoism was less a religion and more a philosophy. Buddhism arrived from India to China in the first century CE but its buildings tended to be constructed within the Chinese secular tradition, with walled enclosures and hall styles. However, Buddhism did contribute some unique architectural forms: the pagoda (based on the Indian stupa); the *p'ai-lou* or ceremonial arch (the most famous being the five-arched example at the Ming tombs near Beijing, 1522–66); and the rock-cut temple and shrine (the Cave of the Thousand Buddhas at Tun-huang, begun 366 CE and the 11th-century Mai-chi Shan, T'ien-shui, Kansu province, span the tradition).

Fine examples of the pagoda are, in date order: Sung Yüeh, Honan province (523 CE), which is the oldest surviving brick building in China; the 'Big Goose Pagoda' (652 CE) of the Tz'u-en monastery in Sian, one of the few surviving buildings of the T'ang dynasty's great capital at Ch'ang-an;

Chinese pagodas. Left: Pagoda of the Sung Yüeh temple, Honan, 523 CE. Center: Big Goose Pagoda, Sian, 701–04 CE. Right: 'Enemy Observation Pagoda', Hopei, c. 1055.

The Duomo, Florence, Italy. The dome was built on to the existing medieval cathedral by Brunelleschi. In order to spread its massive weight (it is 138 ft / 46 m in diameter) he used a double-shell construction.

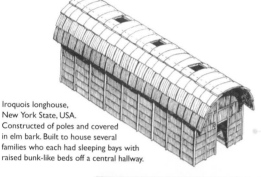

Iroquois longhouse, New York State, USA. Constructed of poles and covered in elm bark. Built to house several families who each had sleeping bays with raised bunk-like beds off a central hallway.

Hôtel-Dieu, Beaune France. Built by Cardinal Rolin, the Duke of Burgundy's Chancellor, as a hospital for the poor of Beaune. Part of it is now a museum but it still houses a functioning hospital.

Frauenkirche, Munich, Germany. Typical of the large South German hall church, the Frauenkirche ('Church of the Madonna') was designed by a local architect, Jorg von Halsbach.

1420–1470

has no right angles in its plan.

1420–36 The Duomo, Florence, Italy.

1428–30 Ca' d'Oro (Golden house) or Palazzo Santa Sofia, Venice, Italy. Built in the Venetian Gothic style with a small inner courtyard, the palazzo combines the features of a medieval church and a Moorish palace. Its name derives from gilt and polychrome decorations that once adorned its walls.

c. 1450 Iroquois longhouse, New York State, USA.

c. 1450 Panagia Paraportiani Church, Mykonos, Greece. An assymetrical conglomeration of four sloping whitewashed chapels built on the ground and a fifth on the roof. This popular shrine mixes Byzantine and vernacular styles and is called 'a confectioner's dream gone mad'.

1452 Hôtel-Dieu, Beaune France.

1461 Bor Namghar (House of Names), Jorhat, Assam, India. Bamboo and thatch structure with a gabled *monikut* (sanctuary) and an assembly hall with the *ghaai khuta* (main pillar), a large column on a raised platform.

1470–86 Frauenkirche, Munich, Germany.

Temple of Heaven, Forbidden City, Beijing, China, 15th century.

and the Sung dynasty 'Enemy Observation Pagoda' at the K'ai Yüan temple in Ting-hsien (completed 1055), built of stone.

Most of the few timber buildings that survive before the Ming dynasty are Buddhist temple halls. From the T'ang dynasty there is the Fo-kuang Temple (857 CE), Shansi province, the earliest surviving wooden building in China. Another fine example is the Kuan-yin hall of the Tu-lo Temple in the walled city of Chi-hsian, Hopei province, 984 CE.

The Great Wall. Built by the engineer Ch'in Shih Huang-ti (221–210 BCE) the Great Wall was in fact a joining together of walls already built by previous feudal states. Nevertheless, it was a colossal undertaking only made possible by conscripted labor. The total length is 2,484 miles (828 km). It was originally built of rammed earth. It was in the 15th and 16th centuries under the Mings that the most extensive repairs and refacing with stone and brick took place.

Imperial Peking (Beijing). 'Pei-ching' the northern capital, had existed since about 2400 BCE when there was a Neolithic settlement. Between 1153–1215 CE it was the capital of the kingdom of the 'Golden Tartars', and from 1215–1368 of the Mongols. In 1403 the Ming dynasty moved its capital to Peking from Nanking and the main lines of the city were laid down then. It has four main parts: the Outer City to the south, the Inner City to the north, and the Imperial City (within the Inner) that contains the Forbidden City. Compared to European cities it is large and the whole complex was planned as a unit. The emphasis is on grouped structures rather than individual buildings. Even the Throne Hall itself (T'ai-ho Tien), for all its size, is rich rather than dominating, which reflects, perhaps, a less pretentious way of expressing the power and prestige of the monarch than would have been found in Renaissance Europe.

Above: *P'ai-lou* (ceremonial arch) to the Ming tombs, Beijing, China, 1522–66.
Facing page: Great Wall of China, 2,484 miles (828 km) of fortification.

AN ENDURING HERITAGE

For much of its history Japan was isolated from outside influences, and those that did have an impact on its cultural, spiritual, and architectural traditions, primarily Korea, China, and Buddhist India, evolved slowly and continuously. Basic forms tended to be constant and changes relatively small. Timber was the main building material because it proved most resistant to the

Matsumoto Castle in central Japan (Honshu) is one of the last remaining original Japanese castles, built for defensive purposes. Nicknamed the Crow Castle, it dates back to 1593, and is built entirely out of wood.

earthquakes to which Japan is prone. A side effect of its use has been the constant reconstruction of old buildings in exact replication of the original, often as frequently as every 20 years. Climate has also had a fundamental role in Japanese building style. The characteristic overhang of the classic Japanese roof enables it to throw off the very heavy annual rainfall. To combat the high humidity of summer, buildings were often raised on open wooden platforms, and movable interior screens (wood or paper-covered frames called *fusuma*) allowed air to circulate throughout the building. As in China, the rigors of cold and dry winters were met with stoicism and extra layers of warm clothes.

Prehistory. The earliest architectural evidence comes from the Neolithic Jomon people who probably reached Japan from north and central Asia via Korea. Their pit-and-post huts (*tateana*) date from *c.* 1000 BCE. The Yayoi culture, originally of Asiatic or Oceanic derivation and centered on Kyushu, marked an advance in building techniques. Their dwellings (second–fifth centuries CE) had pile-supported high floors entered by steps or a ladder, typical of Oceanic cultures. Some of the main monuments that survive are great funeral tumulii around the plain of Yamato, southeast of Osaka, which are probably inspired by the stupas of Buddhist India. It is also from this period that the traditional form of Shinto (a pantheistic nature-centered religion) shrines was established, the two greatest being the Ise Naiku and Ise Geku, dating from the third quarter of the fifth century CE. With its emphasis on natural building materials and the relationship of buildings to nature, Shinto has had a continuously profound effect on Japanese architecture.

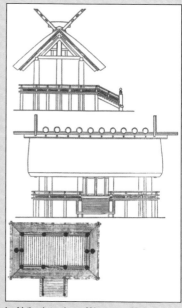

Ise Naiku shrine, Japan, fifth century CE.

Asuka Period (538–645 CE). The imperial clan became established, with close ties to both Korea and northern China, and it was from Korea that Buddhism was introduced in 538 CE. By the end of the sixth century it had been embraced by the imperial house. Under imperial patronage were founded the great Buddhist temples of Haiyu-ji, Hokyi, Hamji, and Horyu-ji, built 607 CE, with the pagoda, gatehouse, and *kondo* (main sanctuary) surviving.

Horyu-ji, Japan, 607 CE.

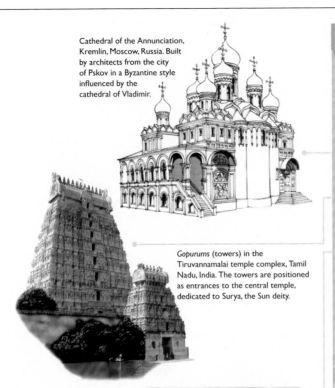

Cathedral of the Annunciation, Kremlin, Moscow, Russia. Built by architects from the city of Pskov in a Byzantine style influenced by the cathedral of Vladimir.

Gopurums (towers) in the Tiruvannamalai temple complex, Tamil Nadu, India. The towers are positioned as entrances to the central temple, dedicated to Surya, the Sun deity.

Machu Picchu, Peru. The terraced Inca site was both a place of habitation as well as a ceremonial and religious complex. The massive granite blocks were cut so accurately that they fitted perfectly without the use of mortar (so strongly bonded that not even earthquakes have managed to dislodge them).

St Peter's, Rome, Italy. In 1503 the newly elected Pope Julius II decided to rebuild the 1200-year-old basilica that had been founded by Emperor Constantine. Many architects were involved but two were to make the major contribution. Bramante took on the initial redesign in 1512. In 1546 Michelangelo took on the job (refusing any payment) and worked on it until his death in 1564.

1475–1513

1475 The Old Queen's Head, Sheffield, England. This double-storied public house is the only remnant of the timber framed medieval town.

1482–9 Cathedral of the Annunciation, Kremlin, Moscow, Russia.

c. 1500 Gopurums (towers) in the Tiruvannamalai temple complex, Tamil Nadu, India.

c. 1500 Machu Picchu, Peru.

1500 Dumfermline Palace, Fife, Scotland. Though in ruins today, it was the favorite residence of many Scottish monarchs. It is attached to the nearby Dumfermline Abbey by a gatehouse over a pond.

c. 1501–06 Hedared Stave Church, Sweden. Sweden's only preserved medieval stave church (see Borgund Stave church, 1150) it has a small, plain interior, originally consisting only of walls without windows, a roof, and an earth floor. The present windows and wooden floor were added later. The kalk (altar) dates from the 13th century.

1506–1612 St Peter's, Rome, Italy.

1513 Catedral Nueva (New Cathedral), Salamanca, Spain. Elaborate yet delicate structure in the Spanish Plateresco style.

Nara Period (645–793 CE). In the seventh century direct relations were established with the Chinese T'ang Dynasty at its capital Ch'ang-an, which was closely copied in the new capital of Nara in 710 CE. Some of the buildings that survive from this period are the temple-monasteries of the Todai-ji (founded 745 CE) and the Toshodai-ji, which, despite much rebuilding, still retain enough original structures to illustrate their style and scale: elaborate roofs of glazed tile; columns painted in vermilion; overhanging eaves and glorious painted decoration; the low Buddha hall; and the pagodas that had superseded the older stupa style. The Todai-ji was the

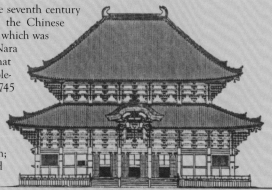

Todai-ji, Japan, founded 745.

largest monastery in Japan, far bigger than anything even in China. The Daibutsuden, or Hall of the Great Buddha of the Todai-ji is the largest wooden building under one roof in the world and contains the largest bronze statue in the world.

Heian Period (794–1185 CE). As was the custom when an emperor died, the capital city was moved, in this case from Nara to Heian-Kyo (now Kyoto) and again the new city was laid out along Chinese lines. It was also in this period that two Buddhist sects were introduced to Japan—Shingon and Tendai—and with them a mass of minor Buddhist divinities that needed to be housed in ever more elaborate shrines and temples. By 898 CE, however, the nobility showed a greater hostility towards foreign ideas and, in opposition to Shingon and Tendai, favored the cult of Amida (Jodo), which embraced anyone who worshipped the Buddha. Many temples were built by emperors and nobility, and of those that survive, the pagoda of Daigoji, the Sangen-in, and the lecture halls of the Koryu-ji and Horyu-ji monasteries are most notable. The palaces of the nobility also became more elaborate in the *shinden-zukuri* style (where interconnected rectangular buildings were set in an intricate series of naturalistic gardens and waterways) that is regarded as one of the typical features of Japanese architecture.

Kamakura Period (1185–1337). The ascendancy of the Minamoto clan brought with it a military-style government of the samurai at Kamakura, just south of Tokyo. The Zen sect of Buddhism, with its emphasis on self-discipline and simplicity, had a particular appeal to the warrior caste, who now sought to cleanse the temples of their multi-deity statues and concentrate on the Buddha figure alone. In their domestic buildings, too, they created a more unified layout of rooms grouped under one roof with public spaces separated from private. This plan, developed in the next period, formed the basis for the Japanese house up to the present day.

A Shinden dwelling, Japan.

Château de Chenonceaux, France. At different times the home both of Diane de Poitiers, Henry II's mistress, and Catherine d' Medici, his wife. The central structure was built on the foundations of a medieval water-mill. The five-arched bridge was designed by Philibert de l'Orme (c. 1510–70) between 1556–59, and the upper gallery by Jean Bullant (c. 1520–78) in 1576.

Château de Chambord, France. Originally intended as a simple hunting lodge for François I, the project grew to a massive size. Domenico da Cortona created the first design, and Leonardo da Vinci may have had some involvement.

Five-arched *p'ai lou*, Beijing, China. The commemorative arch (p'ai lou) is a gateway to an avenue leading to the tombs of Ming emperors. It is built of white marble with a blue-glazed tile roof.

Cour Carrée, Louvre, Paris, France. The wing to the left (as we look at it) of the central building (Pavillon de l'Horloge) is by Pierre Lescot (c. 1510–78) and built between 1546–55. The Pavillon and the wing to its right are by Jacques Lemercier (1585–1684) and built 1624–54.

1515–1546

1515–76 Château de Chenonceaux, France.

1515–21 Belém Tower, Lisbon, Portugal. Late Gothic Portuguese style, also called Manueline, which uses nautical elements such as anchors, cables, and the armillary sphere with sea motifs like shells, pearls, and seaweed. The tower was meant to be a ceremonial and defensive gateway to the city.

1516 Church of Our Lady of Light, Chennai, India. Built in 1516 by the Portuguese, it combines Gothic arches and Baroque ornamentation. The altars are gilded with silver and gold leaves and the ceiling is decorated with painted frescoes.

1519–47 Château de Chambord, France.

1520 Chigi Chapel, Church of Santa Maria del Popolo, Rome, Italy. Octagonal chapel designed by Raphael. The dome has a spectacular mosaic depicting the Creation of the World.

1522–66 Five-arched *p'ai lou*, Beijing, China.

1526–31 Palazzo del Te, Mantua, Italy. Built by Giulio Romano in the Mannerist style.

1546 Cour Carrée, Louvre, Paris, France.

77

Nijo Castle, Japan, 16th century.

Muromachi Period (1338–1573). In 1339 Shogun Ashikaga Takauji of the Minamoto clan moved the capital to a part of Kyoto known as Muromachi. Zen Buddhism, supported by the shogunate, found its fullest expression in the *cha-no-yu*–the tea ceremony, which dictated not only the equipment but also the layout on the room with its *tokonoma*, or recess for the display of paintings and flower arrangements. The shoguns also built themselves splendid retirement palaces, particularly the Kinkaku-ji (Golden Pavilion) and the Ginkaku-ji (Silver Pavilion).

Momoyama Period (1573–1638). The Ashikaga shoguns were overthrown by three of the most important figures in Japanese history: Oda Nobunaga, Toyotomi Hideyoshi, and Tokugawa Ieyasu, who between them, unified the country. The greatest architectural legacy of the period is the splendid feudal castles like Osaka (built by Hideyoshi in 1587); Yedo, now part of the imperial palace at Tokyo; Matsumuto of the early 16th century; and Nagoya, completed in 1611, to name only the most famous. They stand on a base of stone or granite (*glacis*) surrounded by a moat, but the buildings themselves, ornate and rather unwarlike by European standards, are made of timber.

Yedo Period (1615–1867). Ieyesu eventually achieved complete control of Japan and moved his capital to Yedo (Tokyo), where he built his great castle. Official building was carried out on a large scale, though as the period progressed it became increasingly uniform. In contrast, domestic building followed the intimacy of the tea-house. The most influential building of the period is the Katsura imperial palace (c. 1620) built under the guidance of the most important tea-masters of the time in a form that has been influential in domestic building down to the present day.

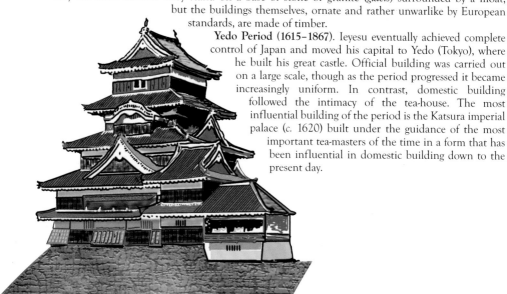

Matsumoto Castle, Japan, 16th century.

Villa Capra, Vicenza, Italy. Also known as the Rotonda due to the round plan of the central salon. Andrea Palladio's circle-within-the-square design became particularly popular in England (see Chiswick House, 1725).

University, Alcalà de Henares, near Madrid, Spain. Architect Gil de Hontañón rebuilt the façade of the University in Spanish Plateresque style.

Hakka houses, Fukien, China. The Hakka people migrated from central to southern China from the third century onwards. Feeling isolated in their new environment, they built multi-story dwellings to accommodate communal living.

Longleat House, Wiltshire, England. Restrained Classicism makes Longleat one of the finest Elizabethan houses in England. It burned down just before completion in 1567 and had to be rebuilt to a new design.

1546–1554

1546–50 Château d'Ancy-le-Franc, Burgundy, France. Strongly influenced by the Italian Renaissance in France, but is also surrounded by a moat in the French tradition.

1550–69 Villa Capra, Vicenza, Italy.

c. 1550 University, Alcalà de Henares, Madrid, Spain.

c. 1550 Hakka houses, Fukien, China.

1550–57 Süleymaniye Camii, Istanbul, Turkey. This Ottoman imperial mosque was designed by the famous architect Mimar Sinan, as an architectural counterpoint to the Hagia Sophia—originally the chief church of Byzantium.

1550–80 Longleat House, Wiltshire, England.

1553 Hadimba Temple, Manali, Himachal Pradesh, India. A four-story structure with intricately carved wooden doors and a wooden *shikhara* (spire), it is typical of the pagoda-style temple architecture of the western Himalayas.

1554 Egeskov Slot, Funen, Denmark. A Renaissance water castle. The name Egeskov (oak forest) comes from the legend that it took an entire forest of oak trees to build the foundation in the middle of a lake.

RENAISSANCE: AN ARTISTIC EXPRESSION

In Italian it is *Rinascimento*, in Spanish *Renacimento*, while in England and Holland it is the French *Renaissance*. The words differ but the meaning is the same: rebirth.

The root of the Renaissance, some argue, is found in the intellectual challenge to the Christian orthodoxy that had dominated Europe since the fourth century. Renaissance scholars of the 14th century, inspired by the traditions of Ancient Greece and Rome, promoted the idea of man as an individual human being, important in his own right: man as the measure of all temporal things. It is a reflection of this view that Renaissance buildings are discussed in terms of their architects, whereas

previously the architect had been almost universally anonymous. With the Renaissance, the artist, whatever his medium, became an important member of society. That this Humanist philosophy should have been born in Italy is not surprising, for it had been the center of the Roman Empire, which itself had looked to Greece for inspiration.

The discovery of the manuscripts of the first century BCE architect and engineer Vitruvius (Marcus Vitruvius

Vitruvius

Pollio) in 1414 inspired the Classic Renaissance (Classical is the adjective describing attributes of Ancient Greece and Rome; Classicism is the noun; Classic refers to styles that reflect some of the characteristics of an original style, whether it is Classical, Romanesque, Byzantine, etc). His books were translated into many languages and certain architects and schools of architecture relied heavily on them. Because they were now available in book form they could travel fast and wide in a way that was impossible in the oral and handwritten tradition of the Middle Ages.

A view of the Vatican at night. Pope Julius asked Bramante for a new design for St Peter's. The work stopped after Bramante's death in 1514 and was resumed under Michelangelo's direction in 1547.

Filippo Brunelleschi (1377–1446) is generally considered to be the first Renaissance architect. His early work, like the Ospedale degli Innocenti (Foundlings Hospital), Florence (begun 1419), shows a new Classical approach with careful proportioning of parts and an overall sense of symmetry. In 1420 he brought all his mathematical skills and the knowledge he had gained from studying ancient Roman vaults to solve the problem of how to create a dome for the medieval Florence cathedral. It stands as one of the great engineering feats of the Renaissance.

Top: The Duomo, Florence, Italy.
Above left: Filippo Brunelleschi.
Right: Pazzi Chapel, Santa Croce, Florence, Italy, 1429–61,
by Brunelleschi.

St Basil the Blessed, Moscow, Russia. Begun by Ivan the Terrible, the cathedral church was designed by two Russian architects, Postnik and Barma. The fabulous coloring of the domes was completed in the 17th century.

Little Moreton Hall, Cheshire, England. Half-timbered houses were built for the expanding middle class who wanted ostentatious decoration without having to pay the higher prices for a similar effect in stone.

The Escorial, near Madrid, Spain. The architect Juan de Herrera (c. 1530–97) established a pure classical style to the point of severity, which was appropriate because the Escorial was a palace and a monastery which his patron, King Philip II, a renowned ascetic, used as a religious retreat.

Cathedral, Mexico City, Mexico. The present cathedral (which replaced a flat-roofed and primitive church built in 1525) is a fine mixture of the Baroque and Classical.

1554–1564

1554–1679 St Basil the Blessed, Moscow, Russia.

1555 Mattancherry Palace, Kerala, India. A mix of Portuguese and the local Nalakettu styles of architecture. The traditional Kerala flooring looks like polished black marble but is actually a mixture of burned coconut shells, charcoal, lime, plant juices, and egg whites.

1559 Little Moreton Hall, Cheshire, England.

1559 Laurentian Library, Florence, Italy. An archetype of Mannerist architecture designed by Michelangelo, and originally the private library of the Medici family. The high entrance hall has an extraordinary staircase with three varying flights of steps.

1559–84 The Escorial, near Madrid, Spain.

1562 Humayun's Tomb, Delhi, India. Example of a garden tomb in the subcontinent, with a Persian *charbagh* plan.

1563–1667 Cathedral, Mexico City, Mexico.

1564 Tuileries Palace, Paris, France. Built by Catherine de' Medici, the widow of Henry II, and designed by architect Philibert de l'Orme. The name comes from the tile

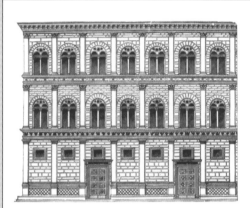

Leone Battista Alberti (1404–72) was chiefly responsible for formulating Renaissance architectural theory in his *Ten Books on Architecture*, itself based on the work of Vitruvius. Alberti's pioneering study helped to establish the status of architecture as an art, rather than a mere trade, as it had been viewed previously. He was a great disseminator of Classical forms and took Renaissance architecture from Florence to the rest of Italy, undertaking buildings in Rimini and Mantua.

Leone Battista Alberti

Left: Palazzo Rucellai, Florence, Italy, begun 1453, by Alberti.
Right: Santa Maria Novella, Florence, Italy, 1470, by Alberti.

The 16th century, the Cinquecento, was the great age of the Renaissance in Italy. Among the wealth of artists three stand above the others: Bramante, Raphael, and Michelangelo. Donato d'Agnolo Lazzari, known as Bramante (1444–1514), came from Urbino and made his reputation in Milan as a strict Classicist. He went to Rome and established himself as the leading architect of the day and, like Brunelleschi, was attracted to the symmetry of the circular church. He experimented with the form in his little temple, Il Tempietto (1502–10), erected in the cloister of San Pietro in Montorio, Rome. In 1505 it was to Bramante that Pope Julius turned for the new design for St Peter's and, in essence, Bramante's design is an elaboration of his work on Il Tempietto. Work started on St Peter's according to Bramante's plan, but his death in 1514 put the project on hold until Michelangelo took it up in 1547.

Bramante

Il Tempietto, San Pietro in Montorio, Rome, Italy, 1502–10, by Bramante.

San Giorgio Maggiore, Venice, Italy. One of the two great churches built by Andrea Palladio, the other being Il Redentore (1577–92).

Raja Birbal's House, Fatehpur Sikri, India. The Moghul emperor, Akbar (1556–1605), probably had this exquisite red sandstone house built as part of his harem.

Matsumoto Castle, Nagano, Japan. Also called Fakashi Castle, Matsumoto is one of only 12 Japanese castles with a multi-story *donjon*, or central fortified tower.

Villa Aldobrandini, Frascati, Italy. Architect Giacomo della Porta's hillside villa looks down majestically over the town of Frascati. The dramatic broken pediment, almost like book-ends in a library, emphasizes a classical balance.

1565–1599

kilns or tuileries which previously occupied the site. Three courtyards set within long, narrow buildings with high roofs, and a squared central dome.

1565 San Giorgio Maggiore, Venice, Italy.

1568 Church of the Gesù, Rome, Italy. "The first truly Baroque façade", this was the model for Jesuit churches all over the world. There is no narthex (entrance or lobby area of a church), just a single nave with arches leading to side chapels.

1572 Raja Birbal's House, Fatehpur Sikri, India.

1580 Red Lodge, Bristol, England. A red stone Tudor house, with lavish oak interiors and a wonderful Elizabethan-style knot garden.

1582 Matsumoto Castle, Nagano, Japan.

1594 Basilica of Bom Jesus, Old Goa, India. The basilica houses the mortal remains of St Francis Xavier. The exterior lime-plaster has been removed to expose the original laterite.

1594 Villa Aldobrandini, Frascati, Italy.

1599 Globe Theater, London, England. Shakespeare's theater was destroyed by fire in

85

MICHELANGELO

Michelangelo Buonarroti

Michelangelo Buonarroti (1475–1564) His work in Florence, particularly the Medici Mausoleum (1519–34), and the Biblioteca Laurenziana (1524–71), with their distortions of the strictly Classical, began the move to Mannerism, a transitional Renaissance style between High Renaissance and the Baroque. In 1547 Michelangelo began what he saw as his greatest work, St Peter's, Rome, on which he spent the last two decades of his life, refusing any payment. He abandoned Bramante's completely symmetrical plan for St Peter's in favor of a Latin cross, and although the basilica is much changed from Michelangelo's original concept, his is still the single greatest contribution. Michelangelo was also interested in large-scale civic works, mostly spectacularly represented by his complete remodeling of the Piazza del Campidoglio (Capitol Hill), Rome (begun in 1540), where he changed a jumble of buildings on a hill into an orderly square approached by a majestic flight of steps.

St Peter's Rome, Italy, with Bramante's plan of 1506 (left) and Michelangelo's plan of 1547 (right).

If Michelangelo had signaled Mannerism other architects of the later 16th century developed it more fully. The most influential was Giulio Romano (1499–1546), a pupil of Raphael, and the creator of the highly idiosyncratic Palazzo del Te (1525–32), Mantua, where novel decorative effect takes precedence over structural necessity. Sebastiano Serlio (1475–1554) is important for his impact (mainly through his treatises) on the Renaissance in France, particularly at Fontainebleau, which was the center of French Mannerism.

Shwe Dagon Pagoda, Yangon, Myanmar. Built over much older foundations and added to regularly, the Shwe Dagon is inspired by Indian stupas but adds its own elegance by elongating the stubby top-knot of the Indian originals into a soaring spire.

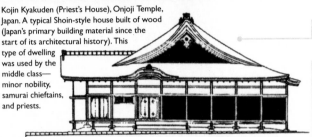

Kojin Kyakuden (Priest's House), Onjoji Temple, Japan. A typical Shoin-style house built of wood (Japan's primary building material since the start of its architectural history). This type of dwelling was used by the middle class—minor nobility, samurai chieftains, and priests.

Masjid-i-Shah (Royal Mosque), Isfahan, Iran. The Safavid dynasty reunited Iran in the early 16th century. Shah Abbas I (1587–1629) moved the capital to Isfahan and was responsible for planning its magnificent cityscape.

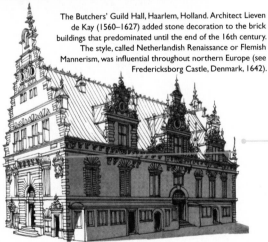

The Butchers' Guild Hall, Haarlem, Holland. Architect Lieven de Kay (1560–1627) added stone decoration to the brick buildings that predominated until the end of the 16th century. The style, called Netherlandish Renaissance or Flemish Mannerism, was influential throughout northern Europe (see Fredericksborg Castle, Denmark, 1642).

1600–1604

1613, though a modern reproduction exists. Originally a three-story, open-air amphitheater approximately 100 ft (30 m) in diameter, it could house up to 3,000 spectators.

c. 1600 Shwe Dagon Pagoda, Yangon, Myanmar.

c. 1600 Kojin Kyakuden (Priest's House), Onjoji Temple, Japan.

c. 1600 Masjid-i-Shah (Royal Mosque), Isfahan, Iran.

1600 Amisfield Tower, Scotland. Four- storied tower with turrets corbeled in the 'billet-and-cable' design, where the stonework imitates logs and rope.

1600 Virabhadra Temple, Lepakshi, Andhra Pradesh, India. Stone structure with pyramidal domed brick towers. Known for its ceiling frescoes and intricately carved columns as well as the large monolithic sculpted Nandi and Nagalinga.

1601 Chùa Thiên Mụ (Thien Mu Pagoda), Huế, Vietnam. Its octagonal 69 ft (21 m) brick tower has seven stories, and is the tallest in Vietnam.

1602 The Butchers' Guild Hall, Haarlem, Holland.

1604 Harmandir Sahib (Golden Temple) Amritsar, Punjab, India.

PALLADIO

Andrea Palladio

Above: Villa Capra, Vicenza, Italy, begun c. 1550, by Palladio.
Below: Cour des Adieux, Fontainebleau, France, 1528–40, by Gilles de Breton.

Andrea Palladio (1508–80) was the greatest architect of the second half of the 16th century, and his strict adherence to Classical Antiquity and the works of Vitruvius is the opposite of the indulgences of the Mannerists. He worked on domestic villas as well as churches in and around Venice. As influential as his buildings were his treatises, *The Four Books of Architecture* and *The Antiquities of Rome*, which were translated into many languages and had a profound impact on architects in France, England, Germany, and America. Two outstanding examples of his work are the Palazzo Chierricati (1550, but not completed until late in the 17th century) at Vicenza, and the Villa Capra (also known as the La Rotonda, c. 1550–69) outside Vicenza, which was to have a particularly powerful appeal to English Palladians of the 18th century. Two of his greatest churches are to be found within Venice itself: San Giorgio Maggiore (1565) and Il Redentore (1577-92).

France was the first European country outside Italy to adopt Renaissance forms, but it was not until the later part of the 16th century that native French architects began to build in the style. King François I was a pioneer patron of architecture, first at the Château of Blois and then at the Château of Chambord (begun 1519). In 1528 he decided to enlarge the medieval castle at Fontainebleau and entrusted Gilles le Breton with the task. The work was to have a decisive affect and encourage French architects to develop their own Renaissance style. One was Philibert de l'Orme (c. 1510-70), a descendant of a long line of master-masons who, with Jean Bullant (c. 1520-78), built the new Tuileries Palace in Paris (destroyed 1871). Pierre Lescot (c. 1510 or 1515-1578) is most famous for his work at the Louvre, again an initiative of François I, where Lescot created, for the first time in France, façades based on Italian lines.

Overleaf: Château de Blois, France.

Sultan Ahmed Mosque, Istanbul, Turkey. Begun 11 years after the death of the greatest Ottoman architect, Sinan, this monumental mosque is a tribute to his lasting influence.

Gold-plated domes and upper floors, and exquisite white marblework in this holiest of Sikh shrines, set in a tank of water.

1605–12 Place des Vosges, Paris, France. An early housing development with terraced houses laid out around a square.

1609–17 Sultan Ahmed Mosque, Istanbul, Turkey.

1613–18 Bodleian Library, Oxford, England. The entrance tower over the gateway is also known as the Tower of Five Orders, as it depicts columns from the five orders of Classical architecture in ascending order: Doric, Tuscan, Ionic, Corinthian, and Composite.

1614 Zuiderkirk, Amsterdam, Holland.

1615 Madrassa-e-Khan, Shiraz, Iran. Brilliant polychrome tilework in the traditional style of *moraq* (mosaic).

1616–35 The Queen's House, Greenwich, England.

1617 Nikkō Tōshō-gū, Nikkō, Japan. A five-storied Shinto shrine with painted carved gates. Each story of the pagoda represents a different element: earth, water, fire, wind, and heaven.

1618 Delft Town Hall, Holland.

Zuiderkirk, Amsterdam, Holland. The first church to be built in Amsterdam after the Reformation. The architect, Hendrik de Keyser (1565–1621) adopted a traditional plan but distinguished it with one of his specialties—the elegant tower. (See also Delft Town Hall, 1618.)

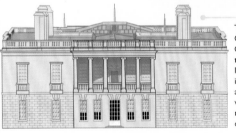

The Queen's House, Greenwich, England. Considered England's first truly Classical building. Inigo Jones (1573–1652), its architect, was a great admirer of Palladio and visited Italy to study and make detailed measurements of his buildings.

Delft Town Hall, Holland. Hendrik de Keyser (1565–1621) was a leading exponent of what is called the Netherlandish Renaissance or Flemish Mannerist school, which had a great influence on 17th-century building styles throughout northern Europe. (See also his Zuiderkirk, 1614.)

Château de Maison Lafitte, Paris, France. Designed by François Mansart, it is one of the best examples of French Baroque. Built on a rectangular platform and surrounded by a dry moat it comprises a central block with side wings and formal terraces.

Taj Mahal, Agra, India. Once described as "a tear on the face of eternity", the Taj was built by Shah Jahan as a mausoleum to his wife Mumtaz Mahal, who died giving birth to their 14th child. It took 20 years to build and was a huge drain on the traeasury.

Santa Maria della Salute, Venice, Italy. The church is one of the glories of the Baroque and was commissioned by the city (architect: Baldassare Longhena 1598–1682) as a thanksgiving for the end of a plague epidemic. The word 'Salute' here means 'health' as well as 'salvation'.

Mauritshuis, The Hague, Holland. Built for Prinz Johan Maurits van Nassau by Jacob van Campen (1595–1657). The house was much copied because van Campen used the limitation of plot size to create a beautifully self-contained Classical building, still much copied.

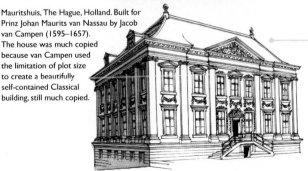

1630–1635

1630–33 Great Synagogue, Vilna, Lithuania. The local laws forbade a synagogue to be higher than a church, so this five-story building has two underground floors. Very little of it survives today.

1630–51 Château de Maison Lafitte, Paris, France.

1631–34 Dominikanerkirche, Vienna, Austria. The third successive church to be built on the same site, it has an impressive façade, topped by a large gable with a pediment.

1632 St Luke's Church (Old Brick Church) Virginia, USA. The oldest existing church of English foundation and the only surviving Gothic building in America, with a square tower, wall buttresses, and lancet-arched windows.

1631–53 Taj Mahal, Agra, India.

1632 Santa Maria della Salute, Venice, Italy.

1633 Naulakha Pavilion, Lahore Fort, Pakistan. A white marble rectangular structure with a curved roof, with exquisite pietra dura work.

1633 Mauritshuis, The Hague, Holland.

1635 Radziwill Palace, Vilnius, Lithuania. The only surviving Renaissance palace in Vilnius, it

Above: Detail of Town Hall in Delft, Netherlands, 1618. Built in the Flemish Mannerist or the Netherlands Renaissance style by Hendrik de Keyser (1565–1621).
Right: Town Hall in Antwerp built in the 16th century.

The Netherlands resisted full-blown Classicism until the end of the 16th century and tended to use Renaissance motifs primarily as decorative elements on medieval buildings—a style known as Flemish Mannerism, which was very influential in England. The outstanding 16th-century example is the Town Hall, Antwerp (1561–65) by Cornelius Floris (1514–75). As with England, a purer classical style did not emerge until the 17th century. Lieven de Key (1560–1627) and Hendrik de Keyser (1565–1621) were the leading architects of their day. De Key designed the Leyden Town Hall (1597) and the Butchers' Guild Hall, Haarlem (1602). De Keyser is best represented by the Amsterdam Exchange (1605), Delft Town Hall (1618), as well as three churches in Amsterdam: Zuiderkerk, Westkerk, and the Noorderkerk. The beginning of pure Renaissance, Classicism came in the second quarter of the 17th century with the advent of Dutch Palladianism, the chief example of which is the Mauritshuis at the Hague (1633) designed by Pieter Post (1608–69) and Jacob van Campen (1595–1657).

In Germany too, it was not until the 17th century that a true Renaissance style became established. The finest example is Elias Holl's (1573–1646) Augsburg Town Hall (1615–20). Holl had traveled to Italy and was a particular admirer of Palladio and Sansovino.

The Red Fort, Delhi, India. The Lal Qila (Red Fort) is a great citadel built by the creator of the Taj Mahal—Shah Jahan.

Fredericksborg Castle, Denmark. The first Renaissance palace built in Scandinavia. The Dutch style is evident with its exuberant towers, gables, turrets, and dormers (see the Butchers' Guild Hall, Haarlem, Holland, 1602).

Val-de-Grâce Church, Paris, France. Begun by F Mansart (1598–1666) but taken over after one year by Jacques Lemercier (c. 1585–1654) who had established himself as the state architect under the patronage of Cardinal Richelieu.

Potala Palace, Lhasa, Tibet. Founded by Ngawang Lobzang Gyatso, the fifth Dalai Lama. The White Palace went up first (1645–48) followed by the central Red Palace (1690–93). More additions were made by later Dalai Lamas, particularly in the 18th century.

1639–1649

combines features of the Netherlands Renaissance with the Manneristic elements of Lithuanian Renaissance architecture.

1639 Brühl Palace, Warsaw, Poland, an excellent example of the Rococo style in Poland.

1639–48 The Red Fort, Delhi, India.

1642 Fredericksborg Castle, Denmark.

1644–46 Bara Katra, Dhaka, Bangladesh. Laid out according to the typical design of a caravanserai (roadside inn) with a courtyard surrounded by shops. It has two gateways, one of them being the main entrance, with three stories and an arched alcove decorated with intricate plasterwork.

1645 St Werburgh's Church, Warburton, England. Though dating to the 13th century it was rebuilt in the 17th century. It has a timber frame with some parts in sandstone, some in brick, and others with wattle and daub. The roof has stone slabs.

1645–67 Val-de-Grâce Church, Paris, France.

1645–93 Potala Palace, Lhasa, Tibet.

1649 The Old House, Southold, New York. Known as 'one of the most distinguished

In England Henry VIII encouraged Italian craftsmen, but his break with the Church of Rome delayed the introduction of Renaissance architectural styles. More influential in England was Flemish Mannerism with its emphasis on surface decoration. The great houses of the period (there was not much ecclesiastical building) are a lively mixture of Elizabethan structures

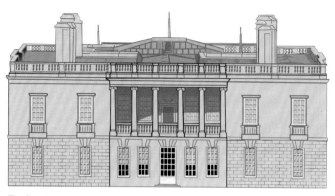

The Queen's House, Greenwich, England, 1616–35, by Inigo Jones.

and Renaissance decoration. Prominent examples are Longleat (1550-80); Hardwick Hall (1591-97), Montacute (1588-1601); and Wollaton Hall (1580-85). It was Inigo Jones (1573-1652), the first truly professional architect in England, who brought the Italian Renaissance to England after having traveled in Italy, where he was greatly influenced by Palladio. His outstanding buildings are the Queen's House (1616-22), Greenwich, and the Banqueting Hall (1619-22), Whitehall, London.

On the Iberian peninsula there were three stages of Renaissance architecture. The first, Renaissance Plateresque (the word comes from the decoration on silver plate), saw the application of surface decoration to what were still medieval-style buildings (the façade of Salamanca University, 1516-29, and the Palacio Municipal at Baeza in southern Spain, 1559, are notable). The second stage retained the rich decoration of the Plateresque but moved towards Renaissance construction (examples are the Ayuntamiento [town hall], Seville [1534-72]; Luna Palace [now the Audiencia], Zaragosa, 1537-52; and the University of Alcalà de Henares near Madrid, c. 1550). The third stage was of a much purer Classical expression and mainly built in the late 16th and early 17th centuries. The architect most responsible for establishing this style was Juan de Herrera (c. 1530-97) who had studied in Italy. His most famous work is the Escorial Palace (1559-84) outside Madrid, a building of awesome severity. Juan Gómez de Mora (1586-1647) followed in Herrera's tradition. His finest achievement is the Plaza Mayor, Madrid, 1617-20 (though initially planned by Herrera).

Previous page: Azay-le-Rideau, France, 1518–29.
Below: Ayuntamiento (town hall), Seville, Spain, begun 1534, by Diego de Riaño.

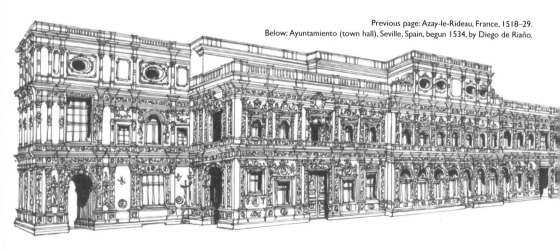

Interior of Rinshunkaku, built originally at Wakayama, now at Yokohama, Japan. A fine example of the Shoin-style house that a samurai family would have lived in. This one was commissioned by a member of the Tokugawa clan, the ruling shogunate until 1868.

Palais de Versailles, France. Louis XIV was an autocrat in every aspect of public life, particularly in architecture, and ensured that his vision was enshrined in his buildings. Louis Le Vau (1612–70) was primarily responsible for the central section. Jules Hardouin-Mansart (1646–1708) added the Galerie de Glace and the de Lotte.

Les Invalides, Paris, France. Designed by Libéral Bruand (1635–97) as a hospital for 4,000 disabled veterans. The church was by Jules Hardouin-Mansart (1646–1708, see also Versailles, 1669). In 1840 the body of Napoleon Bonaparte was brought back from St Helena for interment here.

St Paul's Cathedral, London, England. After the Great Fire of 1666 it was impossible to salvage the old St Paul's. Sir Christopher Wren (1632–1723) prepared two designs which were rejected before the final plan was accepted. However, during the course of construction Wren made many modifications.

1649–1675

surviving examples of English domestic architecture in America'.

1649 Interior of Rinshunkaku, built originally at Wakayama, now at Yokohama, Japan.

1650–56 Jama Masjid, Delhi, India. A historic and grand mosque, it is 261 ft (80 m) long and 90 ft (27 m) wide, while the two minarets are 130 ft (41 m) high. The three domes have alternate stripes of black and white marble.

1661–82 Palais de Versailles, France.

1669 Hasht Behesht (Eight Paradises) Palace, Isfahan, Iran. Timurid in inspiration, a central domed space is flanked by four octagonal rooms opening out to large porches on three sides, and an *iwan* (vaulted hall) in the north.

1671–1708 Les Invalides, Paris, France.

1672 Bonde Palace, Stockholm, Sweden. An H-shaped plan with the central building covered by a tall steep-pitched, copper dressed roof. The façade has Ionic pillars, festoons, and portraits of Roman emperors.

1675–1710 St Paul's Cathedral, London. England.

95

BAROQUE: THEATRICS IN ARCHITECTURE

The word Baroque derives from the Portuguese *barroco*, for 'misshapen pearl' (Spanish *barrueco*) and, like Gothic, was originally a derogatory term referring to what was seen as the bizarre, sometimes bulbous, curves that characterized the style.

The Baroque originated in Italy, more specifically Rome, as an expression of the religious fervor associated with the Catholic Counter-Reformation, and it was in other European Catholic countries that it had the most impact, particularly Spain, Portugal (and through them their South American colonial possessions), Bavaria, Austria, and France.

Its main characteristics were the free use of curves within a classical framework; the use of dramatic lighting effects; and the combination of painting and sculpture to create the 'theater' of the architectural experience, often using *trompe l'oeil* ('cheating the eye') painting techniques. At its best the Baroque is rich, sensuous, and dramatic; at its worst, insufferably hysterical.

Top: Detail of the imposing Abbey of Melk on the River Danube in Austria, remodeled in 1702 by the architect Jacob Prandtauer.
Above: Palais de Versailles, France, 1669, built by Louis XIV.
Overleaf: The baldacchino at St Peter's, Rome designed by Bernini (1598–1680).

Clemence Irons House, Johnston, Rhode Island, USA. The extensions to the left and right are later additions. The stone chimney was originally built into the end wall. The walls were clad in shingles—tile-like pieces of wood that overlapped each other.

Parson Capon House, Topsfield, Massachusetts, USA. The second story overhang and the grouped chimneys are a direct reference to the English Elizabethan houses that were the model for many early American Colonial dwellings.

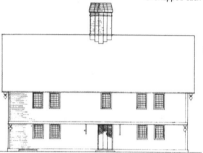

Groot Constantia, Cape Province, South Africa. Built for Simon van der Stel (1639–1712), the first governor of the Cape Colony, Groot Constantia became a blueprint for Cape Dutch houses of wealthier landowners.

Grand Place, Brussels, Belgium. A wonderful exuberance of Baroque, tall slender façades fitting into the small land plots of their medieval predecessors.

1677–1691

1677 Clemence Irons House, Johnston, Rhode Island, USA.

1678–79 Moor Park, Hertfordshire, England. This mansion is an example of the Palladian style, popular in 17th-century England.

1683 Parson Capon House, Topsfield, Massachusetts, USA.

1684 Old Indian Meeting House, Mashpee, Massachusetts, USA. The oldest extant Native American church in the USA, built in a Colonial, Greek Revival style.

1685 Groot Constantia, Cape Province, South Africa.

1689 Basílica de Nuestra Señora de Zapopan, Mexico. Franciscan church with a large vestibule with Ionic columns and sculptured reliefs. Houses an important collection of art.

1690s Grand Place, Brussels, Belgium.

1691 Canongate Kirk, Edinburgh, Scotland. The Kirk has a Dutch-style end gable and a Doric portico. Although rectangular on the exterior, the interior has a cruciform layout, very unusual for a post-Reformation, pre-Victorian building of the Church of Scotland.

Schönbrunn Palace, Vienna, Austria. Fischer von Erlach (1656–1723) became the official architect to the Imperial Court at Vienna. His original design (even more ambitious and flamboyant than the final building) was finished by his son, Josef Emmanuel.

Castle Howard, Yorkshire, England. The architect, Sir John Vanbrugh (1664–1726) was first a soldier and playwright before turning to architecture at the age of 35. Castle Howard was his first commission (and a stupendous undertaking for an inexperienced architect).

Annamese floating houses, Vietnam. The itinerant people of the Annam mountain lakes built their dwellings on rafts so they could be towed to different parts of the lake. Local hardwoods make them rot-resistant and the thatched roofs reduce the effects of humidity.

Melk Abbey, Austria. Jacob Prandtauer (1660–1726) extensively reconstructed an existing medieval building to create this magnificent Baroque landmark perched high over a bend of the Danube.

1695–1703

1695 Schönbrunn Palace, Vienna, Austria.

1698–1707 Stadtschloss, Berlin, Germany. An impressive example of Baroque classicism, this palace was destroyed in World War II.

1699–1777 Castle Howard, Yorkshire, England.

c. 1700–present Annamese floating houses, Vietnam.

1700 Gondhla Fort, Lahaul, Himachal Pradesh, India. The eight-story riverside fort was built in the indigenous timber bonded stone style of the western Himalayas, with alternate layers of stone and wooden beams cemented together with wet clay. The building is topped by a wooden veranda running all the way round the upper story.

1701–04 New Schleissheim Palace, Bavaria, Germany. One of three palaces set in a large garden. Contains some of the most important examples of German Baroque architecture in its Grand Hall, Grand Gallery, Maximilian's Chapel, and the four state apartments.

1702 Melk Abbey, Austria.

1703–1920s Buckingham Palace, London, England. The official London residence of the British monarch by John

Sant'Agnese, begun 1652, Piazza Navona, Rome, Italy, by Rainaldi and Borromini.

Two of the greatest exponents of Baroque were Gianlorenzo Bernini (1598–1680) and Francesco Borromini (1599–1667). Both were painters, architects, and poets, but considered sculpture as their true calling. In 1629 Bernini became architect of St Peter's, Rome, and designed the baldacchino (canopy) over the high altar. He also built the great embracing double-curve arms of the colonnaded piazza in front of St Peter's. In 1645 he designed the sensationally theatrical Cornaro Chapel in Santa Maria della Vittoria, Rome, and between 1648 and 1651 laid out the fountains of Piazza Navona, Rome. His finest work is Sant'Andrea al Quirinale (1658–70), which was to have a great impact on Baroque church building in central Europe.

Borromini went much further than Bernini in challenging Classical norms. San Carlo alle Quattro Fontane (1638–40) was his first church and it caused a sensation. He went on to remodel St John Lateran and created a fine Baroque exterior for Sant'Agnese in the Piazza Navona (1652–56). His use of opposing curves was an important influence on the exuberant Rococo of southern Germany and Austria.

The last great buildings of Venice were also influenced by the Baroque. A good example is the Salute Church, Venice (1632) by Baldassare Longhena (1598–1682), with its dome seemingly supported on elaborate scrolls. The dome for the Chapel of the Holy Shroud, Turin, by Guarino Guarini (1624–83) deserves its place among the Baroque masterworks of Italy.

Blenheim Palace, Oxfordshire, England. The palace was a gift to the great soldier, the Duke of Marlborough, from a grateful nation. The only problem was that his formidable wife, Sarah, detested the architect, Sir John Vanbrugh (1664–1726), and banned him from the site! After Vanbrugh's death the house was completed by Nicholas Hawksmoor (1661–1736).

Mission Church, Santa Anna Pueblo, New Mexico, USA. The irregular outline is due to the constant erosion by wind and rain of the adobe construction.

Cathedral of Sts Peter and Paul, St Petersburg, Russia. Built within a fortress on an island on the River Neva, and the burial church of the czars. The architect Domenico Tressini (1670–1734) was the first important architect employed by Peter the Great.

Cape Cod cottage, Massachusetts, USA. These cottages are as sturdy as a well-made ship. Indeed, they were constructed to withstand the gales pounding in from the northeast. The rooms were clustered around a central chimney that could contain as many as four separate fireplaces.

Upper Belvedere, Vienna, Austria. Architect Lucas von Hildebrandt (1668–1745) was half Austrian, half Italian, and infused the building (for Prince Eugene of Savoy) with what has been described as a mixture of Teutonic discipline and Mediterranean charm.

Nash comprises three wings around a central courtyard. The interior has an ornate suite of state rooms, including the Green Drawing Room and the Throne Rome.

1705–24 Blenheim Palace, Oxfordshire, England.

1708 Intercession Church, Vytegra, Russia. A traditional wooden church of north Russia, built by carpenters working without hammer and nails. Burnt in an accidental fire in 1963.

1710–20 Mission Church, Santa Anna Pueblo, New Mexico, USA.

1711–22 Zwinger, Dresden, Germany. Extravagantly decorated pavilions with the Kronentor, a Baroque gate topped by a large crown with statues representing the four seasons.

1714–25 Cathedral of Sts Peter and Paul, St Petersburg, Russia.

c. 1715 Torre Tagle Palace, Lima, Peru. A stone and plaster façade. Sevillian tiles, Moorish arches, and two finely carved *miradors* (balconies) in dark wood show the blend of European Baroque and local Peruvian tradition.

1720 Cape Cod cottage, Massachusetts, USA.

1721–23 Upper Belvedere, Vienna, Austria.

France produced some exceptional Baroque architecture, if more tempered and less excitable than its Italian neighbor. The chief architect of the early 17th century was Salomon de Brosse (1571–1626) whose pre-eminent work is the Palais de Luxembourg (started 1614) built for Marie de' Medici, wife of Louis XIII. The middle years of the 17th century saw the rise of a number of great French architects: Jacques Lemercier, c. 1585–1654 (Church of the Sorbonne, Paris, and the church of the University of Paris); François Mansart, 1598–1666 (the Baroque central block of the Château de Blois, the church of Val de Grâce, Paris, completed by Lemercier); Louis Le Vau, 1612–70 (Institut de France in refined Baroque, Château de Vaux-le-Vicomte, and substantial parts of Versailles); Jules Hardouin-Mansart, 1646–1708 (church of St-Louis des Invalides, the Place Vendôme, and Place des Victoires, as well as extensive work at Versailles, particularly the royal chapel, stables, Orangery, and Grand Trianon).

Above: The garden front, Château Vaux-le-Vicomte, France, by Louis Le Vau. Right: Les Invalides, Paris, France, 1671–1708. Instituted by Libéral Bruand as a hospital for 4,000 disabled veterans. The dome was designed by Jules Hardouin-Mansart.

Bom Jesus do Monte, Braga, Portugal. Like many pilgrimage churches in Portugal it is at the top of a hill reached by long flights of stairs adorned with many sculptural details—no doubt designed to make the visitor who has to climb them reflect on the redemptive nature of suffering!

Chiswick House, London. Lord Burlington (1694–1753) was the most influential of the aristocratic patron / architects of the 18th century. During his two trips to Italy he was greatly influenced by Palladio, and Chiswick House owes much to Palladio's Villa Capra near Vicenza (see 1550).

Santiago de Compostela, Spain. During the 18th century Baroque elements were often added to medieval buildings (the original cathedral at Santiago was begun in 1077). The architect of these Baroque 'improvements' was Fernando Casas y Nuova.

The Royal Palace, Madrid, Spain. In 1734 the old fortress-like palace was destroyed by fire and the king commissioned Filippo Juvara (1678–1736) of Turin, Italy, to build a new one. Juvara died soon after work began and his plan was executed on a more modest scale by Giovanni Battista Sacchetti (1700–64).

1721–1738

1721–32 El Transparente, Toledo Cathedral, Spain. A wall of marble and florid Baroque alabaster sculpture depicting the Last Supper and the Virgin in Ascension behind the church's main altar, illuminated by a skylight in the vaulted ceiling.

1723 Bom Jesus do Monte, Braga, Portugal.

1723 Mereworth Castle, Kent, England. Designed by Colin Campbell, it is modeled on Palladio's Villa Rotonda, and has a windowless central hall and portico. It is situated in a landscaped valley and surrounded by a moat.

1725 Chiswick House, London.

1726–40 Frauenkirche, Dresden, Germany. Designed by George Bahr in the German Baroque style. In an engineering feat, a 12,000 ton sandstone dome soared to a height of 314 ft (96 m). Destroyed in World War II, the church was reconstructed later.

1738 Façade of Santiago de Compostela, Spain.

1738–64 The Royal Palace, Madrid, Spain.

1738 Lungshan Temple, Taiwan. Built by immigrants from Fukien Province as a branch of the original Lungshan

THE BAROQUE IN ENGLAND

In England the outstanding architect of this period, and perhaps the greatest of any period of English history, was Sir Christopher Wren (1632–1723). His most famous work is, of course, St Paul's Cathedral, London (1675–1710) with its restrained Baroque features. He was also responsible for a large number of London churches (St Bride's, Fleet Street, 1680–1701; St Stephen Walbrook, 1675–87; and St Lawrence Jewry, 1670–86, are outstanding examples). Wren's finest secular works are the Royal Hospital, Greenwich (completed 1752), a "palace of Baroque monumentality", and the Royal Hospital, Chelsea (1682–92). Other significant architects of the time were Sir John Vanbrugh (1664–1726) and Nicholas Hawksmoor (1661–1736). Vanbrugh, playwright, soldier, and wit (though, like many, not a formally trained architect), designed Castle Howard, Yorkshire (1699–1712). At Blenheim Palace (1705–22) Vanbrugh was allowed free rein and the huge edifice stands as the pinnacle of English Baroque. Nicholas Hawksmoor had worked with Wren on many of his greatest projects and assisted Vanbrugh on Castle Howard and Blenheim. He is best remembered for six highly original churches in London, of which Christ Church, Spitalfields (1714–29) is probably the finest.

St Paul's Cathedral and plan, begun 1675, London, England, by Sir Christopher Wren. Facing page: The west façade of the cathedral.

104

Above: Interior of the cathedral at Passau, Germany, built in the Italian Baroque style, c. early 18th century.
Below: The Zwinger, Dresden, Germany, 1711–20, by Daniel Pöppelman.

Germany had suffered terribly during the Thirty Years War (1618–48) and Austria was under pressure from invading Turks until the 1680s. As a consequence, the Baroque did not fully develop in these countries until about 1700, but once it did there was a flowering of some of the greatest Baroque building in Europe. At first it was architects of Italian origin—Barelli, Zuccali, Viscardi—who worked in Italian Baroque forms (typical examples are the Cathedral of Passau and the Theatinerkirche, Munich). Of Austro-German architects the outstanding practitioners were: Matthias Daniel Pöppelman (1662–1736) in Dresden (The Zwinger, 1711–20); Balthasar Neumann (1687–1753) in Würzburg (the Residenz, 1719–53 in collaboration with the painter Tiepolo, and, perhaps his masterpiece, the Vierzehnheiligen Pilgrimage Church, Franconia, of 1743–62); the Austrian Johann Bernard Fischer von Erlach (1656–1723) in Vienna (Karlskirche, 1716; the Palace of Schönbrunn—the Versailles of Austria; National Library, begun 1722; Imperial Chancellery wing of the Hofburg, 1729); Lucas von Hilderbrandt (1668–1745) in Vienna (Upper Belevedere, 1721–23); and Jacob Prandtauer (1660–1726), whose chief building was the remodeling of the great Abbey of Melk on the River Danube in 1702.

In Spain and Portugal, following the austerity of the early Renaissance, Baroque was adopted with a passion. One of the greatest monuments to Spanish Baroque is the Transparente altar in Toledo Cathedral (1721–32) by Narciso Tomé (c. 1694–1742), which has been described as a "fricassee of marble." But even this was mild compared to the work of José de Churriguera (1650–1725) and his family and followers (Pedro de Ribera's Hospicio San Fernando, Madrid, begun 1722, and Francisco Izquierdo's sacristy in the Cartuja, Granada, 1713, are good examples of Churrigueresque, as the high-octane decorative style was called).

Rococo (from the French *rocaille* or seashell) was a lighter and more playful extension of the Baroque. It originated in France and was taken up enthusiastically in Germany, Austria, and Russia, but had little impact in Protestant Europe or America. The French architect François Cuvilliés (1695–1768) was one of the leading designers in the idiom, especially in Bavaria where he was court architect. His Amalienburg hunting lodge of the Nymphenburg Palace, Munich (1734–39) is a Rococo jewel.

The Radcliffe Camera, Oxford, England. In 1714 Dr Radcliffe left provision in his will for the University of Oxford to build a library (architect: James Gibbs (1682–1754). The cylindrical building, covered with a cupola, was much influenced by the buildings he had seen in Rome when he had lived there as a young man.

Peterhof, near St Petersburg, Russia. The original building was designed in 1716–17 by Jean-Baptiste Le Blond (1679–1719) but was then remodeled by Bartolommeo Rastrelli (1700–71) for Elizabeth, Peter the Great's daughter, who had become Empress of Russia in 1741. (See also Winter Palace 1754–56.)

King's Chapel, Boston, Massachusetts, USA. Designed by Peter Harrison (1716–75), a self-taught architect who had been born in England but emigrated to America in 1740. Built in stone and much grander than other Colonial-era churches, King's Chapel is the first in New England to depart from the tradition of church as austere meetinghouse.

Navaho stone hogan, New Mexico, USA. Hogans began as turf-built conical dwellings but by the mid-18th century had dry-stone walls and turf-covered roofs supported on a lattice of stout poles.

1739–1750

Temple in Fukien. Three large halls contain ornate dragon pillars, remarkable wooden carvings, a well, and a shrine.

1739–49 The Radcliffe Camera, Oxford, England.

1744 Vierzehnheiligen Church, Germany. The exterior has the form of a basilica with a twin-tower façade. The plan consists of overlapping ovals separated by three-dimensional transverse arches which create an impression of infinite space.

1747–52 Peterhof, near St Petersburg, Russia.

1749 Liverpool Town Hall, Liverpool, England. This elegant stone building has two fronts, each with a row of Corinthian columns supporting a pediment. On the pediment of the grand front is a sculpture representing Commerce, and mounted on the dome on the roof is a 10-ft (3-m) high statue of Minerva, the Roman goddess of wisdom, covered in gold leaf.

1749–58 King's Chapel, Boston, Massachusetts, USA.

c. 1750 Navaho stone hogan, New Mexico, USA.

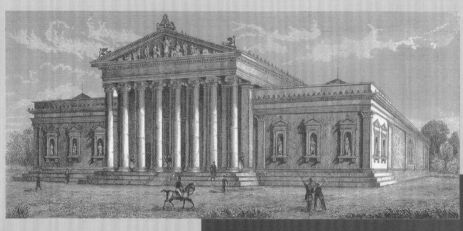

THE PALLADIAN MOVEMENT

The turn to strict Classical forms in European and American architecture involved many factors, but foremost was the realization that Baroque and Rococo had only one way to go—towards greater and greater elaboration—until its inevitable expiration in a swirl of clouds and cherubim. The mid-18th century witnessed the emergence of archaeology and with it a renewed interest in the ancient civilizations of Egypt, Greece, and Rome: the birthplaces of the Classical (Napoleon's campaigns in Egypt also stimulated a huge passion for things *Egyptienne*). In an Age of Reason the Classical order seemed a suitable outward expression of control, something the use of Classical forms in the French Revolution and later under Napoleon only served to reinforce. In France we can see such examples as the Ste-Geneviève, Paris (1756, renamed the Panthéon) by Jacques-Germain Soufflot (1713–80), and the Temple de la Gloire, Paris (1806, renamed the Madeleine in 1813) by Alexandre-Pierre Vignon (1762–1828).

In England the Palladian movement also championed Classical principles. Leading proponents were patron and architect Lord Burlington (1694–1753) whose Chiswick House (1723–29), has been called the "manifesto of English

Far Left: The Glyptothek, Munich, Germany, begun 1815, by Leo von Klenze.
Left: The Panthéon, Paris, France, 1756, by Jacques-Germain Soufflot.
Below: Tympanum from the Temple de la Gloire, Paris, built in 1806 by Alexandre-Pierre Vignon (1762-1828). It was renamed the Madeleine Church in 1813.

VOC·S·M·MAGDALENAE

Above: Chiswick House, England, 1725, by Lord Burlington.
Below: Schauspielhaus, Berlin, Germany, 1819–21, designed by Karl Friedrich Schinkel.

Palladians"; William Kent (1685-1748) represented by Holkham Hall (begun 1734); Robert Adam (1728-92) by Kenwood House (1767-68) and Syon House (1761-70); and the remodeling of Regent's Park and other parts of central London by John Nash (1752-1835).

Some of the most outstanding Neo-Classical works of the early 19th century were to be found in Germany: the Glyptothek, Munich (1815-34) by Leo von Klenze (1784-1864), and perhaps the greatest of all, Karl Friedrich Schinkel (1781-1841) who, apart from being the architect of genius of his age, was also a painter, stage-designer, intellectual, and gifted draughtsman. His Neue Wache (New Guard House, Berlin, 1816-18), the Schauspielhaus (1819-21), and the Altes Museum, his masterwork (1823-30), were built for the Prussian state as national treasures.

North America. As might be expected Colonial America took its architectural lead from England. On the Eastern Seaboard buildings had the simple integrity of the Puritan founders, while in Virginia, where the English settlers had come from more aristocratic origins, the principal buildings tended to be more grandiose. Both, however, reflected the influence of their

Winter Palace, St Petersburg, Russia. The empress Elizabeth commissioned Bartolommeo Rastrelli (1700–71), the leading architect working in Russia at the time, to build an immense palace on the banks of River Neva. He was also to build her two other great palaces, at Petrodvorets and Tsarkoe Selo.

The Panthéon, Paris, France. When Louis XV fell ill in 1744 he vowed that if he recovered he would replace Ste Geneviève Abbey with a grander edifice. The result is one of the great masterpieces of Neo-Classicism, a return to simple, monumental symmetry: the Panthéon, designed by Germain Soufflot (1714–80).

Monticello, Virginia, USA. Thomas Jefferson (1743–1826), third president of the USA, was also one of its most influential architects. He was American Minister to France (1785–89) and his travels in Europe filled him with admiration for Classicism, particularly that of Palladio. Monticello was begun when he was only 24 but he continued to work on it for the rest of his life. Although a Classicist, Jefferson loved modern conveniences—he put toilets on each floor and had a wine hoist from the basement directly to the dining room!

Mount Vernon, Virginia, USA. The original house was built by George Washington's father in a simple 'Elizabethan medieval' style. George Washington bought the property in 1752 and added a story for his bride, Martha Custis. In 1774 he began the extensive changes we see today. This view, from the lawn side, shows the niggling disorder of the windows that disrupt the symmetry.

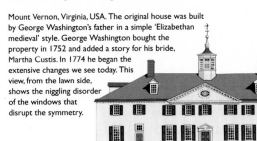

1752–1774

1752 Regia di Caserta, Caserta, Italy. Enormous Baroque palace with 1,200 rooms, 24 state apartments, and a royal theater, designed by Luigi Vanvitelli.

1754 Kordopulova Kashta, Melnik, Bulgaria. A large house built for wine production. Two floors are of stone and two of wood. The lower windows are Bulgarian in style, while the higher ones of Venetian glass, showing a unique mix of Venetian and Ottoman styles.

1754–56 Winter Palace, St Petersburg, Russia.

1755–64 Chinesisches Haus, Sanssouci Park, Potsdam, Germany. A garden pavilion designed by the architect Johann Gottfried Büring in the popular Chinoiserie style.

1756–92 The Panthéon (formerly Ste Genevieve), Paris, France.

1769–1826 Monticello, Virginia, USA.

1770 Yusopov Palace, St Petersburg, Russia. This colonnaded palace is famous as the site of Grigori Rasputin's murder in 1916. An interesting highlight is the 180-seat Rococo private theater and the tiled Moorish Room.

1774–86 Mount Vernon, Virginia, USA.

INVOC·

Mount Vernon, Virginia, USA, 1774-86, by George Washington.

colonial overlord, with the town of Williamsburg (though now much restored) as the single greatest monument of the Colonial era. It was not until the 18th century that named American (though often English-born) architects began to appear: people like Peter Harrison (1716-75), the builder of King's Chapel, Boston (1749) among others. Thomas Jefferson (1743-1826) was not only one of the co-authors of the Declaration of Independence and the third president of the fledgling republic but also a superb Classically-inspired architect, as attested by his own home at Monticello (begun 1769); the State Capitol of Virginia (1785-99); and the University of Virginia (1817-26). Charles Bullfinch (1763-1844) was also an architect inspired by the Classical (Massachusetts State House, 1793-1800), as was another English-born architect, Benjamin Henry Latrobe (1764-1820), the first Surveyor of Public Buildings in the USA, who had advised Jefferson on the University of Virginia and worked on the Capitol, Washington, DC. His finest building is probably the Roman Catholic Cathedral of Baltimore (1804-18).

Thomas Jefferson

Virginia State Capitol, USA, center building, 1785–92, by Thomas Jefferson (wings added 1904–06).

Petrovsky Palace, Moscow, Russia. To celebrate Catherine II's victory over the Turks MF Kazakov (1738–1813) was commissioned to build a palace which combined a Classical plan with a mixture of Gothic and traditional Russian styles (like the bulbous columns along the base).

Turkanoan Clan House, Amazonia, Colombia. The *maloca* is a rectangular building (about 100 ft / 30 m long) that housed a number of families who lived in enclosed spaces at the rear. Men only used the center and front. The façade is decorated with religious symbols.

The Capitol, Washington, DC, USA. The first building was designed by William Thornton (1759–1828), an amateur architect from England, much influenced by Palladio. During the war of 1812 the British badly damaged the building and it was restored first by Benjamin Latrobe (1764–1820) and then Thomas Ustick Walter (1804–88), who designed the flanking wings and central rotunda.

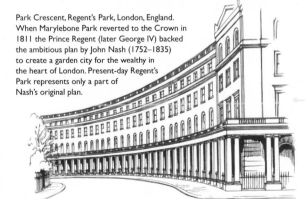

Park Crescent, Regent's Park, London, England. When Marylebone Park reverted to the Crown in 1811 the Prince Regent (later George IV) backed the ambitious plan by John Nash (1752–1835) to create a garden city for the wealthy in the heart of London. Present-day Regent's Park represents only a part of Nash's original plan.

1775–1815

1775 Midford Castle, Somerset, England. A 'folly castle' with three conjoined semi-circular towers in a trefoil plan.

1775–82 Petrovsky Palace, Moscow, Russia.

1777 Catedral de San Cristóbal de La Havana, Havana, Cuba. Baroque cathedral set in the former Swamp Plaza. One of the towers is deliberately wider than the other to allow the water that tended to accumulate on the plaza to flow through the streets.

c. 1790–present Turkanoan Clan House, Amazonia, Colombia.

1793–1867 The Capitol, Washington, DC, USA.

1799 Hawa Mahal (Palace of the Winds), Jaipur, India. Built in the shape of the crown of Krishna, the red and pink sandstone building has a ventilated honeycomb-like façade with 953 small windows. From here the royal women observed city processions without being seen themselves.

1804 Kemper Log House, Cincinnati, Ohio, USA. A traditional handcrafted log house made from unmilled logs.

1812–27 Park Crescent, Regent's Park, London, England.

1815–23 Brighton Pavilion, Brighton, England. A

Reading Room, Bibliothèque Nationale, Paris, France, begun 1854, by Henri Labrouste.

THE INDUSTRIAL AGE

Towards the end of the 18th century two political revolutions—the American and the French—as well as the onset of the Industrial Revolution—set in motion forces that would transform our world to an extent unprecedented in recorded history. Now at the beginning of the 21st century we are so conscious of the enormous changes of the past few decades that it is sometimes difficult to accept that these earlier revolutions were far greater yet. For the first time in history communications were not limited to the speed of a horse or a wind-driven sailing vessel. Steam-powered machinery revolutionized transportation, communications, and manufacturing, and by the 1830s the transformation of western societies from static to dynamic was well underway. For example, nails used in building construction were no longer forged by hand but produced by machines a hundred times faster. Wrought iron became available for structural use in buildings, and by the 1880s steel made possible the structural cage—skeleton construction—that freed walls from their traditional task of supporting floors and roofs.

Above: Traditional meets the Modern: the Plaza Hotel, 1907, by Henry J Hardenbergh, and 9 West 57th Street, New York, USA, 1972, by Skidmore, Owings & Merrill.
Left: St Pancras Station, London, England.

In response to these enormous changes it would have been only natural to see the emergence of a new and revolutionary kind of architecture. What happened instead was a retreat into eclecticism: the copying of the outward forms of past historical styles so that by the mid-19th century it appeared as if an architect's first decision on a project was whether to imitate Gothic or Classical forms. While Gothic had some forceful advocates (notably AWN Pugin, 1812–52, in England) it was Classical that became the dominant architectural style. All over the world, irrespective of the building's function, the

Houses of Parliament, London, England, 1836–65.

local climate, or any other considerations, many public buildings were sheathed in the respectability of Classical forms.

Modern architecture came into being as a reaction against this retrograde nostalgia. It sought to create a new architectural language that reflected the changing needs of society and of the materials and building technologies that had become available. In the later stages of its evolution, Modernist architecture became increasingly concerned with responding to local climate.

In the centuries-old traditional way of building (which culminated in the 1820s), technology had remained essentially unchanged. The load-bearing envelope was the defining characteristic of the

Piazza Vittorio Veneto, Turin, Italy. Turin, close to France, had always felt its neighbor's architectural influence. Central Turin, designed by Giuseppe Frizzi and Carlo Promis, reflects that proximity in its great squares and arcaded streets.

Schauspielhaus, Berlin, Germany. Designed by Karl Friedrich Schinkel (1781–1841) in a very boldly stated Neo-Classical style.

Altes Museum, Berlin, Germany. Another great example of Neo-Classicism. Schinkel's design is often compared to the British Museum in London (Sir Robert Smirke 1781–1867) and built almost at the same time. The Altes Museum is superior in its bold handling of Classical forms and the execution of its detailing.

Houses of Parliament, London, England. Much of the original medieval Palace of Westminster burnt down in 1834. Ninety-six architects submitted plans for a replacement building and Sir Charles Barry (1795–1860) won the competition with his elegantly simple Perpendicular Gothic design that blended sympathetically with the nearby medieval Westminster Abbey and St Margaret's Church.

1818–1837

British royal palace built in the Indo-Saracenic style of 19th-century British India. John Nash extended and redesigned the existing Neo-Classical building, and added domes and minarets. To do this, he used the newly available technology of the time, superimposing a cast-iron structure over the building.

1818 Piazza Vittorio Veneto, Turin, Italy.

1818 Hazuri Bagh Baradari, Lahore, Pakistan. White marble with pillars, cusped arches, and a mirrored ceiling. It is located in a garden and Raja Ranjit Singh often held court here.

1819–21 Schauspielhaus, Berlin, Germany.

1823–30 Altes Museum, Berlin, Germany.

1825 Tuskulénai Manor, Vilnius, Lithuania. The Neo-Classical manor was designed by Karol Podczaszyński. The façade has three serlianas.

1836–65 Houses of Parliament, London, England.

1837–41 Potemkin Stairs, Odessa, Ukraine. The massive stairway leads from the sea harbor to the city of Odessa, built upon a high steppe plateau. The steps vary in width in an optical illusion designed to make

Above left: Bayard (originally Condict) Building, New York, USA, 1898, by Louis Sullivan.
Above right: The Guaranty Building, Buffalo, New York, USA, 1895, by Louis Sullivan.

structure, and the hand of the craftsman shaped everything. This is what had given buildings their authenticity and integrity. To a large extent the movement that gave birth to modern architecture was driven by a need to recapture that quality of genuineness. Modern architecture, so often thought in terms of an avant-garde rejection of tradition, in fact strove to return to a focus on functionalism. In fact, modern architecture should be seen as an effort to recapture the traditional values that had given buildings their authenticity. (It is interesting that the title of Le Corbusier's most famous book, *Vers une Architecture (Towards an Architecture)* was not, as an early translator called it, *Towards a New Architecture.*) The primary goal of the Modern Movement was to return to basic principles rather than blindly copy external forms. No wonder that Mies van der Rohe's favorite quotation was drawn from St Augustine: "Beauty is the radiance of truth." All these precepts are found in the writings of the intellectual father of modern architecture, the French architect and theoretician Eugène-Emanuel Viollet-le-Duc (1814–79). Most of his professional career was dedicated to the restoration of some of the greatest of Gothic buildings (Notre Dame and Sainte Chapelle in Paris, for example). In his writings (*Lectures on Architecture*, 1860, and *Dictionnaire Raisonné de l'Architecture*, 1854–68) he advocated a structural rationalism that would provide the foundation for a new kind of architecture that was responsive to "the nature of the materials employed, to the climate, to the customs of an era, and to the necessities of the moment." Those architects and theorists who followed in the 20th century would mostly do no more than elaborate on Viollet-le-Duc's ideas.

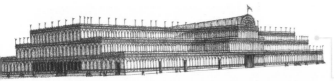

The Crystal Palace, London, England. Sir Joseph Paxton (1803–65) had designed the great greenhouse at Chatsworth House and used this skill to win a competition for a building to house the Great Exhibition of 1851. The rules of the competition stated that the building must be able to be dismantled and re-erected on another site. Paxton's solution, an iron and glass structure, was to have a profound influence on later building techniques and styles.

Opera House, Paris, France. A then unknown architect, Charles Garnier (1825–98), won the competition (beating 170 other contestants) to create an opera house on a site recently cleared during Baron Haussmann's restructuring of the city. The building has a flashy nouveau-riche exuberance perfectly in keeping with the spirit of Napoleon III's Second Empire.

Law Courts, London, England. Architect: George Edmund Street (1824–81). In 13th-century castellated Gothic, Street managed to give variety to his long façade.

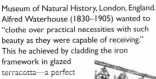

Museum of Natural History, London, England. Alfred Waterhouse (1830–1905) wanted to "clothe over practical necessities with such beauty as they were capable of receiving." This he achieved by cladding the iron framework in glazed terracotta—a perfect material in the soot-laden air of Victorian London.

1851–1874

the staircase look longer than it is.

1851 The Crystal Palace, London, England.

1856 The Round House, Somerville, Massachusetts, USA. A cylindrical wood-frame residence built by Enoch Robinson. Two stories are of the same diameter, while a smaller third one is encircled by military features like battlements and embrasures. Within, a glass skylight tops a central rotunda, and interconnected rooms branch off on each floor.

1862–75 Opera House, Paris, France.

1862 Cold Spring Cemetery Gatehouse, Nelsonville, New York, USA. A granite cottage with Gothic lancet windows. Part of the Gothic Revival style in America.

1867–72 Vladimir Palace, St Petersburg, Russia. The last imperial palace to be constructed in St Petersburg. Its 360 rooms are all decorated in disparate historic styles ranging from Neo-Renaissance to Russian Revival. The façade is of rusticated stucco.

1868–82 Law Courts, London, England.

1873–79 Museum of Natural History, London, England.

1874 Mark Twain House, Hartford, Connecticut,

Carson Pirie Scott building, Chicago, Illinois, 1899, designed by Louis Sullivan.

One of the earliest exponents of this new architecture was another Frenchman, Henri Labrouste (1801–75), with his Bibliothèque Ste-Geneviève (1830–50), and the reading room and book stacks of the Librairie Nationale (1854–75). Perhaps even more prophetic was the prefabricated iron-and-glass Crystal Palace built for the 1851 Great Exhibition in London from a design by Sir Joseph Paxton (1803–65). However, in an age of great engineering feats, it was the bridges, railroad sheds, factory and mill buildings that proved to be the most influential of all.

Modern architecture can be said to have been born in Chicago in the 1880s. The steel skeleton structure was first used by William LeBaron Jenney (1832–1907) in the Home Insurance Building, Chicago, in 1884. Three architectural firms: Adler and Sullivan, Burnham and Root, and Holabird and Roche, played a major role in shaping an architectural language for this totally new building type: the office block. The towering figure among them was Louis H Sullivan (1856–1924) who proclaimed that a skyscraper should be a "proud and soaring thing" and proceeded to demonstrate how it could be done in a succession of increasingly articulated and expressive office towers, culminating in the Guaranty (also known as the Prudential) Building (1895) in Buffalo, New York. Then, following the dissolution of his partnership with Adler, he demonstrated how the steel structural cage should be expressed in the Carson Pirie Scott store building (1899–1904) in Chicago.

Sullivan's disciple, Frank Lloyd Wright (1869–1969), showed that space in a building could be flowing and dynamic rather than compartmentalized and static. After Wright, the two most influential architects of the 20th century were Mies

Below: Interior of Johnson Wax Building, 1936, by Frank Lloyd Wright.
Right: National Gallery, Berlin, Germany, 1962–68, by Mies van der Rohe.

Sacré Coeur, Paris, France. Designed by Paul Abadie (1812–84). Sitting atop the hill of Montmartre, Sacré Coeur echoes the Byzantine / Romanesque cathedral of St Front, Périgueux.

Sagrada Familia, Barcelona, Spain. Antoni Gaudí (1852–1926) drew on Spanish Gothic and Islamic traditions, among others, in designing this votive church to the Holy Family. He foresaw it as the work of generations, and to this day it still has the feeling of a construction site.

Factory Building, New York, USA. The JP Hale Piano Factory is representative of the utilitarian architecture demanded by an age of expanding industrialization: "form should ever follow function".

The Auditorium Building, Chicago, USA. Architects: Louis H Sullivan (1856–1924) and Dankmar Adler (1844–1900). A powerful expression of a multi-use complex, it houses one of the finest auditoriums in the USA (Adler was an acoustics expert).

1875–1886

USA. Architect: Edward Tuckerman Potter. Famous for its whimsical style and the variety and unpredictability of its elements, it is built in Victorian Gothic Revival style, and was, according to legend, designed to look like a riverboat.

1875–1919 Sacré Coeur, Paris, France.

1882–89 City Chambers, Glasgow, Scotland. The headquarters of Glasgow City Council, built by architect William Young. The buildings are a good example of Victorian civic architecture.

1883–present Sagrada Familia, Barcelona, Spain.

1884 JP Hale Piano Factory Building, New York, USA.

1884–86 National Assembly of Bulgaria, Sofia, Bulgaria. Situated in Sofia's very center, it was constructed in Neo-Renaissance style by Konstantin Jovanović, a Serbian-Bulgarian architect.

1885 Home Insurance Building, Chicago, USA. Considered the first skyscraper in the world, due to its height (138 ft / 42 m) and unique weight-bearing frame. It was the first building to use structural, fireproof steel in its frame, though most of it was composed of cast and wrought iron.

1886–89 The Auditorium Building, Chicago, USA.

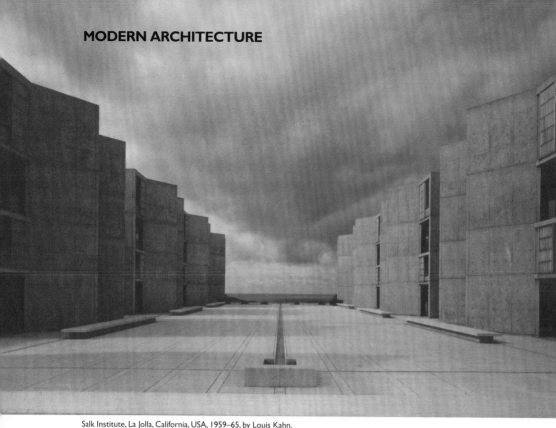

Salk Institute, La Jolla, California, USA, 1959–65, by Louis Kahn.

Lever House, New York, USA, 1952, by Skidmore, Owings & Merrill.

van der Rohe (1886-1959) and Le Corbusier (1887-1965), both of whom created seminal works in the 1920s and achieved a position of pre-eminence after World War II. By then modern architecture had emerged from its heroic period of struggle and achieved acceptance and recognition. The generation of Mies van der Rohe and Le Corbusier, as well as Walter Gropius (1883-1969) and Alvar Aalto (1898-1976), was succeeded by a new generation of architects, including among many others, Eero Saarinen (1910-61), Louis Kahn (1901-74), Oscar Niemeyer (1907-2012), and Arne Jacobsen (1902-71). In fact, so overwhelming was the new modernist orthodoxy that it was embraced by the great majority of architects. No longer was it the province of an elite group of idealistic, deeply committed individuals. Now it was practiced by almost everyone—from the very good to the utterly derivative—which, in its turn, lead to a counter-movement, Post Modernism, spearheaded by Robert Venturi's *Complexity and Contradiction in Architecture* (1966) and Philip Johnson's AT&T Building (1978) in New York City. But modern architecture, still rooted in the principles of structural rationalism, clarity, and integrity, as well as the concerns of sustainability, is still alive and thriving in the work of architects such as Richard Rogers, Norman Foster, IM Pei, Renzo Piano, James Stuart Polshek, Zaha Hadid, Rem Koolhaas, Daniel Liebeskind.

New Scotland Yard, London, England. Richard Norman Shaw (1831–1912) mimed many styles in this highly eclectic work: corner 'tourelles' derive from French castles, the gables from the Netherlands, the door surrounds are Baroque, and over all it has a Scottish baronial feel.

Galerie des Machines, Paris, France. Architects: Victor Contamin (1840–93) and Charles Dutert (1845–1906). Built for the Paris Exhibition of 1889, it was one of the most important steel and glass buildings of its age, with an unprecedented unsupported steel span of 375 ft (114 m). Demolished 1910.

Eiffel Tower, Paris, France. Although many thought it an aesthetic abomination, over two million visited it in the first year (it now receives close to seven million a year).

GUM Department Store, Moscow, Russia. Within a Renaissance-inspired exterior is a network of iron and glass balconies, walkways, and domes.

1887–1889

1887–90 New Scotland Yard, London, England.

1887–91 Galleria Umberto, Naples, Italy. A high, spacious, cruciform structure topped by a cast-iron roof and a glass dome. Architect: Emanuele Rocco (1852–1922). It is an important forerunner of the modern glazed and enclosed shopping mall.

1888 Bee Building, Omaha, Nebraska, USA. Built to house the Omaha Bee newspaper. The detailing of the seven-story red granite structure has carved beehives as exterior ornaments and miniature beehives on the doorknobs. Demolished in 1966.

1889 Galerie des Machines, Paris, France.

1889 F Scott Fitzgerald House or Summit Terrace, St Paul, Minnesota, USA. It is part of rowhouses designed by William H Willcox and Clarence H Johnston, Sr. The rowhouse was in the 'New York Style', where each unit was given a distinctive character.

1889 Eiffel Tower, Paris, France.

1889 GUM Department Store, Moscow, Russia.

1889 Cambridge, Massachusetts City Hall, Cambridge, Massachusetts, USA.

Detail of a palace wall in Bukhara, Uzbekistan. The historic center at Bukhara is a UNESCO World Heritage Site.

"THE INTENTION IN CONSERVING AND RESTORING MONUMENTS IS TO SAFEGUARD THEM
NO LESS AS WORKS OF ART THAN AS HISTORICAL EVIDENCE."
Venice Charter, 1964

History has left behind a legacy of marvelous buildings and sites all over the world, which are invaluable as sources of information on the canvas of artistic and civilizational development. All heritage assets are, however, vulnerable or at risk in some way, whether due to weathering or ageing, desertion or overuse, natural disasters or man-made causes. In the entire spectrum of conservation efforts, the restoration of architecture has been an area of concern and attention from ancient times. Emperor Hadrian renovated the Parthenon as early as the second century CE. Places as old as the pyramids of Egypt and uniquely different from one another as the cathedrals of Europe and Latin America, temples and tombs of India, historic walled cities, and palaces and stately homes, are all in need of special care. In the past monuments have been demolished and their spoils used to construct new buildings, as was done extensively when Christianity spread in the Roman empire and churches were built. Heritage sites are fortunately now listed and under the watchful gaze of national and international charters that seek to ensure their protection.

Monadnock Building, Chicago, USA. Architects: DH Burnham (1846–1912) and John Wellborn Root (1850–91). The last high-rise in Chicago to have load-bearing walls. Absence of ornament make this a milestone in the emergence of modern architecture.

Guaranty Building, Buffalo, New York, USA. The Guaranty demonstrates what Louis Sullivan, its architect, meant when he said "a skyscraper should be a proud and soaring thing."

Carson Pirie Scott Store, Chicago, USA. The Sullivan-designed building bears some of his trademark elements: 'Chicago' windows (a fixed pane flanked by ventilating panes), terra-cotta cladding, and exquisite cast-iron detailing.

Paris Métro station entrance, France. Hector Guimard (1867–1942). Between 1899 and 1913, Guimard designed the Paris Métro station entrances in high Art Nouveau style, with prefabricated modular construction and entwining metal decoration.

1889–1900

Built in Richardsonian Romanesque, the three storied building is marked by load-bearing walls of granite and brownstone, and a 158-ft (48-m) conical bell tower.

1889–91 Monadnock Building, Chicago, USA.

1893–94 Hôtel Tassel, Brussels, Belgium. Victor Horta built this town house, generally considered the first Art Nouveau building in the world because of its innovative plan and the way in which the curved lines of decoration are joined with the structure.

1895–96 Guaranty Building, Buffalo, New York, USA.

1896–98 Queen's Cross Church, Glasgow, Scotland. A masterpiece of the architect Charles Rennie Mackintosh, it combines Norman, Gothic and even Japanese influences.

1899–1904 Carson Pirie Scott Store, Chicago, USA.

1900 Grand Palais, Paris, France. Built to house the Paris Exhibition of 1900, it is the largest existing ironwork and glass structure in the world. Its most striking features are the glass-domed roof and Art Nouveau ironwork.

c.1900 Paris Métro station entrance, France.

ADAPTIVE REUSE

Bernard Feilden, noted British conservationist, said, "Interventions are known to cause some loss of cultural property values but are justifiable in order to preserve the essential integrity of cultural property for future generations." Since the time of Viollet-le-Duc renowned for his work on restoration of historic French buildings (mid-19th century), the approach and methodology of conservation / restoration has evolved to its present thinking of a multi-disciplinary approach. Established guidelines are now considered at the planning stages of national cultural agendas. Not pastiche, not mere stylistic restoration, the aim of preservation of architectural heritage is aimed at authenticity, the survival of traditional cultures, and environmentally sustainable human development.

The highly specialized process of building restoration covers cleaning and repair of the exterior or interior of buildings—as has been done with St Paul's Cathedral in London—to reconstructing damaged or ageing buildings. Intervention methods that employ original techniques and materials as far as possible

Hallway in Hermitage Museum at the former Winter Palace, St Petersburg, Russia.

are advocated. These may have been state-of-the-art in their time, but updating them is a necessity. For instance, it was important that new methods of heating and cooling be installed in the St Petersburg complex of palaces in Russia, and sand-blasting, commonly used for cleaning external surfaces in the UK in the 1960s, was subsequently found to have damaged soft stone façades. Colors, also, cannot always be replicated through the same ingredients as the original. Though many 18th-century greens had arsenic in them, it is now a banned material. Newer materials that are gentler on ageing structures are being regularly developed. Glass-fiber reinforced concrete or gypsum, and polyurethane molds that can be used in situ to replicate components, are two examples. Most of all, modern techniques of restoration have realized the importance of planning and management before hands-on work begins, so that the object of restoration is viewed as part of a consolidated whole; and the methods of adaptive reuse ensure stability and easier maintenance.

House with Chimaeras or Gorodetsky House, Kiev, Ukraine. Originally an upmarket apartment building, designed by Vladislav Gorodetsky, regarded as the Gaudí of Kiev. It is marked by the extensive use of ornate decoration, featuring exotic animal figures.

Unity Temple, Oak Park, Illinois, USA. Described as the "world's first modern church", architect Frank Lloyd Wright (1869–1959) rejected historical styles in favor of a masterful interplay of spaces.

Casa Milá, Barcelona, Spain. Beneath the naturalistic cliff-like façade of Gaudí's apartment block is a steel framework. The medieval looking chimney pots show the influence of Gothic/Moorish on Gaudí's aesthetic.

Robie House, Chicago, USA. This Frank Lloyd Wright house has been called "one of the most influential designs in the history of architecture." Horizontal planes and dynamic flowing spaces are Lloyd Wright trademarks.

1902–1910

1902 Flatiron Building, New York City, USA. Designed by DH Burnham & Co, the Flatiron (named after the triangular shape of an old smoothing-iron) was the first building in New York to be supported by a steel skeleton.

1901–02 House with Chimaeras or Gorodetsky House, Kiev, Ukraine.

1904–06 Unity Temple, Oak Park, Illinois, USA.

1906 The Great Mosque of Djenné, Djenné, Mali. The largest mud brick or adobe building in the world. The *qibla* (prayer hall) is dominated by three large, box-like minarets and a cone-shaped spire topped with an ostrich egg. Vents in the roof have removable ceramic caps to ventilate the interior.

1906–08 Banca de Scont, Timişoara, Romania. Designed by Marcell Komor and Dezso Jakab, it is in typical Hungarian-style Art Nouveau. The curved walls are studded with turquoise tiles forming patterns drawn from folklore.

1906–10 Casa Milá, Barcelona, Spain.

1909 Robie House, Chicago, USA.

1910 Jacir Palace or Qasr Jacir, Bethlehem, central West Bank. The large

CONSERVATION TIMELINE

16th century Intensive efforts at architectural conservation begin with the papal administration of Rome taking charge of Rome's heritage assets.

18th century New concepts of aesthetics and picturesqueness are highlighted. Napoleon Bonaparte is particularly concerned with the idea of "monuments of history", especially after his expedition into Egypt and discovery of its grand architectural legacies.

1843–67 Restoration of Notre Dame de Paris by Viollet-le-Duc.

1877 Foundation of Society for Protection of Ancient Buildings.

19th century The Colosseum (built in 80 BCE) is the first restoration project on a large scale. It is saved from total collapse by the efforts of the Pope.

1869 Turkey passes legislation on historic monuments. Its Waqf Board becomes responsible for Islamic buildings.

1920s With the formation of the League of Nations following World War I, countries come together for the first time to share their concerns. The urgency of restoration is expressed, and it is increasingly felt that there should be an independent body of specialists for this task.

1931 The International Museums Office organizes the First International Congress of Architects and Technicians of Historic Monuments in Athens. This signals the formation of a global forum on restoration of historic buildings.

1933 The Athens Charter for the Restoration of Historic Monuments. The Charter at the fourth Congrès International d'Architecture Moderne (CIAM, International Congress of Modern Architecture). For the first time, ideas and recommendations on architectural restoration are articulated and published (in edited form) by Le Corbusier in 1942.

1957 The devastation of World War II leads to the formation of the United Nations in 1945. United Nations Educational, Scientific and Cultural Organization (UNESCO) ushers in a new era of cultural internationalism. Under its aegis, in Paris, all member states are urged to join the International Center for the Study of the Preservation and Restoration of Cultural Property (ICCROM), based in Rome.

The Colosseum, Rome, Italy, 70 CE.

1964 The Venice Charter. Wrapping up the proceedings of the Second Congress of Architects and Specialists of Historic Monuments, it also results in the creation of the International Council on Monuments and Sites (ICOMOS) in 1965, which remains at the forefront of the movement today. The Charter, recognizing that historic monuments and their settings are symbols of universal human values, to be looked upon as the common heritage of all men irrespective of the country in which they are located, continues to be a benchmark for conservationists around the world.

1966 USA passes the National Historical Preservation Act.

1972 UNESCO's World Heritage Convention (comes into force in 1975) defines the landmark "World Heritage Site". Sites are selected based on having cultural, historical, scientific or natural significance and they are legally protected by international treaties.

1982 Sir Bernard Feilden writes authoritative book on the subject, *The Conservation of Historic Buildings*,

1987 The Washington Charter on Historic Areas and Towns fills an important gap in the Venice Charter by going beyond individual monuments to historic urbanscapes.

1988 DOCOMOMO (International Committee for the Documentation and Conservation of buildings, sites and neighborhoods of the Modern Movement), a non-profit organization, is initiated by Hubert-Jan Henket, architect and professor, and Wessel de Jonge, architect and research fellow at the Eindhoven University of Technology, the Netherlands. Its mission is to preserve the architectural heritage of the Modern Movement that appears to be "more at risk than during any other period", and which

Le Corbusier

The Masarykovo School, Zlin, Czech Republic (top) and Majestic Theatre, Christchurch, New Zealand (above) are two significant buildings of the Modern Movement that have been lost through demolition.

"glorifies the dynamic spirit of the Machine Age".

1990 Lausanne Charter for Archaeological Heritage highlights: collaboration between professionals of different disciplines; participation of the government as well as local cultural groups in heritage protection; the role of legislation; and training of conservationists. It also reiterates the need to preserve sites in situ.

1992 onward Conservation of cultural landscapes, which includes monuments, under the aegis of UNESCO's World Heritage Committee.

1994 Nara Document on Authenticity, drafted at Nara, Japan, by experts emphasizes the importance of cultural diversity versus homogenization in a rapidly globalizing world. It supports the value of traditions and techniques, location and setting, spirit and feeling of all societies in their methods of restoration, and cautions against the blind use of universal methods, materials, and design as scientific knowledge advances.

2000 The State Administration of Cultural Heritage (SACH) formulates, in cooperation with the Getty Conservation Institute and Australian Heritage Commission, the Principles for the Conservation of Heritage Sites in China. From over 3,00,000 registered sites, 1,268 are designated National Priority Protected Sites.

2001 The UNESCO World Heritage Centre, ICOMOS and DOCOMOMO launch a joint program for the identification, documentation and promotion of the built heritage of the 19th and 20th centuries. This program focuses on raising awareness concerning the heritage of architecture, town planning and landscape design of the modern era.

2008 The 10th International Conference on the Study and Conservation of Earthen Architecture in Mali; sub-Saharan Africa is very rich in this form of architecture.

2008 ICOMOS publishes the Charter for the Interpretation and Presentation of Cultural Heritage Sites (also known as the Ename Charter). The charter aims to facilitate the understanding and appreciation of cultural heritage sites and to foster public awareness of the need for their protection and conservation. The charter broadens the view from the individual heritage object to considering heritage sites in their natural and cultural settings and social context for understanding their tangible and intangible values.

2010 onwards The interest for heritage redevelopment in place of heritage conservation steadily increases. In many countries heritage revitalization agreements (HRAs)—formal, voluntary, written agreements negotiated between property owners and local governments—recognize and provide protection to a heritage building, while allowing for redevelopment of the property. Through programs like HRA, many of the world's minor heritage structures are being saved from vanishing.

2014 Getty Foundation launches a fund for conservation of 20th-century architecture with grants assigned to 10 significant buildings. The Keeping it Modern initiative grows with a second round of funding for 14 new buildings around the globe in 2015.

2016 World Monuments Fund launches a campaign backed by a $1.3 million private grant to restore the Edicule at the Church of the Holy Sepulchre, Jerusalem, Israel, the most sacred site in Christianity.

Edicule, Holy Sepulchre

2016 The World Heritage Convention stands ratified by 192 state parties, making it one of the most adhered to international instruments. There are 1,052 World Heritage Sites located in 165 States.

NOTABLE RESTORATIONS

Abu Simbel, Egypt. A set of two temples near the border of Egypt with Sudan, Abu Simbel was built by the pharaoh Ramesses II in the 13th century BCE. In the 1960s, owing to the construction of the Aswan High Dam, the flood waters of the Nile rose to submerge these monuments. Spearheaded by a UNESCO campaign, bolstered by $80 million donated by 50 countries, a massive rescue operation was undertaken. The temples were dismantled and reassembled on the cliffside in exact relationship to each other and the sun as before, and surmounted with a man-made 'mountain'.

Humayun's Tomb Gardens, New Delhi, India. Among the most important Moghul monuments in India, Humayun's Tomb is significant not only because it served as a model for the Taj Mahal but because the gardens surrounding it are an almost perfect example of the *charbagh* (four-part Paradise Garden) concept that became a hallmark of Moghul design. The gardens, pathways, fountains, and water channels were restored according to the original plans, including details such as planting the same species of trees and vegetation as far as possible.

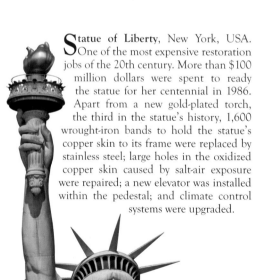

Statue of Liberty, New York, USA. One of the most expensive restoration jobs of the 20th century. More than $100 million dollars were spent to ready the statue for her centennial in 1986. Apart from a new gold-plated torch, the third in the statue's history, 1,600 wrought-iron bands to hold the statue's copper skin to its frame were replaced by stainless steel; large holes in the oxidized copper skin caused by salt-air exposure were repaired; a new elevator was installed within the pedestal; and climate control systems were upgraded.

The White House, Washington, DC, USA. A major process of restoration in the modern period was undertaken when Jacqueline Kennedy refurbished the rooms in different periods of the early republic and world history, and had it declared a museum to help preserve it. Adding stature to the presidential mansion, this effort set the trend for subsequent inmates, each of whom contributed to maintaining the building's structure and exterior. In the early 1990s, extensive repairs to the exterior involved repainting after about 40 layers of paint were removed.

Windsor Great Hall, Windsor Castle, London, England. In 1992, in a major fire that raged for 15 hours, Windsor Great Hall was among the rooms severely damaged in Windsor Castle. Its restoration was included in the total cost of repair of £37 million. Seventy per cent of this was funded through ticket sales for Buckingham Palace's state rooms which were opened to the public for the first time. A perfect restoration job in the Gothic style, where there was little distinction between old and new, it improved upon the original arrangement of public rooms and service quarters.

Heijo Palace, Nara, Japan. The eighth century imperial residence's walled palace and its structures, including the imperial living quarters and administrative buildings, fell into disuse after the capital moved to Heian. Degraded by natural disasters, eventually the palace totally disappeared as the land was reclaimed for agriculture. Excavations started in the 1970s, and in 1998, the palace and its surrounding area were proclaimed a UNESCO World Heritage Site. Large-scale reconstruction began in 2000, and in 2010, to coincide with the 1300th anniversary of the capital city of Nara, the Heijo Palace had been restored using traditional material and building methods.

The Elbe Philharmonic Hall, Hamburg, Germany. An example of the new-found élan for heritage redevelopment, the building was originally a factory storage for cocoa beans. Now it is a multifunctional complex with a state-of-the-art concert hall—the roof of which is built to resemble a series of glassy waves on the Elbe River—a wellness and conference zone, apartments and a five-star hotel. Opened in 2016, it is designed by the architectural firm Herzog & de Meuron.

Alte Pinakothek, Munich, Germany. Old Pinakothek was commissioned by King Ludwig I as an art gallery for the royal collections. Architect Leo von Klenze built it in 1826-36. After its destruction during the Second World War, Hans Dollgast rebuilt it, partly using reclaimed bricks from bomb sites in the city. More remarkable, however, was his creative reinterpretation in a modern idiom of the missing parts of the structure. Countering opposition for his divergence from a conservative approach, Dollgast succeeded in changing the layout and thus introducing some bold innovative elements. The gallery, one of Munich's major art museums, thus represents the entire architectural trajectory of the museum's history from its origins to post-war reconstruction.

Castelvecchio Museum, Verona, Italy. Now a museum housed in a medieval castle, Castelvecchio was the most important military construction of the 13th-14th century Scaliger dynasty. Napoleon also stayed here but it was damaged by French troops (1796-97) partly in retaliation to his arbitrary high-handed policies. The first effort at rebuilding took place in 1923, but the notable work of alteration was carried out by Carlo Scarpa between 1963-65. Seventeen years of historical research and haphazard archaeological discovery were instrumental in the final open-ended state of completion, considered by many as an ideal example of interventionist design.

Rijksmuseum, Amsterdam, the Netherlands. Architect Pierre Cuypers' masterpiece in the neo-romantic style opened for the public in 1885. Seen as "too elaborate" and" too decorated", it was rebuilt in 1962, when extra space was added and the original interior, and some exterior, destroyed or painted over—a project criticized as "the most violent abuse" in the history of museum building. In 1995, a new master plan envisaged a profound renovation of the museum. In 2000, the Dutch cabinet decided on a total renovation, with Cruz y Ortiz from Spain as the main architects, and Van Hoogevest responsible for the restoration. The clear layout of Cuypers was, wherever possible, restored, and the monumental decorations were brought back in the Hall of Fame, the Vestibule, the Night Watch Gallery and the stairwells.

SOME WORLD HERITAGE SITES

Site of Palmyra, Syria, inscribed in 1980.

The Medina at Marrakesh, Morroco, inscribed in 1985.

Fountains Abbey, UK, inscribed in 1986.

Venice, Italy, inscribed in 1987.

Jesuit missions of the Chiquitos, Bolivia, inscribed in 1990.

Kremlin and the Red Square, Moscow, Russia, inscribed in 1990.

Antique Mayan ruins in Uxmal, Mexico, inscribed in 1996.

Historic center of Riga, Latvia, inscribed in 1997.

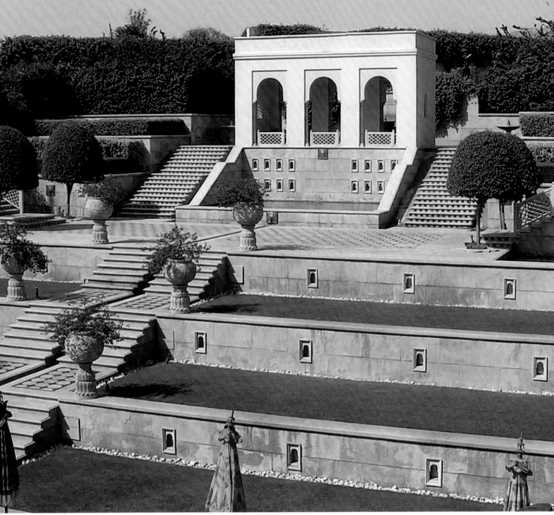

Moghul Gardens at Pinjore, India.

Landscape architecture is defined as the art, planning, design, management, preservation, and rehabilitation of the land and the design of habitats. The scope of the profession encompasses site planning, environmental restoration, recreation and regional planning, landscape urbanism, and historic preservation.

It was not until recent times that the term 'landscape architecture' came into common usage; it was first employed by the Scotsman Gilbert Laing Meason in the title of his book *The Landscape Architecture of the Great Painters of Italy* (1828). The book was about the type of architecture found in landscape paintings. This term was then taken up by others such as Loudon and Downing

Much of the documented material dealing with the evolution of landscape architecture has tended to focus on the 'western' or the 'formal' approaches to the discipline. These typically encompass the Greco-Roman world, post Renaissance Europe, and the United States. Such a tendency has been primarily due to the predilection to classify landscape architecture closely with 'garden' design. Equally valid—and in some cases, more relevant—are the approaches of other cultures throughout history.

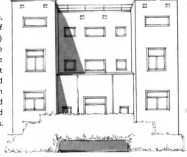

Steiner House, Vienna, Austria. Adolf Loos (1870–1933) reacted against the heavily decorative Jugendstil (Art Nouveau) and countered with an architecture pared down to unadorned essentials.

Fagus factory, Alfeld-an-der-Leine, Germany. Walter Gropius's first, and perhaps most important building proclaimed the advent of a new kind of architecture.

Woolworth Building, New York City, USA. Designed by Cass Gilbert (1859–1934), the Woolworth was the tallest building in the world until 1930. Frank W Woolworth admired the Gothic Revival style and had Gilbert reflect this in his design.

Hearst Castle, San Simeon, California, USA. A fairytale fantasy designed by Julia Morgan (1872–1957), one of the few women to ever succeed in the profession, for the publishing magnate William Randolph Hearst.

1910–1919

hotel building's design is based on the Louvre, but it also incorporates the characteristics of an Arab household.

1910 Steiner House, Vienna, Austria.

1910 Meseritz Synagogue, New York, USA. An unusually narrow building, remarkable for its Neo-Classical façade. It has balconies extending almost to the middle of the sanctuary.

1911 Fagus factory, Alfeld-an-der-Leine, Germany.

1911 Taliesin, Wisconsin, USA. Frank Lloyd Wright's summer home explored his ideas of organic architecture. The limestone chimneys and piers were inspired by Wisconsin's Driftless Area, and sand from the Wisconsin River mixed into the stucco walls evoked the river's sandbars.

1911–13 Woolworth Building, New York City, USA.

1911–13 Centennial Hall, Wrocław, Poland. With a cupola of reinforced concrete it became a key reference for the development of reinforced concrete structures in the 20th century.

1919–47 Hearst Castle, San Simeon, California, USA.

1922–24 Chilehaus (Chile

GRECO-ROMAN

The Greek expression of landscape was defined largely by topographic influences in term of siting of buildings and their inter-relationships. The grid-iron division of land over a rolling terrain gave rise to interesting surface modulations. An outstanding example of the transformation of a rocky hill into one of the great architectural sites of the world is the Acropolis, Athens (fifth century BCE). The formal planning methodology of the Greeks was taken further by the Romans on a much larger scale with the integration of forums (squares placed by different emperors at strategic spots and often named after them) with a series of public buildings. A well documented formal landscape of the period is that of Hadrian's Villa, Tivoli (second century CE).

Hadrian's Villa at Tivoli, second century CE.

PERSIAN

The Persians developed landscapes which were very different from that of contemporary Romans. These were essentially hunting parks surrounded by mud brick walls, with water systems running through them—these walled enclosures began being called the 'Paradise Garden' (*pardeiza*, 'a wall around'). The gardens contained a lot of animals, plants, and water, deemed essential for survival in harsh desert conditions. With the advent of Islam, these enclosed gardens were interpreted for their religious reference to the 'four rivers of Paradise' and the garden as symbolic of Paradise. From them evolved the classical Islamic gardens, later called *charbagh* (sets of four gardens in rectangular grids) by the Moghuls, although there is no mention of this term in Achaemenid times (sixth century BCE). With few built or hardscape elements, these gardens were defined by the irrigation canals and the system of planting mainly fruit trees, leaving little evidence for later interpretations. Among the best surviving examples of the influence of Persian design are the gardens of the Alhambra palace at Granada (mid 14th century).

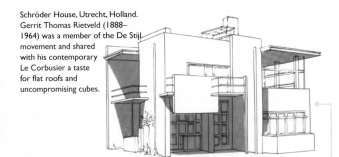

Schröder House, Utrecht, Holland. Gerrit Thomas Rietveld (1888–1964) was a member of the De Stijl movement and shared with his contemporary Le Corbusier a taste for flat roofs and uncompromising cubes.

Bauhaus, Dessau, Germany. Headquarter of the most radical design school of the 20th century, designed by its founder and director, Walter Gropius (1883–1969).

Chrysler Building, New York City, USA. The architect William van Alen (1882–1954) surpassed 40 Wall Street, New York City, as the highest building in the world by bolting on the famous Art Deco spire at the last moment.

PSFS Building, Philadelphia, USA. Architect: Howe & Lescaze. The first truly modern and distinctively 20th-century skyscraper in America.

1922–1929

House) Hamburg, Germany. A huge, 10-story office building spanning an entire street. Famous for its top, resembling a ship's prow, and the façades, which meet at a very sharp angle.

1924 Schröder House, Utrecht, Holland.

1925–26 Bauhaus, Dessau, Germany.

1927 Weissenhof Estate, Stuttgart, Germany. An estate of working-class housing built for the Deutscher Werkbund exhibition. All of its 21 buildings, designed by 16 European architects, have simplified façades, flat roofs used as terraces, and open plan interiors.

1928–30 Chrysler Building, New York City, USA.

1929 Barcelona Pavilion, Barcelona, Spain. Designed by Ludwig Mies van der Rohe, as the German Pavilion for the 1929 International Exposition. An important building in the history of modern architecture, combining a simple form with extravagant materials like marble and onyx.

1929 PSFS Building, Philadelphia, USA.

1929 Seattle Tower, Seattle, Washington, USA. This 27-story Art Deco skyscraper's ziggurat

JAPANESE LANDSCAPE ARCHITECTURE

The evolution of Japanese landscape architecture is known to have been in close conjunction with developments on the Chinese mainland. This is true more specifically of the post seventh century CE period, when Buddhism arrived from China into Japan. Prior to this, for close to 1,000 years of recorded history, there is ample evidence documenting the vision of Shinto concepts in the perceptions and design of temples and burial mounds.

Buddhism's infusion into Japanese culture led to a distinctive architecture and a more abstract interpretation of landscape than what it was before, both at the small and large scale. By about 1000, Japanese landscape design was a highly evolved discipline, codified into a set of design principles that led to a superb abstraction of nature. The garden was to be created in the likeness of nature; it had to flow with the natural lay of the land, be asymmetrical, and reflect awareness of the location and context. Japanese gardens displayed a great love for rock arrangements, not just for their aesthetic appeal but also for the philosophical ideas they could engender. Examples include the Daitakuji, Ginkakuji, and Ryonji temples at Kyoto (eighth–15th century), and the Kyoto Imperial Palace complex.

Above: Kinkakuji Temple (Golden Pavilion Temple), Kyoto, Japan, listed as a World Heritage Site.

Empire State Building, New York City, USA. The Empire State Building rose at the amazing rate of over two stories a week and was finished in less than the scheduled time and under budget.

exterior, said to have been inspired by local rock formations, is in 33 shades of brick designed to form a gradient that lightens from the bottom to the top.

1929–31 Empire State Building, New York City, USA.

1929–31 Communal House of the Textile Institute, Moscow, Russia. Architect: Ivan Nikolaev. A landmark of the Soviet Union's Constructivist architecture.

1929 Rusakov Workers' Club, Moscow, Russia.

1930 Château Montebello, Quebec, Canada. With 186 guest rooms, this hotel is supposed to be the world's largest log 'cabin'. Its centerpiece was a hexagonal rotunda, containing a six-sided stone fireplace, and completely encircled by two mezzanines.

1930 Tugendhat House, Brno, Czech Republic.

1932 Gulf Tower, Pennsylvania, USA. A neon-illuminated structure at the top of the building changed colors based on barometric pressure to provide a weather forecast, visible from a considerable distance.

1932 Swiss Student Center, Paris, France.

Rusakov Workers' Club, Moscow, Russia. One of the few buildings of the Soviet avant-garde to get off the drawing board. Architect Konstantin Melnikov (1890–1974) made this proletarian cultural center an innovative expression of Russian Constructivism.

Tugendhat House, Brno, Czech Republic. Mies van der Rohe (1886–1969). The spatial concepts of Mies's earlier Barcelona Pavilion were applied to a family house where retractable windows allowed interior and exterior to merge.

Swiss Student Center, Paris, France. Le Corbusier's light steel cage was perched on an elevated concrete base.

INDIA

From the third to the ninth century CE, which includes the classical period of Indian architecture, the making of cities laid great emphasis on integral landscape development. Though not clearly classifiable in the European framework of understanding landscape design, it dealt mainly with the attitude of the built habitat with the natural, in both physical and visual terms. This is expressed in the siting and design of temple towns, river edges (*ghats*), sacred groves, and some other locations. Examples include the temple complexes of Madurai, Tanjavur, and Chidambaram, built under the Pallavas and Cholas (sixth–10th century CE); Ajanta (fourth–sixth century CE) and Ellora caves (seventh–ninth century CE); and some of the *ghats* on the Ganga at Varanasi.

Moghul landscape design is a distinct genre. The words over the entrance to Emperor Akbar's tomb at Sikandra explain the reasoning: "These are the gardens of Eden: enter them to dwell therein eternally." The tomb-garden became a microcosm of the world. The three types of gardens made by the great Moghul emperors (1526–1707) were the tomb gardens (Humayun's Tomb, Delhi, and the Taj Mahal, Agra); palace gardens (Red Forts, Delhi and Agra); and the encampment gardens (Shalimar Bagh at Srinagar, Lahore, and Delhi). Each type was conceived, in an Islamic context, as the making of an earthly paradise.

Above: The formal *charbagh* gardens at the Taj Mahal, Agra, India.

Garden at Versailles, France.

The highly structured Renaissance gardens of Italy and France during the 16th–18th centuries redefined not only the approaches to setting buildings in designed environments, but in relating artifice to nature. These followed the grand plans of the era where architecture and city form expressed the power and reach of the ruling elite, and was extended to highly structured and formal garden layouts. Closely following the Romanesque model of Piazza San Marco, Venice (1177), later Renaissance examples like the Villa d'Este, Tivoli (1570) and Bernini's Piazza San Pietro (1656) created the benchmark in private and public open space design.

The anthropocentric attitude in all spheres of life was reflected in the control of nature, evident from the very formal planting seen in classical gardens like the works of André Le Norte in Vaux-le-Vicomte, Versailles (1722), and others. These monumental landscapes not only redefined the approach to open space design but also had a huge influence on subsequent city planning. The inspired plans for Washington, DC, by Pierre Charles L'Enfant in 1791, and Edwin Lutyens's New Delhi in 1929 are examples of the influence of Baroque gardening on urban design.

A detailed plan of the formal gardens at the Villa d'Este, Tivoli, Italy.

ENGLAND AND THE GARDEN CITY MOVEMENT

In the 18th century, England became the focus of a new style of landscape design, heralding what came to be known as the English Garden. Inspired by the Romantic Movement sweeping arts and literature, pioneers like Charles Bridgeman, followed by Humphry Repton and Lancelot 'Capability' Brown, remodeled the great estate parks of the English gentry to resemble a clean and romantic version of nature. Bridgeman's remodeling of Hampton Court (1720) and Brown's Villa for Alexander Pope at Twickenham (1730) exemplify this genre.

Through the 19th century, a unique focus developed out of the combination of urban planning and the tradition of landscape gardening. Designers like Fredrick Law Olmsted, Calvert Vaux, and others considered landscape as a way of recreating nature. Olmstead completed a series of parks which continue to have huge influence on the practices of landscape architecture today. Among these were Central Park, New York; Prospect Park, Brooklyn; and Boston's Emerald Necklace park system.

The Garden City movement is an approach to urban planning that was conceptualized in 1898 by Sir Ebenezer Howard. Garden cities were to be self-contained communities surrounded by green belts, containing carefully balanced areas of residences, industry, and agriculture. Inspired by the Utopian novel *Looking Backward*, Howard published *Tomorrow: a Peaceful Path to Real Reform* in 1898. Two cities based on Howard's ideas were the Letchworth Garden City and Welwyn Garden City, both in England. Howard's successor, Sir Frederic Osborn, extended the movement into regional planning.

During the first three decades of the 20th century, the idea of the garden city was influential in the United States (Radburn, New Jersey; Jackson Heights, Queens; Forest Hills, New York; and Baldwin Hills Village, Los Angeles), Canada, and Argentina. Scandinavian examples include the garden city of Bromma, Stockholm, and the internationally acclaimed functionalist garden city area of Södra Ängby. The Garden City movement also influenced the Scottish urbanist Sir Patrick Geddes in the planning of Jerusalem's expansion, and of Tel Aviv (1925). Contemporary town planning charters like *New Urbanism and Principles of Intelligent Urbanism* find their origins in this movement. At the other end of the spectrum were the domestic landscapes in America, shifting the focus once again from the public to the private, exemplified by the works of Thomas Church in the 1940s.

Above: Gardens at Stourhead, UK.

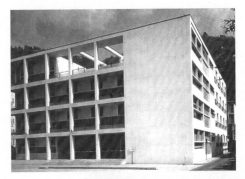

Casa del Fascio, Como, Italy. Under Fascism architecture was meant to discard 'bourgeois' decorative baggage. Giuseppe Terragni (1904–43) created this local Fascist headquarter as a perfect example of Italian Rationalism.

'Fallingwater', Bear Run, Pennsylvania, USA. Frank Lloyd Wright's most famous building and an icon of modern architecture. The relationship between building and landscape seems to echo Japanese traditions.

SC Johnson & Son HQ, Racine, Wisconsin, USA. Frank Lloyd Wright's forest of concrete mushrooms supports a ceiling of illuminated glass that fills the workspace with light.

Gropius House, Lincoln, Massachusetts, USA. Gropius's own house remains faithful to the principles he had formulated in the Bauhaus, while adapting traditional New England materials like wood siding.

1932–1939

1932–36 Casa del Fascio, Como, Italy.

1933 House of Tomorrow, Chicago, Illinois, USA. Designed by George F Keck for the *Century of Progress* exposition in Chicago. Intended as the house of the future, this octagonal house with plate glass walls even had its own airplane hangar.

1936 'Fallingwater', Bear Run, Pennsylvania, USA.

1936 SC Johnson & Son HQ, Racine, Wisconsin, USA.

1937 Casa Malaparte, Capri, Italy. The house, both admired and hated in equal measure by architects, is a red masonry box with reverse pyramidal stairs leading to the roof patio. It is located on a cliff 105 ft (32 m) above the sea.

1937–46 Notre-Dame de Toute Grâce du Plateau d'Assy, Passy, France. Designed by Maurice Novarina. Some of the best known artists of the 20th century contributed to the decoration of this church, considered an important landmark in the development of modern sacred art.

1938 Gropius House, Lincoln, Massachusetts, USA.

1939 Jefferson Memorial, Washington, DC, USA. A Neo-Classical building designed by John Russell Pope. With its circular marble steps, portico, colonnade of Ionic columns, and shallow dome, it echoes the Roman Pantheon.

CONTEMPORARY DEVELOPMENTS

It was during the Post Modern era that landscape designers started to extend their role to produce stand-alone works which did not need the support of an architectural framework to justify the context, approach, or need for the expression of landscape. Early defining works by pioneers like Roberto Burle Marx and Luis Barragan amply illustrated the point that landscape architecture had evolved from several sources and disciplines, and encompassed a wider frame of reference than that provided by architecture. The shift was further highlighted in the 1970s when Ian McHarg emphasized the need for ecological ethics, while Garrett Eckbo raised the importance of the element of time (landscape being composed of living, i.e., perishable elements).

Landscape architecture continues to develop as a discipline, and has responded to many of the movements of design and architecture through the 20th century. Some examples that break new ground and further the horizons of exploration include Parc de la Vilette (Bernard Tschumi, 1983); NMB Bank, Amsterdam (Copijn & Rawstorne, 1987); and IBM Solana (Peter Walker, 1990). Today, the Landscape Urbanism theory propagates the predominant capability of landscape over architecture in organizing the city and adding to the urban experience.

In the 21st century environmental concerns are compelling sustainable landscape, urban and building design to be integrated as an answer to increasing climate, overpopulation and pollution problems. An example is the Qinhuangdao Beach Restoration project in China (2008). A work not just of landscape design but also of eco engineering, it turned a deserted, eroding and garbage-ridden beach into a place of beauty. The renewed beach also features a recovered wetland that will encourage wildlife to return and use the new habitat.

Above: A view of Central Park, New York, USA.

Jacobs House, Madison, Wisconsin, USA. One of a series of Frank Lloyd Wright buildings in his 'Usonian' phase: Modernist houses for the middle class.

Farnsworth House, Plano, Illinois, USA. Architect: Mies van der Rohe. It seems to float effortlessly above the ground, a testament to Mies's concern for the relationship between site and building.

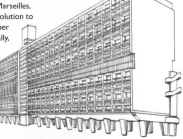

Unité d'Habitation, Marseilles, France. A futuristic solution to housing a large number of people economically, in keeping with Corbusier's belief that "the house is a machine for living in."

UN Secretariat, New York City, USA. The design committee included, among others, Le Corbusier and the Brazilian Oscar Niemeyer. The bold slab form is set in counterpoint to the sinuous General Assembly building below it.

1944–1949

1944 Jacobs House, Madison, Wisconsin, USA.

1945–51 Farnsworth House, Plano, Illinois, USA.

1946 Kaufmann Desert House, Palm Springs, California, USA. One of the last and most famous of Richard Neutra's projects. Its features connect to the desert environment, as well as offer protection against the harsh climate.

1946–52 Unité d'Habitation, Marseilles, France.

1947 Avenel Cooperative Housing Project, Los Angeles, USA. A 'cooperative experiment' in limited-space low-cost urban housing by architect Gregory Ain, it consists of 10 three-bedroom units with sliding glass walls, built along a common path.

1947–50 UN Secretariat, New York City, USA.

1949 Baker House, Massachusetts, USA. A dormitory at MIT designed by Alvar Aalto. Its undulating shape gives many of the rooms a wedge layout. The dining hall has a very distinctive 'moon garden' roof.

ECO ARCHITECTURE

Before industrial technology made materials and resources easy to obtain, people had to work with the limited means at their disposal to build their habitations. This may be seen in the villages of the Anasazi Indians, for example, which were built facing south to take natural advantage of the warmth and light of the sun.

However, powerful civilizations exploited nature at a scale that could not get naturally replenished as the need arose, as was the case with the deforestation caused by the Romans in North Africa for timber.

Doorway in Pueblo Bonito Great House, Chaco Canyon National Park, New Mexico. USA.

THE INDUSTRIAL ERA (c. 1780–1962)

'Fallingwater', Bear Run, Pennsylvania, USA, designed by Frank Lloyd Wright, 1938.

In response to the crisis brought about by depleting forests and rising population, in addition to changes in cultural habits and norms, 18th-century Europe saw a dramatic increase in the use of fossil fuels to generate energy: notably coal, at a non-renewable rate. The consequent prosperity in turn seeded the environmental crises that came two centuries later. With oil moving people and goods and electricity grids carrying energy conveniently into buildings, industrial economy went global by the 20th century. Architecture responded with grand gestures enabled by the development of steel, glass, and concrete: stronger, more durable, lighter, or transparent materials. Engineers adopted them in projects such as the Crystal Palace (1851) and the Eiffel Tower (1889). Later, architects, too, shed their outdated styles and embraced these materials to fashion the Modern era, led by architects such as Mies van der Rohe and Le Corbusier, both of whom developed new industrial materials to a mature level and integrated them into architecture. However, the thread of natural architecture, even in a modern idiom, was kept alive by the most senior of the three masters, Frank Lloyd Wright, whose organic architecture was based on the philosophy of working with nature, not dominating it. Mature examples of this attitude, still not consciously ecological, are seen in the regional Modernist examples of the 1950–80s by practitioners such as Eero Saarinen in the USA, Joseph Allen Stein in India, and Geoffrey Bawa in Sri Lanka.

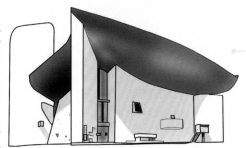

Pilgrimage Chapel, Ronchamp, France. A building unlike anything else in Le Corbusier's architectural output. Some critics saw it as the greatest piece of sculpture of the 20th century.

SR Crown Hall, Illinois Institute of Technology, Chicago, USA. Mies van der Rohe came to the IIT in 1938 and was commissioned to design a new campus, of which Crown Hall is considered the outstanding building.

Lever House, New York City, USA. Architects: Skidmore, Owings & Merrill. Until 1952 Park Avenue, New York, was a barren canyon of brick. Then came Lever House and its glass curtain-wall that created a revolution in commercial architecture.

Brasilia, Brazil. Lúcio Costa was the principal urban planner and Oscar Niemeyer the principal architect for Brazil's new capital city. When seen from above, the city's plan resembles a cross (or an airplane or a bird with wings outstretched).

1950–1958

1950–55 Pilgrimage Chapel, Ronchamp, France.

1950 Lansbury Estate, London, England. One of the largest public housing estates built in post-war London, it was based on the idea that new development should comprise self-sufficient neighborhoods.

1950 Thomas E Keys Residence, Rochester, Minnesota, USA. Another example of Frank Lloyd Wright's Usonian style of architecture (see Jacobs House, 1944).

1950–56 SR Crown Hall, Illinois Institute of Technology, Chicago, USA.

1952 Lever House, New York City, USA.

1953 Geodesic dome, Ford Motor Company Headquarters, Detroit, USA. Designed by R Buckminster Fuller.

1956–60 Brasilia, Brazil.

1958 Seagram Building, New York City, USA. Seagram Building, New York City, USA. Architect: Mies van der Rohe. "The lesson of the Master"——an exercise in enriching the urban environment with bronze, amber-tinted glass, elegant proportions, and a generous open plaza.

ECO ARCHITECTURE

THE POST MODERN WORLD (1962–1980)

Concerns over chemical pollution in the 1960s and the first oil crisis of 1973 brought energy conservation and ecological preservation into public discourse. While mainstream architecture was slow to respond, niche architecture immediately experimented with resource concerns and how they might inform the design of space. The American architect R Buckminster Fuller inquired how humanity could last on planet Earth. He became influential for his geodesic domes, which dominated early ecological architecture by creating a philosophical groundwork for 'doing more with less' and working with integrated systems. (Lightweight construction was a starting point of ecological architecture, and domes represented this at its most sophisticated though they were never adopted at a large scale and went extinct.) The 'flower children', representative of the 1960s' counter culture in the USA, started building a range of autonomous, renewable energy-based houses, especially in the region of Arizona. They integrated passive solar harnessing with heat storage, insulation, and orientation to make buildings comfortable without much energy. For example, the widely used Trombe wall technique (after the French engineer Felix Trombe) obviates or reduces the need for artificial heating by trapping and moderating winter heat into the interior of a building, using only masonry and glazing.

In the 1970s, Sim Van der Ryn founded the Farallones Institute, Berkeley, California, to explore ecological lifestyles. Meantime, a spiritual community, the city of Auroville, was founded in India. Its stated purpose was not so much 'ecology' as the evolution of 'consciousness'; still, its seminal homes resemble those made at Arizona. Auroville is now a community of 2,000 with a culture of resource consciousness, energy conservation, water harnessing, and waste treatment.

Geodesic dome of a botanic garden in Milwaukee, USA.

NEW-AGE MATERIALS

Interest in embodied resources, that is, topsoil, water, or energy (fire), consumed to extract, manufacture, transport, and assemble materials led to a resurgence of building in raw earth, this time in a modern, engineered way. This was brought back into architectural parlance by the Egyptian architect Hassan Fathy. In New Gourna resettlement village, Fathy revived ancient ecologically appropriate techniques of building walls and roofs in earth, using vaults and domes without any timber. Engineering of earth materials was advanced in the late 20th century by practitioners such as Gernot Minke and architectural teams at Craterre (Grenoble, France) and Auroville. In the southern Indian state of Kerala, Laurie Baker's fired brick, low cost, high quality, beautiful buildings turned frugality into a style statement.

There is increasing use of industrial and agricultural wastes such as coal fly-ash from power plants to make concrete and lightweight masonry blocks, or sawdust and agro-wastes to make boards. Insulating straw bale houses in various parts of the world has been an invention. Vegetated 'living' building skins, where the surface of the building is made up of biological material, such as grasses and herbs growing in peat and moss and irrigated with nutrient solutions, have been developed. Efforts have been devoted to growing, rather than mining materials. A switch is being made to timber from sustainable forests, and grasses, such as bamboo, are being employed. Residues from old buildings are being

Laurie Baker

recycled as aggregate for new concrete in mega-cities like Tokyo. The latter exemplifies the 'cradle to cradle' approach of William McDonough. This approach considers the life cycle of all material in a building like tracing flows in an ecosystem: from extraction, through manufacture and assembly, to dismantling, followed by reusing and recycling, or allowing it to biologically degrade.

The beginning of the 21st century is characterized by eco- and energy saving architecture becoming mainstream. More projects are incorporating landscape, building and materials into the vision of sustainability. Architect Renzo Piano's California Academy of Sciences, San Francisco (2008), endowed

Interior of a bamboo roof structure.

with a huge, dynamic green roof featuring grassy meadows and hillocks, is an outstanding representation of this approach.

California Academy of Sciences, USA.

1980s ONWARD

In the mid-1980s, with advances in glass and insulation technology, increasing environmental awareness and energy cost, 'passive', 'natural', bio-climatic, or solar building design became widespread amongst architects in colder climates. At one stage, in the mid-1980s some Scandinavian homes were three times better insulated than the typical suburban American home, thereby barely requiring any energy for heating.

In terms of trapping heat, William McDonough's work with glass claddings is regarded as a classic, while the French architect Jean Nouvel's work displays the maturing craft of handling tall glazed façades. With homeowners demanding ecological features, mainstream environment-sensitive projects are becoming commercially

Torre Agbar, Barcelona designed by Jean Nouvel uses multiple louvres and shading devices according to time of day and orientation.

possible. An example is the well-known carbon neutral BedZED community, Bedfordshire, UK, who live in houses with built-in natural ventilation, solar heating, garbage separation, water conservation, and green energy generation.

By the 1990s, practitioners in warm climates also developed their own vocabulary and authored new trends. Water and vegetative cooling were implemented in the public spaces of the International Expo (Seville, 1992). The Malaysian architect Ken Yeang spearheaded concepts of the tropical city and the tropical skyscraper, interspersing unconditioned vegetated space with air-conditioned space.

Besides looking at running energy costs, architects started working on water management, using wastes and embodied resources. In India, this manifests in Ashok B Lall's institutional buildings for Development Alternatives and SM Sehgal Foundation. While the early 20th-century masters exhibited Internationalism or universally applicable design, the new practitioners of ecological design are creating parallel regional dialects, while working within the grammar of a globalized modern architecture. The beginning of the 21st century has seen the environmentally friendly way of building become a necessary part of the architectural process. It is exemplifed in projects such as the head office

of Manitoba Hydro in Canada (2009). Using bioclimatic principles, the building's various design elements enable a 70 per cent energy saving compared with typical office towers.

Eco-apartments in Adelaide, Australia.

Palazzetto dello Sport, Rome, Italy. Pier Luigi Nervi (1891–1979) was an Italian civil engineer and one of the 20th century's pre-eminent architects working in reinforced concrete.

Dulles Airport, Virginia, USA. Architect Eero Saarinen (1910–61) declared "I think this airport is the best thing I have ever done."

Beijing Railway Station, Beijing, China. Combines 1950s design with traditional Chinese architecture. It was the largest modern passenger terminal in China at the time.

Solomon R Guggenheim Museum, New York City, USA. Frank Lloyd Wright's only building in Manhattan and one of the world's most distinctive architectural shapes. Wright had started working on the plan as early as 1942.

1958–1959

1958 Tokyo Tower, Tokyo, Japan. This 1,091-ft (332.6-m) orange and white lattice tower, similar in design to the Eiffel Tower, is the largest self-supporting steel structure in the world.

1958 Atomium, Brussels, Belgium. Built for the 1958 Brussels World's Fair. Designed by André Waterkeyn, it is 335 ft (102 m) tall. Nine connected steel spheres impart to it the shape of a unit cell of an iron crystal magnified 165 billion times.

1958–59 Palazzetto dello Sport, Rome, Italy.

1958–63 Dulles Airport, Virginia, USA.

1959 Beijing Railway Station, Beijing, China.

1959 State Kremlin Palace, Moscow, Russia. A glass and concrete structure, nearly half of which is submerged underground. Controversial for being out of place among the older buildings of the Kremlin.

1959 Solomon R Guggenheim Museum, New York City, USA. Louis Kahn (1901–74). Research facility built for Dr Jonas Salk of polio vaccine fame. Kahn's cool and lyrical juxtaposition of buildings and site achieves an almost poetic quality.

1959–65 Salk Institute, La Jolla, California, USA.

IMPROVING ECOLOGICAL PERFORMANCE

The World Commission on Environment and Development (WCED) popularized the concept of Sustainable Development in its report *Our Common Future* (1987). The Intergovernmental Panel on Climate Change (IPCC), a scientific body, asserted the reality of man-made global warming for which it shared the Nobel Peace Prize in 2007. Between these 20 years, however, energy, climate, material, and environmental concerns remained on the fringes of architectural practise, and were brought into the limelight by the unlikely vehicle of a market mechanism: voluntary rating systems.

Rating systems, such as the widely disseminated Leadership in Energy and Environmental Design (LEED) by the US Green Building Council, are designed to encourage investment in environmental performance beyond the minimum enforced by local codes. Besides energy and water conservation, rating systems have promoted emerging concerns for daylight, views, occupant health, and indoor air quality.

However, though better sealing of buildings has reduced heat loss, it has also created the 'sick-building syndrome'. To combat this, designers are reducing volatile organic compounds—typically in paints, carpets, and particle boards—in interiors.

Above: Natural building materials in an eco-friendly house in Tulum, Mexico.

Green office building utilizing the latest environmental technology. The solar panels provide energy for electricity and shade over the windows to help lower ambient temperature.

THE FUTURE

New bio- or nano-materials, such as dust-free glass or ultra capacitors that can store very large quantities of energy in a small volume, promise to revolutionize our buildings. Learning from nature is becoming common as ecological design scales up: landscape design and cycles of energy and water dominate healthy city planning today. Freiburg in Germany (1986 onwards) and Viikki near Helsinki (1990 onwards) are examples. Recent directions include New Urbanism with 'smart neighborhoods', distributed heat and power co-generation utilities, and intelligent multi-modal public transport, while urban designers establish ecological principles that should generate sustainable cities for an otherwise barren future.

Opera House, Sydney, Australia. Danish architect Jørn Utzon won an international competition with his elegant and witty evocation of sails, the highest of which is almost 200 ft (60 m) above the natural stone deck.

Cary House, Mill Valley, California, USA. Architect: Joseph Esherick (1914–98). Use of wood, light, play with space, and adaptation to site made Esherick the leader of West Coast Modernism.

National Gallery, Berlin, Germany. Architect: Mies van der Rohe. His final and crowning masterpiece.

Deere & Co Administrative Center, Moline, Illinois, USA. Architect Eero Saarinen thought his Dulles Airport (see 1958) one of his finest achievements, while many others have hailed his Deere HQ as "one of the great American mid-century buildings."

1959–1966

1959–73 Opera House, Sydney, Australia.

1960 Cary House, Mill Valley, California, USA.

1960 National Theater, Singapore. Architect: Alfred Wong. It had a massive 150-ton steel roof with five points representing the five stars of the Singapore flag. There were no side or rear walls. Demolished in 1986.

1962 Place Ville-Marie, Montreal, Canada. A cruciform International-style office tower, it is 617 ft (188 m) high and has a rotating beacon on the roof.

1962–68 National Gallery, Berlin, Germany.

1962 Space Needle, Seattle, Washington, USA. Built for the 1962 World's Fair, it is 605 feet (184 m) high and 138 feet (42 m) wide, weighs 9,550 tons and can withstand winds of up to 200 mph (320 km / h).

1963 Deere & Co Administrative Center, Moline, Illinois, USA.

1966 Kaden Tower, Louisville, Kentucky, USA. Designed by William Wesley Peters, a protégé of Frank Lloyd Wright, it shares features with Wright's plan for the unbuilt Calico Mills building in Ahmedabad, especially in the grillwork over the windows.

Mass housing implies the assumption of responsibility by the government to provide housing for families who cannot afford to access housing in the open market. Consequent to industrialization, and as manufacturing, trading, and business activities grew, and cities and towns emerged as growth centers, more and more people required government assistance in finding housing.

ENGLAND, THE WELFARE STATE

England is a typical example of the government having engaged in large-scale mass housing and its continuation as an evolving concept under changing circumstances. The Housing Act of 1890 had made local authorities responsible for improving existing conditions that had deteriorated substantially. In 1930, the Housing and Town Planning Act emphasized large-scale clearance of slums and rebuilding efforts. By 1945, England had turned into a truly welfare state, going by the commitment to social housing building programs on a mass scale that characterized enormous expansion in inner city estates.

Above: A council housing block in inner London.

Kimbell Art Museum, Fort Worth, Texas, USA. Louis Kahn described his building as a 'friendly home'. The 16-barrel-vaulted roofs with their plexiglass panels bathe the works of art in indirect sunlight to create "a harmony of spaces and light."

East Wing, National Gallery of Art, Washington, DC, USA. Architect: IM Pei & Partners. A stunning complex of joined triangular buildings that create surprisingly intimate spaces for the art inside.

Centre National d'Art et de Culture Georges Pompidou, Paris, France. The 'Brutalism' of the 1960s and 1970s in which ventilation ducts, electrical conduits, stairs, etc., were given forefront exposure found dramatic expression in Richard Rogers' and Renzo Piano's museum—"an oil refinery for modern art."

Lloyd's Building, London, England. Richard Rogers (see Pompidou Center, 1971) again inverted the usual order. Those 'service' elements that had traditionally been hidden are here paraded in all their stainless-steel glory.

1966–1978

1966 Kimbell Art Museum, Fort Worth, Texas, USA.

1967 Habitat 67, Montreal, Canada. A housing complex by Moshe Safdie, built for Expo 67. Aiming to combine the features of disparate private homes and a modern apartment building, it consists of interlocking, modular units in concrete.

1971 East Wing, National Gallery of Art, Washington, DC, USA.

1971 Azadi Tower, Tehran, Iran. Built to mark the 2,500th anniversary of the Persian empire, it combines Sassanid and Islamic architecture styles. Architect Hossein Amanat also integrated some of the symbology of his religion, the Baha'i faith, in the design.

1971–77 Centre National d'Art et de Culture Georges Pompidou, Paris, France.

1974–76 Church of the Holy Trinity or Wotruba Church, Vienna, Austria. This startling building, made according to a model by Fritz Wotruba, consists of 152 asymmetrically arranged concrete blocks, and resembles a piece of abstract sculpture.

1978–86 Lloyd's Building, London, England.

155

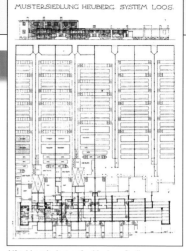

MUSTERSIEDLUNG HEUBERG. SYSTEM LOOS.

ARCHITECTS' INITIATIVES IN EUROPE

While parallel development took place in other northern European countries, the scale and continuity did not match that in England. However, in terms of architecture, many early models had been established. Supporters of modern architecture believed that industrialization would raise the quality and volume of mass housing construction. The Finnish architect Alvar Aalto engaged himself with mass housing in the 1920s and 1930s. He set out to redefine the place of the individual in society, which was perceived as having been denied or suppressed in mass production housing schemes. His designs were more organic, allowing for variations in spatial geometry in response to individual needs. The stepped workers' housing in Kauttua, Sweden (1938) and

Alfred Loos's designs for Heuberg Siedlung Housing, 1920s.

Boston public housing (late 1940s) are early examples of Aalto's work.

In Austria, Adolf Loos supported the International modern style based on the minimalism of Walter Gropius's architecture. As the architect to the Housing Department in Vienna (1920-22), he had perfected the art of making complex split-level houses such as the Moller House (1928), which was close in spirit to Corbusier's villas.

Appointed architect to the city of Rotterdam, Holland, in 1918, JJP Oud (1890-1963) firmly reacted against Mannerist elements of the 'Amsterdam School'. The simplicity of his design solutions resulted in white, cubist housing blocks, as is evident at Hock of Holland housing (1924-27), and the now famous Kielbok Estate in Rotterdam (1925).

In Italy, Aldo Rossi's housing complex at Gallaratese Quarter in Milan, in collaboration with Carlo Aymoneno is an example of collective social living with an accent on well-articulated collective social spaces.

Adolf Loos

THE WEST, POST WORLD WAR II

Le Corbusier advocated the Utopian City that relied on mass housing on a grand scale—numerous slab blocks that would characterize the city fabric. This idea culminated in his Unité d'Habitation projects in Marseilles (1947-52) and in Berlin (1956-58). Similar examples can be found in the works of Atelier 5 in their terrace housing at Flamatt (1957) and the housing complex at Halen, both in Switzerland. Their works incorporated terrace gardens and landscape in a substantial way.

Large-scale destruction caused by the war had made mass housing a priority in the process of rebuilding cities across

Erskine Gyttorp terrace houses.

Europe. The need for economy and speed of construction ushered in prefabrication as a solution. Both western and socialist eastern Europe, particularly countries like the Soviet Union and East

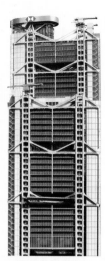

Hong Kong and Shanghai Bank, Hong Kong, China. Architect Norman Foster (with structural engineers Ove Arup & Partners) opened up the interior space by suspending floors from trusses.

The Louvre Pyramid, Paris, France. IM Pei's glass entrance to the Louvre extension is at once regal (the pyramid as ancient symbol of royalty) yet democratically transparent.

Rose Center for Earth and Science, Natural History Museum, New York City, USA. Architect: Polshek Partnership. The cube that houses the Hayden Planetarium is the largest glass curtain-wall in the USA. Its 736 panes add up to 36,000 sq ft (3,969 sq m).

Burj al-Arab is located on an artificial island, 918 ft (280 m) off the shore of Dubai, UAE. Rising to 1053 ft (321 m), it is the tallest hotel building in the world. The architect, Tom Wright, intended it to resemble the sail of an Arabian boat.

1979–1999

1979 Xanadu houses, USA. A series of experimental homes built at different sites. They contained home automation systems, were ergonomically designed, and made of polyurethane insulation foam. Demolished by 2005.

1986 Hong Kong and Shanghai Bank, Hong Kong, China.

1988 The Corinthian, New York City, USA. The city's largest apartment building at the time. This 55-story structure designed by Michael Schimenti has towers of an unusual 'corn-cob' design.

1989 The Louvre Pyramid, Paris, France.

1990 Cherkizovskaya, Moscow, Russia. This Moscow Metro station is designed by architects VA Cheremin and AL Vigdorov. It has a single vault, with a curved ceiling and a platform without pillars decorated with stained glass panes at the ends, above the exits.

1990 Bank of China, Hong Kong, China.

1999 Rose Center for Earth and Science, Natural History Museum, New York City, USA.

1999 Burj al-Arab, Dubai, UAE.

Germany, engaged in large-scale prefabricated high-rise housing. After some time, however, in western Europe, growing affluence, a desire for individual freedom of expression, and the consequent choice available for open dissent resulted in dissatisfaction with the monotonous and repetitive designs that prefabrication predicated. General public apathy became a strong reaction to such mass produced housing blocks.

The growing indifference was contested by Ralph Erskine in his design of the Byker Redevelopment in Newcastle-upon-Tyne, England (1969–82). Erskine viewed the problem of social housing as one of pubic participation and social unity. The process of designing housing should, he believed, allow residents a say in the establishment of their communities. The estates he designed were not large monolithic blocks, but were composed of smaller units, each with a particular identity. Separation of vehicular and pedestrian movement and exploitation of site peculiarities assumed importance in his design. The projects became immensely popular with residents and visiting architects, and the influence is apparent in recent housing projects all over the world.

In the late 1960s and early 1970s, the Dutch architect NJ Habraken formulated his idea of 'Supports' and 'Infill' as an alternative way to look at social housing. While relying on prefabricated production, he advocated that the shell of the building and of dwelling units be standardized but wider options be made available for internal configurations.

Portugal's transition to a modern democracy in the early 1970s saw social housing emerge as governmental policy to deal with long neglected housing needs, particularly those of the deteriorated Illias (inner city traditional slum housing clusters) in cities like Porto and Lisbon. A large number of architects subsequently engaged in a community participation approach to design. Amongst them was Alvaro Siza, who designed low-rise, medium-density projects in Lisbon and Evora, that related to the lives of people not just as individual families but as communities. These projects also had a strong bearing on local context and explicit regard for urban history.

In the US, mass housing never assumed serious proportions. Existing cities were not destroyed in the war and the accent was on suburbanization, a move away from cities. This left large sections of poor people to inhabit vacated central city housing. The Pruitt Igoe housing built in St Louis, Missouri (1954) was an attempt at a larger urban housing project. It turned out to be a massive failure as it degenerated into a slum and was seen as a symbol of poverty. It was dynamited in 1972 (in the 1980s, housing super-blocks had to be demolished for similar reasons at Bijlmer, on the outskirts of Amsterdam).

Tom Collins House, Byker,
Newcastle-upon-Tyne,
by Ralph Erskine.

The Reichstag Dome, Berlin, Germany. Architect: Norman Foster. A large glass dome on the top of the parliamentary building allows passersby to view the Reichstag proceedings, thus symbolizing transparency in government. Natural light from above radiates down to the parliament floor.

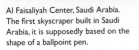

Al Faisaliyah Center, Saudi Arabia. The first skyscraper built in Saudi Arabia, it is supposedly based on the shape of a ballpoint pen.

Jewish Museum extension, Berlin. Architect Daniel Libeskind has connected this modern extension to the existing Baroque Berlin Museum building through underground axial roads which take the visitor along a narrative path.

Modern Art Museum of Fort Worth, Texas, USA. Architect: Tadao Ando. Five long pavilions constructed in glass, steel, and concrete, set into a reflecting pond. An effortless balance between letting in natural light and ensuring the security of museum exhibits.

1999–2002

1999 The Reichstag Dome, Berlin, Germany.

2000 Tate Modern, London, UK. Architect: Herzog & de Meuron. Previously a power station, it was converted to a national museum to display international modern art. Leaving the original building largely intact, the architects have combined the old with the new in a sensitive yet powerful manner.

2000 Al Faisaliyah Center, Saudi Arabia.

2001 Jewish Museum extension, Berlin.

2002 Modern Art Museum of Fort Worth, Texas, USA.

2002 The American Folk Art Museum, New York, USA. This eight-story structure by architects Tod Williams and Billie Tsien stands solemn and proud in the heart of Manhattan. Tombasil, the white bronze alloy used for external cladding, changes appearance with daylight and the seasons.

2002 Sendai Mediatheque, Sendai, Japan. Architect Toyo Ito devised a new sculptural concept using plates and tubes. While the 'plates' constitute the floor slabs, the 'tubes' are the columns that vertically penetrate the plates.

THE DEVELOPING WORLD

As the developed countries rebuilt their war-torn cities with industrialized mass housing, the newly independent countries in the developing world had to cope with large numbers of refugees and poor migrants flocking the cities. In addition, a rationalized, industrialized system of construction was unavailable to them, and middle-income people did not possess the ability to organize and build their own cheap affordable dwellings.

In such a scenario, governmental policies oscillated between providing fully built and serviced apartment dwellings to making available 'sites-and-services' plots, and leaving people to build on them on their own. Addressing the phenomenal housing shortage became a numbers game. Design quality was relegated to the background. Providing complete dwelling solutions was expensive and unsustainable, requiring huge subsidies—something governments could not afford in the face of other pressing priorities such as food, clothing, education, and health. The few sporadic exceptions that materialized did so through the accidental convergence of policy makers and competent architects.

South America. Mass housing was done on a large scale in Mexico, Brazil, Colombia, and other Latin American countries. In Mexico, Louis Barragan was involved in the design of a satellite town on the outskirts of Mexico City that had a large proportion of lower-income mass housing. On the outskirts of Bogota, Columbia, fairly large low-rise walk-up blocks, within the 'shells' of which inhabitants could organize their dwellings, were built for 120,000 low- and middle-income families. In the early 1970s, the Peruvian government organised the Previ Design Competition among a hand-picked group of architects, including Christopher Alexander and Charles Correa. The participants had to design and execute demonstrations at the site, considering the responses of future dwellers as one of the criteria, and which would then be evaluated by the government. Many Latin American governments used mass housing as an instrument to contain popular dissatisfaction and even popular movements.

Contemporary pueblo-style condominiums in Mexico painted in bright colors.

Taipei 101, Taipei, Taiwan. This 101-story landmark skyscraper was the tallest in the world when built. It combines traditional Asian with modern, international stylistic features.

Crown Fountain, Chicago, Illinois, USA. Artist Jaume Plensa's interactive work of public art is part of the Millennium Park in Chicago. It consists of a black granite reflecting pool between two glass block towers, which use light-emitting diodes to show digital videos.

The Swiss Re tower, London, UK. Architect: Norman Foster. Nicknamed the Gherkin for its tall, rounded, pickle-like shape. A novel system of structural glass and automated building systems in one of London's first environmentally sustainable skyscrapers.

The Scottish Parliament Building, Holyrood, Edinburgh, Scotland. Architect Enric Miralles cleverly captures the spirit of a somber institution in a manner that is anti-classical and non-hierarchical, as well as being obviously environmentally benign.

2003–2005

2003 Selfridges Building, Birmingham, UK.

2003 Simmons Hall Student Residence, MIT, Boston, USA. Architect: Steven Holl. A radical design in which a number of individual buildings form a porous membrane of light and transparency.

2003 Taipei 101, Taipei, Taiwan.

2004 Crown Fountain, Chicago, Illinois, USA.

2004 The Swiss Re tower, London, UK.

2004 The Scottish Parliament Building, Holyrood, Edinburgh, Scotland.

2005 BMW Central Plant, Leipzig, Germany. Architect: Zaha Hadid. Several auto assembly buildings are threaded together with actual production lines carrying half-built vehicles in a modern design that reflects the flow of ideas, people, and components that constitute BMW's commitment to excellence.

2005 Milan Trade Fair, Milan, Italy. Architect Massimiliano Fuksas derived the form from constant altimetric variations in 'craters', 'waves', and 'dunes'. The whole complex is covered by a vast roof—an undulating lightweight structure, with a surface area exceeding 54,740 sq yards (46,000 sq m).

Mass housing in Guangzhou, China.

Public housing, Astillero, Spain.

India and China. In India, in the 1960s, Maxwell Fry and Jane Drew were inspired by traditional living patterns in which dwelling and activities spilled over to the outdoor community space in an informal continuum; one which blurred the strict division between the public and the private. Their low-rise clustered housing in Chandigarh is a fine example of designing in a hot, arid climate for poorer communities. BV Doshi designed the World Bank financed Aranya project—a sites-and-services scheme for 50,000 economically weaker section (EWS) families in Indore. In communist China, mass housing was the only option available for families as the 'market' was practically non-existent. The government

Berlin Hauptbahnof, Berlin, Germany. Part of the transport plan for reunified Berlin, this is the main central station for Berlin, with a light and spacious design. The soaring glass hall of the Stadtbahn line (section through the city) running from east to west is intersected by the 160-m long, 40-m wide station building, running in a north-south direction.

2006–2010

2006 Berlin Hauptbahnof, Berlin, Germany.
2008 Beijing Airport, Beijing, China,
2008 Beijing National Stadium (Bird's Nest), Beijing, China.
2008 New Acropolis Museum, near Acropolis, Athens, Greece. Architect: Bernard Tschumi. Built just next to the Parthenon the museum makes a humble yet powerful statement by the straightforward use of three materials—marble, concrete, and glass.
2010 Burj Khalifa, Dubai, UAE.
2010 Strata, London, UK. Nicknamed 'the Razor' because of its sharp edges and sleek profile, the residential building has three turbines installed at its top to generate its own energy.
2010 Monterrey Housing, Nuevo León, Mexico. The government-commissioned 70-homes project was a turning point in social housing. The units are designed to incorporate the necessary parts of a house (kitchen, bathrooms). The rest of the complex is self built by the owners. Architects: Elemental, Santiago, Chile.

Beijing Airport, Beijing, China. Architects: Foster and Partners. The world's most advanced airport building evokes traditional Chinese symbols and colors, especially with its soaring dragon-like form.

Beijing National Stadium (Bird's Nest), Beijing, China. Architects: Herzog & de Meuron. Inaugurated at the 2008 Olympic Games, this is the largest steel construction in the world and has a striking resemblance to a bird's nest. At first glance the lines might seem random; however, each half of the stadium is consciously designed to be almost identical to the other.

New Acropolis Museum, Athens, Greece.

provided basic 'complete' homes with shared facilities such as kitchens and toilets, on a need-based system.

Privatization and the market-place. In the last two decades, government policies have shifted from the traditional role of housing provider to that of an enabler. The focus now is on regulating the housing market through planning and land policies which would ensure supply of land for social housing and permit private developers to provide the stock. This has hindered the production of housing for the urban poor and those who really need them in a speculative market. Architects now face the fresh challenge of adapting to the changed circumstances in this shifting paradigm of being social players in a market place.

Million Programme housing, Rinkeby, Sweden.

The Kanagawa Institute of Technology's Glass Building, Tokyo, Japan. Junya Ishigami and Associates' ultimate take on open-space office planning. The building's 305 white pillars create the sensation of zoned spaces and provide a flexible layout.

2010–2012

2010 The Kanagawa Institute of Technology's Glass Building, Tokyo, Japan.

2010 The Seed Cathedral, Shanghai, China.

2011 Pearl River Tower, Guangzhou, China. One of the world's most energy-efficient skyscrapers incorporates wind turbines, solar collectors, photovoltaic cells and underfloor air distribution.

2011 Metropol Parasol, Seville, Spain.

2011 Ordos Museum, Ordos, Mongolia. Inspired by the ever-rising sun on the grassland, the Chinese architectural firm MAD designed this museum located in the Gobi desert. The building combines local traditions with modern urban needs and context.

2012 Gardens by the Bay, Singapore. A nature park spanning 101 hectares over reclaimed land is part of a strategy of the government to transform Singapore from a "Garden City" to a "City in a Garden". Designed by Grant Associates and Gustafson Porter architects.

2012 The Shard, London.

2012 Heydar Aliyev Center, Baku, Azerbaijan.

Seed Cathedral, Shanghai, China. Thomas Heatherwick's sculptural creation comprises 60,000 acrylic rods, each bearing a plant seed at its inner tip. This building's dual role is to inform visitors and to act as a seed bank to archive Earth's ecological history.

Metropol Parasol, Seville, Spain. German architect Jurgen Mayer's wooden structure is claimed to be the largest such in the world.

The Shard, London. The tallest building in the UK. Its architect, Renzo Piano, was inspired by the railway lines next to the site and the masts of a sailing ship.

DECONSTRUCTIVISM

Bjarke Ingels' Mountain Dwellings residential complex in Copenhagen, Denmark, climbs on the back of the diagonal-roofed car park, evoking the slope of a mountain.

Based on the ideas of International Style of architecture which evolved in the 1920s–'30s in the USA and Europe, and the Japanese Metabolist movement of the 1960s–'70s, a new style in architecture started developing in the early 1990s. More than designing, this approach involves 'solving problems'. The focus lies on function and movement of people using the building. The pragmatism of this architectural idiom and the disaffection

with established norms of aesthetics has earned it another name: deconstructivism. Once again, the guiding principle is "form follows function". This approach is evident in the work of architect such as Frank Gehry, in its early phase, and Zaha Hadid, Bjarke Ingels and many others, more recently.

One of the most important theorists and urbanists of his generation is the Dutch architect Rem Koolhaas (b. 1944). In addition to his architecture, Koolhaas has also introduced the concept of the 'generic city' in urbanism, in which he examines and defines the organically developing nature of megacities in the 20th and 21st centuries.

The CCTV Center, Beijing, China, designed by Rem Koolhaas.

ARCHITECTURE WITH SOCIAL INTEREST

In a large part of Latin America the adoption of neo-liberal economics and policy in the early 1970s resulted in major social and housing problems during 1990–2000. The solution to successfully fight poverty and inequality has been sought through collective action, community involvement and individual initiative. A new generation of activists, social pragmatists and idealists emerged, and very soon, their efforts have become visible in architecture and urbanism.

A more democratic, equitable and inclusive form of urban development

is being practiced jointly by residents, politicians, architects and activists. Projects like the redevelopment of Torre de David, the empty and half-built office complex in downtown Caracas, and the Vivienda housing complex, where half the houses have to be finished by the residents themselves are pioneering examples. The work of architects like Alejandro Aravena of the Chilean architectural firm Elemental, Alfredo Brillembourg and Hubert Klumpner of Urban-Think Tank, and activist-politicians such as Antanas Mockus are setting the tone in this architectural movement.

Louvre-Lens, Lens, France.

Community In A Cube
(CIAC), Middleborough, UK

Fogo Island Inn, Newfoundland,
Canada Architect Todd
Saunders' light-on-its-feet
building, raised on a stilted
foundation, is rooted in
Newfoundland's outport
settlers' tradition of not
building permanent structures
or dwellings when sailing off
shore for fishing. Use has been
made of local materials and
craftsmanship to create this
"restorative space" for guests.

Queen Alia Terminal,
Amman, Jordan.
Composed of concrete
domes with roofs inspired
by Bedouin tents.

2012–2013

2012 CCTV Tower, Beijing,
China.

2012 Louvre-Lens, Lens,
France. SANAA and
Imrey Culbert architects
broke the design into
several spaces to
maintain the openness
of the site and evoke its
mining history.

2012 Community In
A Cube (CIAC),
Middleborough,
UK A mixed-use
scheme forming part
of the Middlehaven
regeneration project,
the building by
FAT Architecture,
communicates with
the surrounding space
though use of specific
local architecture.

2013 National Aquarium
Denmark, Kastrup,
Denmark.

2013 Louisiana Sports Hall
of Fame & Northwest
Louisiana History
Museum, Natchitoches,
USA. The louvered
copper exterior is
styled on the shutters of
plantation houses while
the interior imagines
the curve of Cane River
Lake.

2013 Tête en l'air
Social Housing, Paris,
France. An existing
building revamped into
inexpensive apartments
with private gardens.

2013 Fogo Island Inn,
Newfoundland, Canada.

2013 Queen Alia Terminal,
Amman, Jordan.

ANTI INTERNATIONAL ARCHITECTURE

The Ningbo Museum in China, designed by Wang Shu, represents a mountain, its valleys, caves, etc, which are key motifs in Chinese culture.

In the second decade of the 21st century, a style of urbanism and architecture has emerged as a reaction to the clean and uniform design of the new international style. A group of young architects have come to the fore. Honoring the local environment, tradition and craftsmanship, buildings are being created by combining modern techniques and traditional materials. Sustainability, reuse of materials and a local environment are taken very seriously. The Chinese architect Wang Shu (b. 1963) claims that globalization and its professionalized, soulless architecture have stripped cities of their special attributes. The works of Boonserm Premthada of Thailand and Kunle Adeyemi of Nigeria are clear examples of this new growing trend.

The Kunle Adeyemi designed Makoko Floating School, Lagos, on the coastline of Nigeria, is built of wood and forms part of a community of inter-locking residences.

Palm Jumeirah, Dubai, UAE. Artificial islands created by reclaiming land.

Museu do Amanhã, Rio de Janeiro, Brazil.

#CIDADEOLIMPICA

One World Trade Center (Freedom Tower), New York, USA. The tallest building in the western hemisphere has a footprint replicating the Twin Towers that once stood on the site. Its chamfered edges, forming eight triangles, climax to a square parapet at the top. With life safety systems far exceeding New York's building codes, the tower is one an iconic symbol of the city's skyline.

Poly Grand Theater, Shanghai, China. A theater box wrapped in a transparent skin of glass, with tunnels and footbridges puncturing the simple elevational geometry.

2014–2016

2014 Palm Jumeirah, Dubai, UAE.

2014 20 Fenchurch Street, London, UK.

2015 Providence Tower, London, UK.

2015 Museu do Amanhã, (Museum of Tomorrow) Rio de Janeiro, Brazil. The museum uses 40 per cent less energy compared with conventional buildings. Solar spines and a fan-like skylight enable it to adapt to changing environmental conditions.

2015 Freedom Tower, One World Trade Center, New York, USA.

2016 Poly Grand Theater, Shanghai, China.

2016 Roy and Diana Vagelos Education Center, New York, USA. A state-of-the-art medical and graduate education building with communal and study spaces distributed along an exposed staircase that extends through the height of the building.

2017 Apple Park, Cupertino, USA.

2020 (expected completion) Jeddah Tower, Jeddah, Saudi Arabia. The mixed-use building featuring a hotel, office space, apartments and the world's highest observatory will have a slender, subtly asymmetrical massing, evoking a bundle of leaves shooting up from the ground. At over one km in height, it will be the world's tallest building.

169

The history of fortification is as old as the human race. A hill top defended by a thick hedge of branches and thorns, perhaps surrounded by a ditch, may have been rudimentary, but those principles of construction, much elaborated, served castle construction for many centuries. As the nature of warfare changed, the shape, height, thickness, and function of the walls also changed, but the essential principle remained the same.

For centuries military techniques altered only very gradually, and so castles remained relevant. In the 15th century, however, the advent of the cannon changed all that. Stone walls could no longer resist the mighty forces of artillery, and so the castle was transformed into something purely decorative. That is not to say that the castle died out completely. For example, the Maginot Line, a series of fortifications built by the French during the 1930s to deter attack from Germany, took the

Château de Pierrefonds, France, 14th century, restored in the 19th century.

8000 BCE Jericho, Israel. The ancient walled city of Jericho was surrounded with a 25-ft (8-m) wide 6-ft (2-m) deep ditch cut from solid rock.

1600 BCE Ashur, present-day Iraq. The ancient capital of Assyria, was protected by 'curtain' walls, the connecting walls linking up towers or bastions.

c. 1300 BCE The Lion's Gate, Mycenae, Greece. The walled city could only be approached by one track and entered through heavily defended gateways.

➤ 600 BCE Babylon, Iraq. Nebuchadnezzar II's Babylon was protected by walls 23 ft (8 m) thick, with towers and a moat.

⋀ 400 BCE Rhodes, Greece. The island fortifications, with the use of arches and piers, were later imitated by the Romans and Byzantines.

300 BCE Maiden Castle, Dorset, England. A concentric circle earthwork, hill-top defense.

c. 221 BCE The Great Wall of China, China. Almost 2,300 miles (4,000 km) long. Much of the present wall was constructed during the Ming Dynasty, 14th–16th centuries CE.

215 BCE Syracuse, Italy. The first use of loopholes or *muertières*, at that time simple vertical slots through which archers could fire.

37 BCE Jerusalem, Israel. Herod the Great constructs the great walls of Jerusalem.

30 BCE Masada, Israel. Herod builds the hill-top fortress of Masada, surrounding the whole of the plateau at the top with a wall 12 ft (4 m) high and 18 ft (6 m) thick. Like many later medieval castles it was an isolated fortress built to defend a leader and his followers. It took the Roman general Flavius Silva many months of intensive siege in 70 CE, including building a huge ramp which is still visible, before the citadel was captured. The Jewish defenders chose suicide over capture.

castle underground. All to no avail, however, as the German army demonstrated decisively at the beginning of World War II.

Archaeology has uncovered extensive fortification throughout those areas of the earliest fixed settlements in our history: Mesopotamia, Egypt, and Greece. For example, the earliest walls of the famed city of Jericho were built c. 8000 BCE, while those of Babylon predate1900 BCE. The strongly fortified hill towns of Mycenae and Tiryns in Greece date from c. 1300 BCE, and in Britain, the great earthwork fortress of Maiden Castle, Dorset (still clearly delineated today), was constructed about 300 BCE.

The Romans were expert fortifiers as well as effective besiegers. Legionaries carried with them the materials needed to construct temporary defenses wherever they camped, and as soon as they had established their rule built camps, outposts, frontier lines (the Limes Germanicus in Germany of about 200 CE and Hadrian's Wall in Britain, 122–25 CE, are the most famous), and fortified cities throughout their empire (Nîmes, Autun, and Senlis in France; Colchester, York, and Chester in England, have particularly good remains).

◀ **c. 15 BCE Roman fortified gates:** For example, Porte Auguste, Nîmes, Porte St André, Autun, both in France.

4 BCE The first mention of the portcullis (a wood and iron gate that could be lowered and raised) by the Roman Aeneas Tacticus.

c. 200 CE The Limes, Germany. A series of Roman fortifications stretching 300 miles (480 km) from the Rhine to the Danube.

122–25 CE Hadrian's Wall, UK. Divided Roman-occupied England from Scotland, 73 miles (117 km) long, about 10 ft (3.5 m) wide and about 20 ft (7 m) high, with fortified camps every 4 miles (6 km) the largest and best preserved being Housesteads.

300 CE Roman Porte Nigra, Trier, Germany.

◀ **413 CE Constantinople, Turkey.** The walls were punctuated every 60 yards (55 m) by towers.

527–565 CE Castles, Byzantine Empire. Emperor Justinian undertook extensive castle building throughout the Byzantine empire.

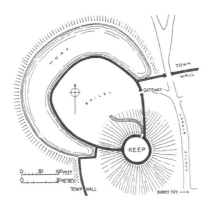

◀ **Mid-11th century Motte-and-bailey castles, Europe.** "It is the custom of the nobles of that neighborhood [northeast France] to make a mound of earth as high as they can and dig a ditch about it. The space on the top of the mound is enclosed by a palisade of very strong logs, strengthened at intervals by towers. Inside the enclosure is a citadel or keep. The entrance to the fortress is by means of a bridge." Jean de Colmieu, 1130.

With the collapse of the Roman empire in the fourth and fifth centuries the history of fortification shifted to the Byzantine Empire under continual attack on all sides. Because timber was scarce in this part of the world the Byzantines tended to build in stone both great walled encirclements of cities (most notably Constantinople in 413) and castles. It was this tradition that the Muslims (particularly Saladin in the 12th century) adapted and from which Crusader invaders learned important lessons, which they took back to Europe. For example, the great Château Gaillard in France was built by Richard I (completed 1198) following his experience during the Third Crusade (1189–92). The Crusaders also built massive fortifications in the Holy Land itself (combining the Muslim tower and Byzantine curtain-wall models). The Krak des Chevaliers in Syria (begun 1150), built by the Knights Hospitaller, is one of the most spectacular and remarkably well-preserved examples (the principle of the double-wall defense employed at Krak was later applied to the still impressive fortifications of the French town of Carcassonne during the 13th century).

The 11th century ushered in a massive expansion of castle building in western Europe. The Normans of France were at the forefront of new developments, and their conquest of England in 1066 initiated many new castles. One of the main types was the motte-and-bailey—essentially an elaboration of the ancient defended hill. The motte or mound (sometimes man-made) on which stood a tower, while a larger area, the bailey, also protected by a ditch-moat and earth palisade or sometimes a wall, protected the locals and their livestock. Another castle type, the rectangular stone keep, was also built throughout northern France and England (the most famous being the White Tower of the Tower of London, built 1070).

Edward I (1272–1307), king of England, undertook one of the greatest building programs in the history of the castle during his pacification of Wales. Caerphilly (1267–77), Conway (1283–87), Caernarvon (1285–1322), Harlech (1285–1290), and Beaumaris (1295–1320), still stand as his legacy.

The Tower of London, UK.

◄ 1150 Krak des Chevaliers, Syria. A Crusader castle built by the Knights of St John (Knights Hospitallers) has been called "the best preserved and most wholly admirable castle in the world." It withstood prolonged sieges by the Muslims until 1271.

1170–82 Citadel, Cairo, Egypt. Saladin builds the great citadel of Old Cairo, among the finest works of military architecture of the medieval period.

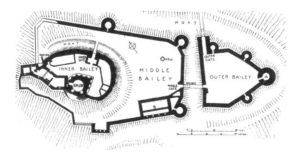

▲ 1180 Gravensteen Castle, Ghent, Belgium. Built by Philip of Alsace, Count of Flanders.

◄ 1196–98 Château Gaillard, France. Richard I (Lionheart) completes the construction of Château Gaillard, France, incorporating many of the lessons he had learned during the Third Crusade. Gaillard was one of the most formidable castles of its day.

c. 1200 Round keeps begin to replace rectangular. Tour de César, Provins, and Etampes, in France; Conisborough and Orford in England are fine examples.

➤ **1230 Eilean Donan Castle, Scotland.** A fortress for the Macrae clan.

∨ **1247 Carcassonne, restored 19th cenutry, France.** The old walls (dating from Roman and Visigothic times) were strongly reinforced with the addition of an outer curtain wall, towers, and gatehouses.

➤ **1310 Rhodes Castle, Greece.** Among the finest military works of the 14th century are the fortifications of the citadel of Rhodes, built by the Knights of St John. It was forced to capitulate in 1523 after a prolonged siege by Suleiman the Magnificent.

Harlech Castle, Wales, UK.

Conway Castle, Wales, UK.

Caenarvon Castle, Wales, UK.

⋀ 1272–1307 Wales, UK.
Edward I, king of England. During his pacification of Wales Edward built a string of formidable castles which, because they were never tested in war, remain today almost intact.

◄ 1308–80 Ponte Valentré, Cahors, France. A fine example of a medieval fortified bridge.

1370–83 The Bastille, Paris France. One of the most powerful fortifications of its time. Destroyed during the French Revolution.

◀ **1386–90 Bodiam Castle, England.**

➤ **1488 Amsterdamsche Poort, Haarlem, Holland.** The gateways to medieval towns were often heavily defended and also served as customs points at which taxes were collected on imported goods.

➤ **1594 Matsumoto Castle, Nagano, Japan.** Many of the finest castles in Japan were built during the Momoyama period (1573–1638). Matsumoto is typical in standing on a stone base (glacis) that is surrounded by a moat. The keep was wooden.

17th century The Pré Carré, France. Sébastian le Prestre de Vauban (1633–1707) was commissioned by Louis XIV of France to build a series of forts (the Pré Carré) on the frontier with the then Spanish Netherlands. His moated star-shaped fortresses left no 'blind spots' where an attacker could hide. Defenders could fire on the enemy with cannons protected by thick walls and rake the moats with handguns fired through slits in the walls. During his career he built 33 forts and strengthened 300 others throughout France.

◄ **1869–8 Neuschwanstein, Bavaria.** The castle as romantic fantasy. Designed by Eduard Reidel (1813–85) and Georg von Dollmann (1830–95) for Ludwig II of Bavaria.

1929 The Maginot Line, France. André Maginot, French Minister for War, starts building the ill-fated Maginot line: a system of 50 forts stretching from the Belgian border in the west to the Swiss border in the east. When Germany attacked France in 1940 key forts were either knocked out by German special forces teams, or simply by-passed.

1931-43 Vallo Alpino, present-day Slovenia and Croatia. The Italians built one of the heaviest defence lines during World War II. When its construction ceased in 1943 a total of 1,475 positions, each with one or more casemates, had been constructed, and 450 more were still under construction.

A PENTHOUSE ADDRESS

The origin of the term penthouse derives from the Roman covered passage *(musculus)*, made of timber and covered in hide and tiles, used to protect soldiers while they were undermining the walls of a besieged fortress or town.

THERE CAN BE LITTLE DOUBT THAT IN MANY WAYS THE STORY OF BRIDGE BUILDING IS THE STORY OF CIVILIZATION. BY IT, WE CAN READILY MEASURE AN IMPORTANT PART OF PEOPLE'S PROGRESS.
Franklin D Roosevelt, 18 October, 1931

Bridges have always had an impact beyond their status as architectural forms or engineering marvels. They have inspired artists and poets; they have stood since primitive times as symbols of connection, of possibility, of making it to the 'other side,' even as their function remains resolutely earthy: linking point A to point B.

A bridge provides a pathway where normal surface construction is impossible or impractical. The earliest bridges were natural—fallen trees spanning gorges, huge rocks arching over streams, or vines joining tree to tree. The first man-made bridges mimicked nature's handiwork: tree trunks laid across streams, flat stones traversing shallow waterways, or vines, twisted and hung in suspension. These three types—beam, arch, and suspension—have existed since ancient times, and remain the prototypes for even the most complex modern bridges.

The Romans were antiquity's greatest bridge builders. Roman engineering went far beyond anything previously seen, primarily through four advances: the discovery of cement; perfection of the semicircular masonry arch; development of the coffered dome; and a commitment to public works. Among the most famous of the surviving Roman bridges are the Pont du Gard (14 CE) near Nîmes, France; the Alcántara Bridge (98 CE) on the Spanish-Portuguese border; and the aqueduct at Segovia, Spain (98 CE).

Asia's history of significant bridge building predates Europe's. China was the source of many bridge forms, including the first chain-link suspension bridge, the Panho (206 BCE), built during the Han Dynasty. After the decline of the Roman Empire, beam, arch, suspension, and cantilever bridge building flourished in China while languishing in Europe for seven centuries. The Anji Bridge (605 CE) is far more sophisticated than anything contemporaneous in Europe.

The medieval period saw a revival of bridge building in Europe, many commissioned and executed by Christian religious orders. The Gothic pointed arch was a distinguishing feature of this era, as was the multi-functional

Tagus Bridge, Lisbon, Portugal, completed in 1966.

bridge, which incorporated shops, houses, chapels, towers, and other buildings into its structure. The legendary Pont D'Avignon (1187) is an example of a bridge built by a religious order, which included a chapel in its overall design.

Bridges as bustling centers of commerce, grand passageways, and / or residences sprung up during the Renaissance, exemplified by renaissance developments on the Ponte Vecchio, which was originally built in 1345, Venice's Rialto (1591), and Paris' Pont Neuf (1607). The greatest architect of the era, Andrea Palladio (1508–80), spawned a wave of Neo-Classical bridge building through his influential books, *Quattro Libri dell' Architettura*. These designs were adopted primarily by English landscape designers.

Iron revolutionized bridge building. Its widespread use during the Industrial Revolution made it the material of choice for early 19th-century engineers like Thomas Telford, Robert Stephenson, and Isambard Brunel. Iron Bridge (1779) in Shropshire, England, was the first all-iron bridge and still stands as a monument to the advent of the Industrial Age. By the turn of the century, a new material was embraced that expanded even further how big, how long, and how mighty (while seeming lighter) bridges could be. Steel was the ticket. It was stronger and more flexible than iron, and made more design variations possible. New York's Brooklyn Bridge (1883), designed by John Roebling, remains one of the world's most famous steel suspension bridges. Leading bridge designers James Eads, Benjamin Baker, and Gustave Eiffel also exploited steel to magnificent effect, making lasting contributions to the world pantheon of spectacular bridges.

⌃ **c. 2000 BCE China.** Crude suspension bridges built in India and China.

➤ **480 BCE Hellespont bridge, Iran.** King Xerxes constructed a huge pontoon bridge across the Hellespont (the straits dividing Asia and Europe), literally and metaphorically bridging East and West.

c. 55 BCE Roman bridges. Julius Caesar spanned the River Rhine with wooden trestle bridges.

∧ **c. 14 CE Pont du Gard near Nîmes, France.** Built by Agrippa as part of a 21 mile (45 km) aqueduct to carry water across the River Gard in cement-lined channels on the top tier.

◄ **c. 100 CE Aicántara, Spain.** This bridge was built by the Roman emperor Trajan.

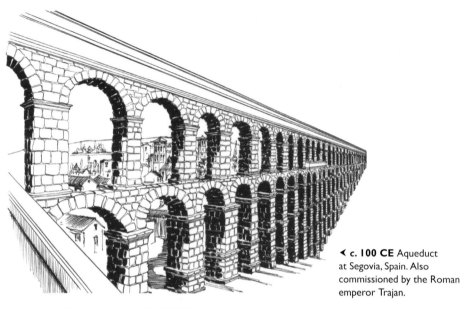

◀ **c. 100 CE** Aqueduct at Segovia, Spain. Also commissioned by the Roman emperor Trajan.

➤ **605–16 CE An-chi bridge, Zhao Xian, Hebei Province, China.** One of the most remarkable stone bridges in the world, predating anything in the West by 700 years.

The 20th century was a Golden Age for American bridge building. The Brooklyn Bridge was followed by a series of ever longer suspension structures: San Francisco's Golden Gate (1937); Michigan's Mackinac Straits (1957); New York's Verrazano Narrows (1964), to name a few. Europe and Asia quickly joined in toward the end of the century, producing astonishing, groundbreaking bridges into the millennium and beyond. Denmark's Great Belt (1998), Hong Kong's Tsing Ma (1997), and Japan's Akashi Kaikyo (1998), are some of the bridges that far exceeded what was once thought possible in terms of sheer length. New materials and new forms continue to alter bridge design the world over. Prestressed concrete, joining steel in popularity in the 20th century, is giving way to experiments with new hybrid materials. New types, like cable-stayed variations, are increasingly popular in the 21st century, contributing to the world landscape quite a few immensely strong but paradoxically delicate-looking structures. Avant-garde architect-engineer Santiago Calatrava's most celebrated bridge, the Puente del Alamillo (1992) in Seville, Spain, is a shining example.

Today's bridges are a testimony to both construction and form. Some of them are truly monuments, hailed for their visual impact and symbolic value as much as for their technology. As the need arises for more and more existing bridges to undergo repair, rehabilitation, and renovation to withstand 21st-century traffic loads—along with newer ones to be built—research also continues on earthquake-resistant design solutions. Appropriate materials that are high strength, high fatigue, and corrosion resistant, lightweight, and cost effective are being explored. Among them are fiber-reinforced polymer and aluminum, and there is even an attempt to transfer technology from the aerospace industry, giving such materials an edge over their traditional concrete and steel counterparts.

Three thousand years of bridge building make it easy to understand why Roosevelt saw in it a parallel to the "story of civilization." It's the story of human achievement, of human stumbling, of human striving. Its history, its present, and its future all speak volumes about who we are and where we are going.

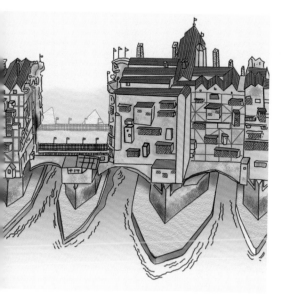

1187 Pont d'Avignon, France. The original length was about 3,000 ft (900 m) and spanned the Petit-Rhône and the Grand-Rhône.

◀ **1210 Old London Bridge, London, UK.** Nineteen arches, none identical, created fierce tidal rips as the River Thames was forced through the narrow openings.

▲ **1345 The Ponte Vecchio, Florence, Italy.** Attributed to Taddeo Gaddi (c. 1300–66), a pupil of the great painter Giotto. The Ponte Vecchio was the first bridge in Europe to use the segmented arch (although it had been used in the An-chi bridge, China, in 605 CE).

1357 Charles Bridge, Prague, Czech Republic. It replaced an older stone bridge destroyed by floods in 1342. Although built by Charles IV, Holy Roman Emperor, the bridge was not named for him until 1870.

1507 Pont Notre-Dame, Paris. This was the first stone bridge in Paris.

➤ **1591 The Rialto, Venice.** Designed by Antonio da Ponte (1512–97). Following a fire in 1512 that destroyed yet another in a succession of wooden bridges, Fra Giovanni Giocondo (the designer of the first stone bridge in Paris, the Pont Notre-Dame) suggested a permanent stone structure. Although designs were submitted by various architects—Palladio and Michelangelo included—until the 75-year-old (and appropriately named) Antonio da Ponte daringly proposed

spanning the Grand Canal with a single arch. He overcame the main problem of the soft canal bed by creating foundations made up of 6,000 alder piles packed tightly within coffer dams. The month it was completed, July 1591, it had to withstand an earthquake—which it did, triumphantly unscathed.

▲ **c. 1650 Khaju bridge, Isfahan, Iran.** Built by Shah Abbas II of Persia. It is a unique combination of dam, bridge, and palace.

1750 Westminster Bridge, London, UK. It took 500 years for a second bridge to span the Thames and relieve the severe congestion of the Old London Bridge.

▼ **1777–79 Ironbridge, Coalbrookdale, UK.** The first cast-iron bridge and one of the first structures to be made from prefabricated parts which cut construction time to only three months. Its single arch spans 100 ft (30.5 m) over the Severn Gorge; its five arch ribs were each cast in two halves. The bridge was so crowded with celebrants on its 200th birthday in 1979 that parts of it actually broke off and plunged into the river. Now visitors are strictly limited to no more than 200 at any one time.

1806 Birth year of two of the greatest bridge builders in history—John Roebling of Brooklyn Bridge fame, and Isambard Kingdom Brunel of the Clifton Suspension Bridge.

1824–31 Old London Bridge replaced with a masonry bridge designed by Sir John Rennie. It was to last until 1972, when it was sold and re-erected at Lake Havasu City, Arizona.

◀ **1864 (completed) Clifton Suspension Bridge, UK.** Although Brunel had built a number of wooden bridges the Clifton Suspension over the Avon Gorge at Bristol, England, was his first—and last—major bridge. Work began in 1835 but repeated delays held up progress. In 1842 Brunel was told to stop work and the iron for the chain was sold. Brunel died in 1859, but the work was finished to his design by colleagues from the Institution of Civil Engineers.

BRIDGES

1866 Cincinnati, Ohio, USA. John Roebling built the then world-record suspension bridge over the Ohio River at Cincinnati.

➤ **1874 St Louis, Mississippi, USA.** James Eads' triple-arch bridge across the Mississippi River at St Louis—the world's first important steel bridge and the longest of its time.

1879 The Tay bridge disaster, Scotland, UK. From the very beginning of work on the Tay Bridge in 1871 there were problems, and a series of accidents cost the lives of 20 workers. In 1878 the rail service started, but at 5pm on Sunday, 28 October 1879, a massive storm smashed into the bridge. A train carrying 75 passengers reached the center just as it collapsed, hurling it into the river. A Court of Inquiry blamed Sir Thomas Beach, the bridge's designer, who had completely miscalculated wind stress on the structure.

➤ **1882–89 Forth Rail Bridge, Scotland, UK.** The designers, Sir John Fowler and Benjamin Baker, attacked the problem of spanning the estuary of the Firth of Forth with the innovative use of steel and cantilevering.

▼ **1883 Brooklyn Bridge, New York City, USA.** John Roebling's brilliant design for his 1,595 ft (486 m) suspension bridge was executed by his son, Washington Roebling, following his father's tragic death from tetanus after his foot was crushed in an accident on site.

∧ 1886–94 Tower Bridge, London, UK.
Designed jointly by the engineer John Wolf-Barry
and the architect Sir Horace Jones. Tower Bridge
is a 'bascule' ('see-saw' or 'rocker') bridge which
allows the roadway to be raised to let ships pass
beneath.

**1927–31 George Washington Bridge, New
York City, USA.** Designed by Othmar Amman
and built by the Roebling Co. The second car deck
was added in 1962.

1932 Sydney Harbour Bridge, Australia.
Designed by English engineer Ralph Freeman, the
arched cantilever bridge is the most massive of its
kind in the world.

**≻ 1933–37 Golden Gate Bridge, San
Francisco, USA.** Designed by Charles Ellis under
the direction of Joseph Strauss. Its suspended
span is 4,200 ft (1,280 m). Two hundred thousand
pedestrians had the free run of the bridge on its
opening day, 27 May 1937. Its grace and majesty
have inspired countless artists and writers, but
it also has the dubious distinction of being the
world's most popular site for suicides.

**1954–57 Mackinac Straights Bridge,
Michigan, USA.** With a suspended span of 3,800
ft (1,158 m), the Mackinac was second only to the
Golden Gate, San Francisco, when it was built.

**≺ 1940 Tacoma Narrows Straights Bridge,
Washington State, USA.** The catastrophic
failure of the Tacoma Narrows Straights Bridge
remains one of the most notorious of all time.
It self-destructed on 7 November 1940, a mere
four months after its opening on 1 July 1940.
Before its demise it was nicknamed 'Galloping
Gertie' because it swayed
and rippled even under light
winds. Official cause of death:
fatal torsional oscillation.

**≺ 1966 Tagus Bridge,
Lisbon, Portugal.** Europe's
first long-span suspension
bridge. The exceptional
deck height of 230 ft (70 m)
allows shipping to pass in
and out of the busy port of
Lisbon.

BRIDGES

1978 New River George Bridge, West Virginia, USA. The world's longest steel arch.

1981 Humber Bridge, UK. For 17 years it held the record for the longest suspended span (4,624 ft / 1,410 m) until superseded by Denmark's Great Belt East Bridge and Japan's Akashi Kaikyo Bridge, both completed in 1998.

1993-2004 Millau Viaduct, Millau, France. The bridge crosses the River Tarn and runs through a spectacular gorge between two high plateaus. It provides a direct route from Paris to Barcelona. Each section of the dramatic yet delicate bridge spans 1,122 ft (342 m) and its columns range in height from 246 ft (75 m) to 803 ft (245 m, equivalent to the height of the Eiffel Tower), with the masts rising a further 295 ft (90 m) above the road deck. Each column splits into two thinner, more flexible columns below the roadway, forming an A-frame above deck level. The tapered form of the columns both expresses their structural loads and minimizes their profile in elevation (see previous page).

1998 Akashi-Kaikyo Bridge, Kobe and Awaji-shima, Japan. The longest, tallest, and most expensive suspension bridge built to date. It stretches 12,828 ft (4,276 m) and cost $ 4.3 billion to construct. Its two towers, at 928 ft (309 m) are the tallest bridge towers in the world. Engineers armed the all-steel bridge to withstand the worst of Japanese hurricanes, tsunamis, and earthquakes. In fact, the bridge did indeed survive the catastrophic Great Hanshin Earthquake of 1995, although when the shaking subsided it had grown 3 ft longer!

2001 Leonardo Bridge Project, Aas, Norway. Leonardo da Vinci's visionary design for a 787-ft (240-m) span granite bridge crossing the Golden Horn as part of a project for Sultan Bayazid II of Constantinople finally saw the light of day 500 years later in a smaller pedestrian reconstruction over the highway linking Oslo and Stockholm. Spearheaded by artist Vebjørn Sand, its final plans were made by Selberg Architects. Built in timber, the bridge resembles a perfect pressed bow, and relies on two structural principals, the keystone arch and the parabolic curve.

▼ 2001 Gateshead Millennium Bridge, Newcastle on Tyne, UK. The world's first and only tilting bridge, it was so designed to allow passing ships up to 82 ft (25 m) high to move up the River Tyne. Every day at 12 pm, the bridge rotates back on large bearings for 4.5 minutes depending on wind speed. It consists of a pair of steel arches, suspended above the river from a series of suspension cables, one comprising the pedestrian and cycle path, and the other a supporting deck forming an arc over the river. As the arc tilts, the pathway rises, with each arch counterbalancing the other. The bridge was

designed by Wilkinson Eyre and installed in one piece by Asian Hercules II, one of the world's largest floating cranes.

2004 Sundial Bridge, Turtle Bay, California, USA. Resembling a bird in flight, this pedestrian bridge over the Sacramento River connects the Redding river trail system with the Turtle Bay Exploration Park and McConnell Arboretum. Santiago Calatrava's unique cantilevering methods, here using a tall pylon (which acts as a sundial telling time on a Spanish tiled garden border on the north) and cable, dispensed with supports in the nearby salmon-spawning water. Made of steel, glass, and granite, it has a beautiful translucent non-skid deck for viewing at night.

2007 Constitution Bridge, Venice, Italy. Calatrava's hi-tech structure was the city's first new bridge to be built in 70 years, and the fourth over the Grand Canal. It links Venice's railway station on one side with Piazzale Roma on the other. Criticized on issues of cost overruns, structural instability, and initial lack of access for the disabled—the bridge had no formal opening. The arc of steel, dubbed a "carpet of light" by some, spans 310 ft (94 m) and is accessed by a flight of glass steps. The final cost was estimated at 11 million euros.

◀ 2010 The Helix Bridge, Singapore. A pedestrian walkway inspired by the double-helix structure of DNA, the bridge looks delicate and intricate, but the two helix constructions act as a strong tubular truss enabling the 280-m span to carry 10,000 people at a time. The bridge has four viewing pods which provide stunning views of the Singapore skyline while glass openings in the floor create a relationship with the water underneath.

2016 Lucky Knot Bridge, Changsha, China. The bridge "with no beginning and no end", described so because of its inspiration from a Mobius ring, is also inspired by the Chinese decorative art of knotting, which is associated with luck. Practically, its shape allows it to not only span the river but connect some of the rapidly developing city's public spaces, like roads, parks and river banks at different points and heights. The roller coaster look of the truss bridge is vivified by its red colour.

THE WORLD'S LONGEST BRIDGES

Rank	Bridge	Location	Ft (m)	Year
1.	Akashi Kaikyo	Hyogo, Japan	6,529 (1,990)	1998
2.	Xihoumen bridge	Zhoushan Archipelago, China	5,412 (1,650)	2007
3.	Great Belt Link	Funen-Zealand, Denmark	5,326 (1,624)	1998
4.	Osman Gazi	Sea of Marmara, Turkey	5,090 (1,550)	2016
5.	Yi Sun-sin	Yeosu, South Korea	5,069 (1,545)	2012
6.	Runyang	Yangtze River, Nanjing, China	4,887 (1,490)	2005
7.	Nanjing Fourth Yangtze	Yangtze River, Nanjing, China	4,652 (1,418)	2012
8.	Humber	Hull, England	4,626 (1,410)	1981
9.	Yavuz Sultan Selim	Straits of Bosphorus, Istanbul, Turkey	4,619 (1,408)	2016
10.	Jiangyin	Jiangsu, China	4,544 (1,385)	1999

• *All bridges are suspension bridges*
• *Length is main span length*
• *Date is year completed*
• *Sources:* Bridges *by Judith Dupre; updated information from http://bridge.aalto.fi/en/longspan.html*

TOWERS

THE FORCE AND POWER OF ALTITUDE MUST BE IN IT, THE GLORY AND THE PRIDE
OF EXALTATION MUST BE IN IT. IT MUST BE EVERY INCH A PROUD
AND SOARING THING, RISING IN SHEER EXALTATION . . .
American skyscraper pioneer, Louis Sullivan, 1896.

From the tower of Babel to the Petronas Towers in Kuala Lumpur, building ever skyward has been a persistent theme in both lore as well as the actual history of architecture. Taller and taller buildings have evolved from practical considerations, to be sure—especially limitations of space—but colossal buildings, soaring higher and higher, carry a powerful symbolism that has been as much a reason for their existence as any other.

Petronas Towers, Kuala Lumpur, Malaysia, 1998.

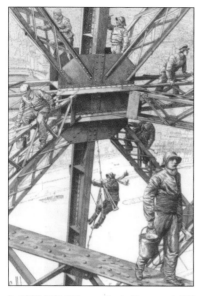

> **1889 Eiffel Tower, Paris, France, 1,063 ft (324 m).** Engineer Gustave Eiffel's colossal edifice was built for the Paris Exposition. Gigantic it was, but beloved it certainly was not, at first. A "truly tragic street lamp" (even Eiffel referred to it as France's tallest flag pole) and an "odious column of bolted metal" were some of the comments of early detractors. It was the tallest structure in the world for 40 years, until the Chrysler Building topped it in 1930.

The term 'skyscraper' was coined in the 1880s in America, just after the first tall buildings appeared, mostly in Chicago and New York. While a decidedly modern art form, the skyscraper can trace its roots to ancient times. The impulse to build toward the heavens has been present in many civilizations. Egyptian pyramids, medieval towers, Gothic spires, Mayan pyramids, Chinese pagodas, although not strictly precursors of modern-era skyscrapers, share the same desire to create high buildings that proclaim power and induce awe.

Steel-framed construction and great height are the primary defining features of skyscrapers. Other innovations were crucial in making them functional: elevator technology, fireproofing, central heating, electrical plumbing pumps, and the telephone, to name some. The rapid growth of metropolitan centers in the late 1800s created the social impetus for high-rise buildings; technology did the rest.

The story of super-tall buildings begins in Chicago, where the great fire of 1871 wiped out much of the city, and rebuilding began on a vast scale. The Industrial Revolution had made iron and steel viable as building materials. Chicago's Home Insurance Building (1885) was the first tall building to be supported by a steel skeleton of vertical columns and horizontal beams, although its 10 stories make it diminutive for a modern skyscraper. The move away from load-bearing walls, along with the advent of elevators meant that buildings could shoot infinitely higher. A new era of building was born.

^ 1885 Home Insurance Building, Chicago, USA, 138 ft (41.4 m). Considered the world's first skyscraper, this 10-story building (demolished in 1931) was the first to be supported by a steel skeleton of vertical columns and horizontal beams. Engineer William Le Baron Jenney's discovery that thin pieces of steel could support a building triggered a revolutionary change in the way tall buildings could be constructed.

⌄ 1902 Flatiron Building, New York City, USA, 285 ft (85.5 m). Designed by Daniel Burnham and John Wellborn Root, the Flatiron (so named because its triangular profile looked like an old smoothing, or flat, clothes iron) is New York's oldest surviving skyscraper. Unlike Burnham's work on Chicago high-rises where he avoided historical references, the Flatiron is loaded with classical detailing from its rusticated base to its corniced top.

Pioneering early skyscrapers included the Wainwright Building (St Louis, 1891) featuring Louis Sullivan's unique stylistic articulation; the Reliance Building (Chicago, 1894) with its revolutionary glass curtain wall; and the Barclay-Vesey Building (New York, 1926), which completed echewed historical motifs in both its massing and its decorative detail.

Other great early skyscrapers did use art-historical motifs. The Flatiron Building (New York, 1902) had its Beaux-Arts design; the Metropolitan Life Insurance Tower (New York, 1909) had a Classical silhouette; and the Woolworth Building (New York, 1913) its glorious Gothic detailing. Whether quoting from the past or trying to break from it, all the great skyscrapers reflect their designers' efforts to find the proper aesthetic for an architectural form that was growing ever taller and was clearly here to stay.

The golden age of skyscraper construction is generally agreed to be the period that gave rise to the Chrysler Building (New York, 1930); the Empire State Building (New York, 1931); the PSFS Building (Philadelphia, 1932); and the Rockefeller Center (New York, 1940), to name just a few. These glorious buildings shattered previous height barriers, exploited flexible materials, and gave new resonance to the concept of buildings as aspirational symbols.

Then came master architect Mies van der Rohe and the Seagram Building (New York, 1958). Mies was prominent in the Modernist movement in architecture decades before the Seagram Building was completed, and the impact of the Seagram on skyscraper design was immense. It was the prototype for the spare, glass-walled, box-shaped office building that has been the dominant form in skyscraper design over the second half of the 20th century and into the 21st.

The end of the 20th century saw a stylistic shift in skyscraper design from Modernism to Post Modernism, to hybrids of the two, mixed with vernacular idioms. More notably it moved away from being an almost exclusively American phenomenon, to a world-wide one. Today, eight out of 10 of the world's tallest buildings are in Asia.

Petro dollars and booming economies at the start of the 21st century are shaping the architectural dreams of oil rich and developing countries. Asian cities are soaring upwards as proof of the new-found wealth of tower-obsessed developers and politicians. From the Middle East to Korea to Taiwan, distinctively designed skyscrapers, not only in the metropolises but smaller cities too have become a must on the built landscape. The Dubai Burj and Guanzhou's skyscrapers, when complete, will give the Chicago Spire good competition in technical and visual mastery, while competing for the title of highest building. And while a great deal of research is going into structural strategies which would withstand assaults similar to the one on the World Trade Center in 2001, the skyscraper keeps shooting flamboyantly upwards.

◄ **1913 Woolworth Building, New York City, USA, 792 ft (238 m).** Retail baron Frank W Woolworth wanted an HQ building worthy of his fortune, even if that fortune had been made in nickels and dimes (he paid for his building in cash—$13.5 million). He chose Cass Gilbert as the architect, who discovered that the verticality of the Gothic allowed him to build tall and yet still keep the building rooted in tradition.

➤ **1925 Tribune Tower, Chicago, USA, 463 ft (139 m).** In 1922 the *Chicago Daily Tribune* held a competition to build "the most beautiful and distinguished office building in the world." Out of 300 entries (including the great Modernists Eliel Saarinen and Walter Gropius) the competition was won by two unkown 'traditionalists', Raymond Hood and John Howells, and their Gothic treatment, complete with flying buttresses.

∨ 1930 The Chrysler Building, New York, USA, 1,046 ft (314 m).
The crowning jewel of Manhattan's skyline, this Art Deco masterpiece reflects the exuberance of the roaring twenties. It was completed after a ferocious race with the Bank of Manhattan to become the tallest building in the world. The Chrysler succeeded with something of a sneak attack: the stainless-steel spire was assembled secretly in the fire shaft and was erected only after the competing building was finished.

◀ **1931 Empire State Building, New York, USA.** On completion it broke multiple records and became the world's tallest office building, surpassing the Chrysler by 204 ft (73 m). It was constructed in record time: its 3,000 workers finished the job in only one year and 45 days. Its 2.5 million sq ft (23,250 sq m) of office space was greater than the Chrysler and the next largest building of the day combined. It consisted of 60,000 tons of steel, 200,000 cu ft (5,663 cu m) of Indiana limestone and granite, 10 million bricks, and 730 tons of aluminum and stainless steel.

▲ **1958 Seagram Building, New York City, USA.** Samuel Bronfman, the owner of the huge Seagram distillery empire wanted a building that would be "the crowning glory of everyone's work." His daughter persuaded him to employ the leading Modernist of his day—Mies van der Rohe. The clarity, serenity, and masterful placement of the building in its urban context led the great architectural historian Lewis Mumford to call the Seagram, the "Lesson of the Master."

▲ **1972–2001 World Trade Center towers, New York, USA.** Once the tallest buildings in the world (although they had been overtaken in 1974 by the Sears Tower in Chicago), the 'twin towers' were demolished when each was hit by a hijacked jumbo jet in a terrorist attack on 11 September 2001. All steel and aluminum, they were 1,353 ft (412.5 m) high. They were structurally innovative in that their outer cladding carried their load, quite unlike most modern skyscrapers. This actually caused the towers to remain standing much longer than might have been expected. The buildings finally collapsed from the intense heat of the jet-fuel fed fire, imploding upon themselves rather than falling over. The horrific event, killing almost 3,000 people, has forever altered the way the image of the towers is now perceived. If ever there was an example of the astonishing power of buildings as symbols, this was it.

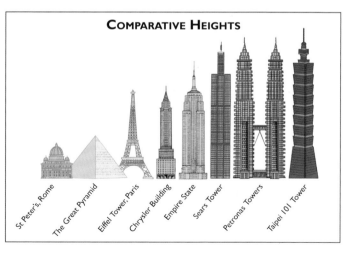

COMPARATIVE HEIGHTS

St Peter's, Rome · The Great Pyramid · Eiffel Tower, Paris · Chrysler Building · Empire State · Sears Tower · Petronas Towers · Taipei 101 Tower

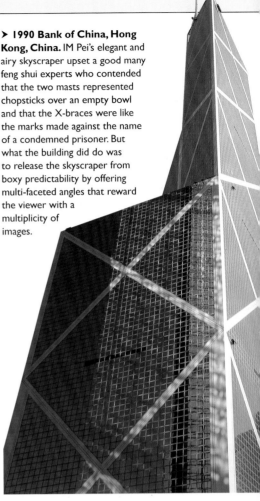

➤ 1990 Bank of China, Hong Kong, China. IM Pei's elegant and airy skyscraper upset a good many feng shui experts who contended that the two masts represented chopsticks over an empty bowl and that the X-braces were like the marks made against the name of a condemned prisoner. But what the building did do was to release the skyscraper from boxy predictability by offering multi-faceted angles that reward the viewer with a multiplicity of images.

⋀ 1974 Sears Tower, Chicago, USA. Fazlur Khan and Bruce Graham, partners in Skidmore, Owings & Merrill, were determined to break out of the plain box approach that had come to dominate skyscraper building. In fact, their Sears Tower is nine skyscrapers of varying heights. Working in the highest floors can, however, be terrifying. Wind stresses have been known to shatter windows, the whole structure sways alarmingly, and the corner columns creak and groan.

1998 Petronas Twin Towers, Kuala Lumpur, Malaysia. This 88-floor building is 1,482.6 ft (451.9 m) high and are designed by Argentine-American architect Cesar Pelli. Super high-strength reinforced concrete was used in the structure to cut down on the use of expensive imported steel.

THE WORLD'S TALLEST BUILDINGS

Rank	Building	City	Ft (m)	Floors	Year
1.	Burj Khalifa	Dubai	2,716.5 (828)	160+	2010
2.	Tokyo Sky Tree	Tokyo	2,080 (634)	32	2011
3.	Abraj Al Bait Towers	Mecca	1,972 (601)	120	2011
4.	One World Trade Centre	New York	1,776 (541)	94	2013
5.	Taipei 101 Tower	Taipei, Taiwan	1,670 ft (509)	101	2004
6.	Shanghai World Financial Center	Shanghai, China	1,614 ft (492)	101	2008
7.	Petronas Towers	Kuala Lumpur, Malaysia	1,483 ft (452)	88	1998
8.	Sears Tower	Chicago, USA	1,450 ft (442)	108	1974
9.	Jin Mao building	Shanghai, China	1,381 ft (421)	88	1999
10.	Two International Finance Center	Hong Kong, China	1,362 ft (414)	88	2003

Source: www.emporis.com

2003 Victoria Towers, Hong Kong, 699 ft (213 m). Standing at the junction of two major thoroughfares in the city, this is a complex of three 62-floor, mixed-use towers, epitomizing the concept of luxury living in a high density area. The architects, Rocco Design Ltd, created a nine-story podium, with the first four floors designated for retail. The granite, glass, and tile-clad complex includes a variety of recreational facilities, mini theater, and extensive children's areas.

2004 Taipei 101, Taiwan, 1,670 ft (509 m). Overtaking Kuala Lumpur's Petronas Towers, Taipei 101 claimed first position for the world's tallest building; the height includes its 197 ft (60 m) spire and the world's highest roof. Built in a seismically volatile region, the 101-floor tower is made of pliant steel, employing steel plates of varying tensile strengths. It is additionally supported by concrete-filled steel piles sunk into the soil to a depth of 262 ft (80 m). Designed by CY Lee and Partners, the tower also boasts the world's two fastest elevators.

2005 Q1 (Queensland Number One), Gold Coast, 1,061 ft (323 m). Flaunted as the world's tallest residential tower, it also claimed to be the tallest building in the southern hemisphere. Q1 was designed by Atelier SDG, inspired by the Sydney 2000 Olympic torch and the Sydney Opera House. It was named after the Australian Olympic sculling team of the 1920s. Levels 77 and 78 house the observation deck, which can accommodate 400 persons and offer 360-degree views, from Brisbane in the north to Byron Bay in the south.

2007 Park Place, Dubai, 768 ft (234 m). The design of this Post Modern office cum residential project was inspired by a perfume bottle, and realized by Cox Architecture Planning Design. The 60-floor building (15 for offices and 45 for residences) uses a heat refracting technology to save on energy required for cooling, and is covered in a 'second skin' to counter the punishing Arabian sun. Its location on the plush Sheikh Zayed Road makes it one of Dubai's exclusive properties.

2008 Shanghai World Financial Center, China, 1,614 ft (492 m). The project, owned by Japan's biggest private real estate developer, took over 14 years to be completed, due to delays on account of southeast Asia's financial crisis. When completed, the building was hailed as the third tallest in the world. It has 101 floors above and

Shanghai World Financial Center.

three below the ground. The prohibitive floor space rental has meant that the tenants include only the topmost financial companies in the world. A hotel, conference centers, and six floors for a sightseeing observatory are expected to attract three million tourists annually.

2010 Burj Khalifa, Dubai, 2,716.5 ft (828 m). The tallest tower in the world (2017) is the centerpiece to a large scale mixed use urban development which includes homes, hotels, parkland, towers, the Dubai Mall, and the 30-acre artificial Burj Khalifa Lake. The tower contains a total of 57 elevators and eight escalators. While the Y-shaped floor plan is inspired by the Hymenocallis flower, the tower draws ideas from Islamic architecture. An innovative buttressed central core and wings support the height of the building designed by Adrian Smith of Skidmore, Owings and Merrill architects.

Burj Khalifa.

Major architects mentioned in the book
and their principal buildings.

AALTO, ALVAR 1898–1976
• LIBRARY, Viipuri, Finland, 1927–34
• SANATORIUM, Paimio, Finland, 1928–33
• FINNISH PAVILION, Paris Exposition, 1937
• VILLA MAIREA, Noormarkku, Finland, 1937–39
• BAKER DORMITORY, MIT, Cambridge, Mass., USA, 1946–49
• TOWN HALL, Säynätsalo, Finland, 1949–59
• HELSINKI UNIVERSITY OF TECHNOLOGY, Espoo, Finland, 1952–57
• FINNISH NATIONAL PENSIONS INSTITUTE, Helsinki, Finland, 1952–56
• CHURCH, Imatra, Finland, 1956–59
• LIBRARY, St Benedict Abbey, Mt Angel, Oregon, USA, 1964–68

ADAM, ROBERT (1728–92); JOHN (1721–92); JAMES (1732–90)
• DUMFRIES HOUSE, Dumfries, Scotland, 1750–54
• KEDDLESTON HALL, Derbyshire, UK, 1759–70
• ADMIRALTY SCREEN, London, UK, 1759–60
• SYON HOUSE, Isleworth, London, UK, 1762–69
• OSTERLEY PARK, London, UK, 1763–80
• LIBRARY, Kenwood House, London, UK, 1767–69
• REGISTER HOUSE, Edinburgh, Scotland, begun 1774
• CULZEAN CASTLE, Ayr, Scotland, 1777–92
• OLD COLLEGE, EDINBURGH UNIVERSITY, Edinburgh, Scotland, 1789
• SETON CASTLE, East Lothian, Scotland, 1789–91
• CHARLOTTE SQUARE, Edinburgh, Scotland, 1791–1807

ALBERTI, LEONE BATTISTA 1404–72
• FAÇADE, Palazzo Rucellai, Florence, Italy, 1446–51
• FAÇADE, Santa Maria Novella, Florence, Italy, 1460–67
• SANT'ANDREA, Mantua, Italy, begun 1470

ARUP, OVE 1895–1988
• SMITHSON'S SCHOOL, Hunstanton, Norfolk, UK, 1950–51
• COLLEGE BUILDINGS FOR CORPUS CHRIST COLLEGE, Cambridge, UK, 1965–71
• SOMERVILLE COLLEGE, Oxford, UK, 1965–75
• FESTIVAL HALL, Liverpool, UK, 1982–84
• LLOYD'S OFFICES, Chatham, Kent, UK, 1983

BEHRENS, PETER 1868–1940
• AEG TURBINE FACTORY, Berlin, Germany, 1909
• AEG SMALL MOTOR FACTORY, Berlin, Germany, 1910
• GERMAN EMBASSY, St Petersburg, Russia, 1911
• IG FARBEN, Hoechst Dyeworks, Frankfurt, Germany, 1920–24
• AEG ADMINISTRATIVE BUILDING, Berlin, Germany, 1937

BERNINI, GIOVANNI LORENZO 1598–1680
• BALDACCHINO, St Peter's, Rome, Italy, begun 1624
• CORNARO CHAPEL, Santa Maria della Vittoria, Rome, Italy, 1645–52
• PIAZZA NAVONA, Rome, Italy, 1648–51
• SANT'ANDREA AL QUIRINALE, Rome, Italy, 1658–70
• PIAZZA, St Peter's, Rome, Italy, 1656
• PALAZZO ODESCALCHI, Rome, Italy, begun 1664
• SCALA REGIA, Vatican, Italy, 1663–66

BORROMINI, FRANCESCO 1599–1667
• SAN CARLO ALLE QUATTRO FONTANE, Rome, Italy, 1634–43
• ORATORY OF ST PHILIP NERI, Rome, Italy, 1638–50
• SANT'IVO ALLA SAPIENZA, Rome, Italy, 1642–49
• COLLEGIO DI PROPAGANDA FIDE, Rome, Italy 1647–64
• SANT'AGNESE, Piazza Navona, Rome, Italy, 1653–57

BRAMANTE, DONATO 1443 / 44–1514
• SANTA MARIA PRESSO SAN SATIRO, Milan, Italy, begun 1482
• ST PETER'S, Rome, Italy, 1517
• CLOISTER OF SANTA MARIA DELLA PACE, Rome, Italy, 1500
• TEMPIETTO OF SAN PIETRO, Rome, Italy, after 1510
• SANTA CASA, Loreto, Italy, 1509 onwards

BREUER, MARCEL 1902–81
• HARNISCHMACHER HOUSE, Wiesbaden, Germany, 1932
• BREUER HOUSE, Lincoln, Mass., USA, 1939
• BREUER HOUSE, New Canaan, Conn., USA, 1947
• (WITH NERVI AND ZEHRFUSS) UNESCO, Paris, France, 1951–58
• HUD BUILDING, Washington, DC, USA, 1967
• WHITNEY MUSEUM, New York, USA, 1966

BRUNELLESCHI SEE FEATURED ARTICLE

BURNHAM, DANIEL 1846–1912
• MONTAUK BUILDING, Chicago, Ill., USA,

1881-82
- (Burnham & Root) Rookery Building, Chicago, Ill., USA, 1885-86
- (Burnham & Root) Monadnock Building, Chicago, Ill., USA, 1889-91
- (DH Burnham & Co) Reliance Building, Chicago, Ill., USA, 1890
- (Burnham & Root) Ashland Block, Chicago, Ill., USA, 1891-92
- (DH Burnham & Co) Fisher Building, Chicago, Ill., USA
- (DH Burnham & Co) Flatiron Building, New York, NY., USA, 1902
- (DH Burnham & Co) Railway Exchange Building, Chicago, Ill., USA, 1903-04
- (DH Burnham & Co) Union Station, Washington, DC, USA, 1907

Calatrava, Santiago, B. 1951
- Zurich Stadelhofen Railway Station, Zurich, Switzerland, 1983-1990
- Bridge Puente Del Alamillo, Expo' 92, Seville, Spain, 1987-1992
- Gare Do Oriente, Lisbon, Portugal, 1993-1998
- The Milwaukee Art Museum, Wisconsin, Usa, 1994-2001
- Science Museum, Valencia, Spain, 2005-2009
- Margaret Hunt Hill Bridge, Dallas, Usa, 2010-2012
- Museum Of Tomorrow, Rio De Janeiro, Brazil, 2010-2015
- The World Trade Centre
- Transportation Hub, New York, Usa, 2003-2016

Callicrates, Fifth century BCE
- Parthenon, Athens, Greece, 447-438 BCE
- Ionic temple of Athena Nike on Acropolis, Athens, Greece, 448-421 BCE

Campen, Jacob van 1595-1657
- Coymans House, Amsterdam, Netherlands, 1624
- Mauritshuis, The Hague, Netherlands, 1633-35
- Noordeinde Palace, The Hague, Netherlands, 1640
- Town Hall, Amsterdam, Netherlands, 1648-55
- Nieuwe Kerk, Haarlem, Netherlands, 1645-
- Accijnhuis Theater, Amsterdam, Netherlands, 1637

Churriguera, Alberto (1676-1750); Joaquin (1674-1724); José Benitio (1665-1725)
- Ayala Chapel, Segovia Cathedral, Spain, 1686-87

- Plaza Mayor, Salamanca, Spain, begun 1728
- San Estaban, San Sebastian, Spain, begun 1731
- Parish Church, Orgaz, Spain, 1738
- Façade, Church of the Assumption, Rueda, Spain, 1738-47

Corbusier SEE FEATURED ARTICLE

Cuvilliés, Jean–François 1695-1768
- Reiche Zimmer, Residenz, Munich, Germany, 1730-37
- Amalienburg, Schloss Nymphenburg, Munich, Germany, 1734-39
- Residenztheater, Munich, Germany, 1751-53
- Façade, Theatinerkirche, Munich, Germany, 1767

Delorme, Philibert c. 1510–70
- Château d'Anet, Dreux, France, 1547-52
- Bridge and gallery, Château de Chenonceaux, France, 1556-59

De Meuron, Pierre, B. 1950 (Herzog & De Meuron)
SEE Jacques Herzog

Eiffel, Gustave 1832–1923
- Eiffel Tower, Paris, France, 1889
- Duoro Bridge, Portugal, 1876-77
- (with Boileau) Bon Marché Store, Paris, France, 1876
- Armature, Statue of Liberty, New York, NY., USA, 1885

Esherick, Joseph 1914–98
- Goldman House, San Francisco, California, USA, 1952
- Cary House, Mill Valley, California, USA, 1960
- (with De Mars and Olsen) Wurster Hall, Berkeley, California, USA, 1964
- (with MLTW) C-Ranch, Sonoma, California, USA, 1965
- Monterey Bay Aquarium, California, USA, 1984

Fischer von Erlach, Johann Bernard 1656–1723
- Dreifaltigkeitskirche, Salzburg, Austria, 1694-1702
- Kollegienkirche, Salzburg, Austria, 1694-1707
- Town Palace of Prince Eugene of Savoy, The Belvedere, Vienna, Austria, 1696-1700
- Johannesspitalkirche, Salzburg, Austria, 1699-1704

- KARLSKIRCHE, Vienna, Austria, begun 1715

FLORIS, CORNELIS 1514–75
- ANTWERP TOWN HALL, Antwerp, Netherlands, 1561-66
- HANSEATENHUIS, Antwerp, Netherlands, 1566
- ROOD SCREEN, Tournai Cathedral, Belgium, 1572

FONTAINE, PIERRE–FRANÇOIS–LEONARD (PERCIER AND FONTAINE) 1762–1853
- ARC DU CAROUSEL, Paris, France, 1806-07
- RUE DE RIVOLI, Paris, France, 1801
- RESTORATION, PALAIS ROYAL, Paris, France, 1814-31
- HOTEL-DIEU, Pontoise, France, 1823-27

FOSTER, NORMAN 1935–
- HONGKONG AND SHANGHAI BANK HEADQUARTERS, Hong Kong, China, 1979-86
- AMERICAN AIR MUSEUM, Duxford, Cambridge, UK, 1987-97
- AL FAISALIAH COMPLEX, Riyadh, Saudi Arabia, 1994-2000
- CHEK LAP KOK AIRPORT, Hong Kong, China, 1992-1998
- CITY HALL, London, UK, 1998-2002
- BEIJING AIRPORT, Beijing, China, 2003-2008
- CRYSTAL ISLAND, Moscow, Russia, 2006
- CAJA MADRID TOWER, Madrid, Spain, 2002-2009

GAUDÍ SEE FEATURED ARTICLE

GEHRY, FRANK, B. 1928
- CHIAT/DAY BUILDING, Venice, California 1985-1991
- DANCING HOUSE, Prag, Chehia, 1994-1996
- GUGGENHEIM MUSEUM, Bilbao, Spain, 1993-1997
- MUSEUM OF POP CULTURE, Seattle, USA, 2000
- THE TOWER IN SPRUCE STREET, New York, USA, 2011

GIBBS, JAMES 1682–1754
- ST MARY-LE-STRAND, London, UK, 1714-24
- THE OCTAGON, Twickenham, UK, 1720
- ST MARTIN IN THE FIELDS, London, UK, 1722-26
- SENATE HOUSE, Cambridge, UK, 1722-30
- DERBY CATHEDRAL, 1723-25
- KING'S COLLEGE FELLOWS' BUILDING, Cambridge University, UK, 1724-49
- THE RADCLIFFE LIBRARY, Oxford University, UK, 1737-49

GILBERT, CASS 1859–1934
- WOOLWORTH BUILDING, New York, NY., USA, 1911
- NEW YORK LIFE ASSURANCE BUILDING, New York, NY., USA, 1925

GRAVES, MICHAEL, 1934–2015
- THE PORTLAND BUILDING, Oregon, USA, 1979-1982
- HUMANA BUILDING, Louisville, Kentucky, USA, 1982
- TEAM DISNEY BUILDING, Burbank, California, USA, 1989-1990
- THE WALT DISNEY WORLD DOLPHIN RESORT, Orlando, Florida, USA, 1987-1990
- NCAA HALL OF CHAMPIONS, Indianapolis, Indiana, USA, 1997-2000
- STEIGENBERGER HOTEL, El Gouna, Egypt, 1997
- THE INTERNATIONAL FINANCE CORPORATION BUILDING, Washington D.C., USA, 1997
- MUSEUM OF THE SHENANDOAH VALLEY, Winchester, Virginia, USA, 2005
- 425 FIFTH AVENUE, New York, New York, USA, 2000-2003

GROPIUS, WALTER 1883–1969
- FAGUS FACTORY, Alfeld-an-der-Leine, Germany, 1911
- ADMINISTRATIVE BUILDING, Werkbund Exhibition, Cologne, Germany, 1914
- BAUHAUS, Dessau, Germany, 1925-26
- SIEMENSSTADT HOUSING PROJECT, Berlin, Germany, 1929
- IMPINGTON VILLAGE COLLEGE, Cambridge, UK, 1934-37
- GROPIUS HOUSE, Lincoln, Mass., USA, 1937
- GRADUATE CENTER, Harvard University, Cambridge, USA, 1949
- BAUHAUSARCHIV, Berlin, Germany, designed 1964, built 1976-78

GUIMARD, HÉCTOR 1867–1942
- CASTEL BÉRANGER, Paris, France, 1894-1912
- METRO STATIONS, Paris, France, 1899-1913
- HÔTEL GUIMARD, Paris, France, 1912

HADID, ZAHA 1950–2016
- VITRA FIRE STATION, Germany, 1990-1993
- SARAGOSA BRIDGE PAVILION, Spain 2005-2008
- SHEIK ZAYED BRIDGE, Abu-Dhabi 1997-2010
- PIVERSIDE MUSEUM, Glasgow, Scotland 2004-2011
- HEYDAR ALIYEV CENTER, Baku, Azerbejian, 2007-2012
- WANGJING SOHO TOWER, Beijing, China, 2009-2014
- PORT AUTHORITY, Antwerp, Belgium 2009-2016

HARDOUIN–MANSART, JULES 1646–1708
• GRAND TRIANON AND CHAPEL, Versailles, France, begun 1678
• DOME OF THE INVALIDES CHAPEL, Paris, France, 1680–91
• PLACE VENDÔME, Paris, France, begun 1698

HARRISON, PETER 1716–76
• REDWOOD LIBRARY, Newport, Rhode Island, USA, 1748–50
• KING'S CHAPEL, Boston, Mass., USA, 1749–58
• TOURO SYNAGOGUE, Newport, Rhode Island, USA, 1759
• CHRIST CHURCH, Cambridge, Mass., USA, 1760–61
• BRICK MARKET, Newport, Rhode Island, USA, 1761–72

HAWKSMOOR, NICHOLAS 1661–1736
• (WITH VANBRUGH) CASTLE HOWARD, Yorkshire, UK, 1699–1712
• (WITH VANBRUGH) BLENHEIM PALACE, Oxfordshire, UK, 1705–24
• ST ALPHEGE, GREENWICH, London, UK, 1712–14
• CLARENDON BUILDING, Oxford, UK, 1712–65
• ST ANNE'S, LIMEHOUSE, London, UK, 1714–30
• CHRIST CHURCH, Spitalfields, London, UK, 1714–29
• ST GEORGE-IN-THE-EAST, Stepney, London, UK, 1714–29
• QUADRANGLE HALL & CODDINGTON LIBRARY, All Souls College, Oxford University, UK, 1716–35
• WEST TOWERS, Westminster Abbey, London, UK 1718

HERRERA, JUAN DE 1530–97
• ESCORIAL, Madrid, Spain, 1559–84
• INFIRMARY AND CHAPEL, Toledo, Spain, 1574–82
• PALACE, Aranjuez, Spain, 1571–86
• EXCHANGE BUILDING, Seville, Spain, 1582
• VALLADOLID Cathedral, Spain, c. 1585

HERZOG, JACQUES, B. 1950 (HERZOG & DE MEURON)
• MUSEUM OF MODERN ART, Duisburg, Germany, 1999
• NATIONAL STADIUM, Beijing, China, 2004–2008
• FORUM BUILDING, Barcelona, Spain, 2001–2004
• TATE MODERN, London, UK, 1995–2000
• DOMINUS WINERY, California, USA 1995–1998

• VITRA HOUSE WEIL AM RHEIN, Germany, 2006–2009
• ELBPHILHARMONIE, Hamburg, Germany, 2006–2016

HILDEBRANDT, JOHANN LUKAS VON 1668–1745
• SCHWARZENBERG PALACE, Vienna, Austria, 1697–1714
• (WITH FISCHER VON ERLACH) BELVEDERE, Vienna, Austria, 1714–24
• PIARISTENKIRCHE, Vienna, Austria, 1714–46
• SEMINARKIRCHE, Linz, Austria, 1717–25
• PARISH CHURCH, Gollersdorf, Austria, 1740–41

HOBAN, JAMES 1762–1831
• STATE CAPITOL, Columbia, South Carolina, USA, completed 1791
• WHITE HOUSE, Washington, DC, USA, 1793–1801
• STATE AND WAR OFFICES, Washington, DC, USA, 1818

HOLABIRD & ROCHE, WILLIAM HOLABIRD 1854–1923; MARTIN ROCHE 1853–1927
• TACOMA BUILDING, Chicago, Ill., USA, 1886–87
• MARQUETTE BUILDING, Chicago, Ill., USA, 1893–94
• McCLURG (CROWN) BUILDING, Chicago, Ill., USA, 1899

HOOD, RAYMOND MATHEWSON 1881–1934
• CHICAGO TRIBUNE BUILDING, Chicago, Ill., USA, 1923–25
• AMERICAN RADIATOR CO. BUILDING, New York, NY., USA, 1924
• DAILY NEWS BUILDING, New York, NY., USA, 1929
• ROCKEFELLER CENTER, New York, NY., USA, 1931–34
• RCA BUILDING, New York, NY., USA, 1934
• McGRAW HILL BUILDING, New York, NY., USA, 1930–32

HOWE, GEORGE 1886–1955
• (WITH LESCAZE) PSFS BUILDING, Philadelphia, USA, 1929–32
• FORTUNE ROCK, Mount Deseret, Maine, USA, 1938

HUNT, RICHARD MORRIS 1827–95
• JNH GRISWOLD HOUSE, Newport, Rhode Island, USA, 1862
• TRIBUNE BUILDING, New York, NY., USA, 1873

- 'BILTMORE', Ashville, N Carolina, USA, 1888-95
- 'THE BREAKERS', Newport, Rhode Island, USA, 1892-95
- JJ ASTOR HOUSE, Newport, Rhode Island, USA, 1893
- ENTRANCE WING, Metropolitan Museum of Art, New York, NY., USA, 1894-1902

IMHOTEP, BETWEEN 2780–2680 BCE
- STEP PYRAMID AT SAQQARA, Egypt, c. 2778 BCE

JACOBSEN, ARNE 1902–70
- BELLAVISTA HOUSING, Klampenborg, near Copenhagen, Denmark, 1934
- TOWN HALL, Aärhus, Denmark, 1938-42
- MUNKEGAARDS SCHOOL, Gentofte, Denmark, 1952-56
- TOWN HALL OF RODOVRE, Copenhagen, Denmark, 1955-56
- SAS HOTEL, Copenhagen, Denmark, 1960
- ST CATHERINE'S COLLEGE, Oxford University, UK, 1964

JEFFERSON, THOMAS 1743–1826
- MONTICELLO, Virginia, USA, 1768-82 and 1796-1809
- VIRGINIA STATE CAPITOL, Virginia, USA, completed 1796
- UNIVERSITY OF VIRGINIA, Charlottesville, Virginia, USA, 1817-26

JONES, INIGO 1573–1652
- THE QUEEN'S HOUSE, Greenwich, UK, 1616-35
- THE PRINCE'S LODGING, Newmarket, Suffolk, UK, 1619-22
- BANQUETING HOUSE, Whitehall, London, UK, 1619-22
- QUEEN'S CHAPEL, St James's Palace, London, UK, 1623-27
- ST PAUL'S CHURCH, Covent Garden, London, UK, 1631-33
- PIAZZA, Covent Garden, London, UK, 1631-37

JOHNSON, PHILIP CORTELYOU, B.1903
- (WITH MIES VAN DER ROHE) JOHNSON HOUSE, New Canaan, Connecticut, USA, 1949
- SEAGRAM BUILDING, New York, NY., USA, 1956
- FOUR SEASONS RESTAURANT, New York, NY., USA, 1959
- AT&T BUILDING, New York, NY., USA, 1979-84

KAHN, LOUIS 1901–74
- YALE ART GALLERY, New Haven, Conn., USA, 1951
- RICHARDS MEDICAL LABORATORY, Philadelphia, Penn., USA, 1957-64
- SALK INSTITUTE, La Jolla, California, USA, 1959-63
- NATION ASSEMBLY, Dhaka, Bangladesh, 1962-74
- EXETER LIBRARY, Oxford University, UK, 1965-72
- KIMBELL ART MUSEUM, Fort Worth, Texas, USA, 1966-72
- CENTER FOR BRITISH ART & STUDIES, Yale, New Haven, Conn., USA, 1969-72

KENT, WILLIAM 1685–1748
- HOLKHAM HALL, Norfolk, UK, 1734
- THE TREASURY, London, UK, 1733-37
- 22 ARLINGTON ST, London, UK, 1741
- 44 BERKELEY SQUARE, London, UK, 1742-44
- HORSE GUARDS, London, UK, 1750-59

KEY, LIEVEN DE 1560–1627
- FAÇADE, Leiden Town Hall, Netherlands, 1594-97
- THE WEIGH HOUSE, Haarlem, Netherlands, 1598
- BUTCHERS GUILD HALL, Haarlem, Netherlands, 1602-03
- TOWER, Nieuwekerk, Haarlem, Netherlands, 1613

KOOLHAAS, REM B.1944
- EURALILLE MASTERPLAN, Lille, France, 1989-1994
- DUTCH EMBASSY, Berlin, Germany, 1997-2003
- PRADA SHOP, Los Angeles, USA, 2004-ongoing
- SEATTLE PUBLIC LIBRARY, Seattle, USA, 2004
- CONCERT HAL CASA DA MUSICA, Porto Portugal, 1999-2005
- DEE AND CHARLES WYLY THEATER, Dallas, USA, 2001-2009
- CCTV HEAD OFFICE, Beijing, China, 2002-2012
- STOCK EXCHANGE, Shenzhen, China, 2006-2013

KUROKAWA, KISHO, 1934–2007
- THE NAKAGIN CAPSULE TOWER, Tokyo, 1970-1972
- SAITAMA PREFECTURAL MUSEUM OF MODERN ART, Saitama, Japan, 1978-1982
- ENTRANCE TO THE NAGOYA CITY ART MUSEUM, Nagoya, Japan, 1983-1987
- THE MUSEUM OF MODERN ART, Wakayama, Japan, 1990-1994
- NEW WING OF THE VAN GOGH MUSEUM,

Amsterdam, The Netherlands, 1990-1998
THE NATIONAL ART CENTRE, Tokyo, Japan,
2000-2006

LABROUSTE, HENRI 1801–75
• BIBLIOTHÈQUE STE GENEVIÈVE, Paris,
France, designed 1838
• BIBLIOTHÈQUE NATIONALE, Paris, France,
begun 1854

LATROBE, BENJAMIN HENRY 1764–1820
• THE CAPITOL, Washington, DC, USA,
from 1803
• BANK OF PENNSYLVANIA, Philadelphia,
Penn., USA, 1799-1801
• BALTIMORE CATHEDRAL, Baltimore,
Maryland, USA, 1804-18
• EXCHANGE BUILDING, Baltimore, Maryland,
USA, 1816-20
• (WITH JEFFERSON) UNIVERSITY OF VIRGINIA,
USA, 1817-26
• LOUISIANA STATE BANK, New Orleans,
Louisiana, USA, begun 1819

LAUTNER, JOHN EDWARD, 1911–1994
• LAUTNER RESIDENCE, Los Angeles, USA,
1939-1940
• MAUER RESIDENCE, Los Angeles, USA,
1945- 1946
• DESERT HOT SPRING MOTEL, Palm Springs,
USA, 1947-1947
• SHEETS APARTMENTS, Los Angeles, USA,
1948-1950
• HARPEL HOUSE, Los Angeles, USA,
1956-1956
• MALIN RESIDENCE, Chemosphere, Los
Angeles, USA, 1958-1960
• REINER RESIDENCE, Silver Top, Los
Angeles, USA, 1963
• SHEATS RESIDENCE, Los Angeles, USA,
1962-1963

LE CORBUSIER *SEE FEATURED ARTICLE*

LE VAU, LOUIS 1612–70
• HÔTEL LAMBERT, Paris, France, 1640-
• CHÂTEAU, VAUX-LE-VICOMTE, France, 1657
• (WITH LEBRUN) REBUILT GALERIE
D'APOLLON, Louvre, Paris, France, 1661-62
• REMODELING OF VERSAILLES, France, 1669
• COLLÈGE DES QUATRE NATIONS (NOW
INSTITUT DE FRANCE), Paris, France,
begun 1661

LEMERCIER, JACQUES 1585–1654
• LOUVRE EXTENSIONS, Paris, France, 1624
• PALAIS ROYAL, Paris, France, 1624-36
• CHURCH OF THE SORBONNE, Paris, France,
begun 1626

• DOME, Val-de-Grâce, Paris, France, begun
1646

LEONARDO DA VINCI 1452–1519
• STUDIES FOR DOME AND CROSSING, Milan
Cathedral, Italy, 1487
• (WITH BRAMANTE *attrib.*) CROSSING AND
CHANCEL, Santa Maria della Grazie, Milan,
Italy, 1490s
• STUDIES FOR ROYAL RESIDENCE, Romoratin,
France, *c.* 1517-19

**LONGHENA, BALDASSARE
c. 1597–1682**
• PALAZZO GIUSTINIAN-LOLIN, Venice, Italy,
1620-23
• SANTA MARIA DELLA SALUTE, Venice, Italy,
begun 1630
• DOUBLE STAIRCASE, monastery of San
Giorgio Maggiore, Venice, Italy, 1643-45
• PALAZZO REZZONICO, Venice, Italy, begun
1667
• PALAZZO PESARO,Venice, Italy, 1649-82
• OSPEDALETTO, Venice, Italy, 1670-78

LOOS, ADOLF 1870–1933
• STEINER HOUSE, Vienna, Austria, 1910
• TRISTAN TZARA HOUSE, Paris, France, 1925
• MOLLER HOUSE, Prague, Czech Republic,
1928

**MCKIM WHITE & MEAD, CHARLES
FOLLEN MCKIM (1847–1909); WILLIAM
RUTHERFORD MEAD (1846–1928);
STANFORD WHITE (1853–1906)**
• VILLARD MANSIONS, New York, NY., USA,
1882-85
• WILLIAM G LOWE HOUSE, Bristol, Rhode
Island, USA, 1886-87
• BOSTON PUBLIC LIBRARY, Boston, Mass.,
USA, 1887-88
• RHODE ISLAND STATE CAPITOL, USA,
1891-1903
• COLUMBIA UNIVERSITY, New York, NY.,
USA, 1893-94
• PIERPONT MORGAN LIBRARY, New York,
NY., USA, 1902-07
• METROPOLITAN MUSEUM OF ART, New
York, NY., USA, 1906

MELNIKOV, KONSTANTIN 1890–1974
• SOVIET PAVILION, Paris Exposition, France,
1925
• RUSAKOV WORKERS' CLUB, Moscow,
Russia, 1927
• MELNIKOV HOUSE, Moscow, Russia, 1927

MIES VAN DER ROHE *SEE FEATURED ARTICLE*

MICHELANGELO, BUONAROTTI 1475–1564
- MEDICI CHAPEL, Florence, Italy, 1519–34
- BIBLIOTECA LAURENZIANA, Florence, 1524–71
- REORGANIZATION OF THE CAPITOL, Rome, Italy, begun 1539
- COMPLETED PALAZZO FARNESE, Rome, Italy, begun 1546
- SFORZA CHAPEL, Santa Maria Maggiore, Rome, Italy, completed 1560
- REMODELING SANTA MARIA DEGLI ANGELI, Rome, Italy, 1561
- ST PETER'S, Rome, Italy, 1546–64

NASH, JOHN 1752–1835
- RAVENSWORTH CASTLE, Gateshead, UK, 1808
- REGENT'S PARK TERRACES, London, UK, 1819
- BRIGHTON PAVILION, Brighton, UK, 1815–21
- HAYMARKET THEATER, London, UK, 1820–21
- ALL SOUL'S LANGHAM SQUARE, London, UK, 1822–25
- UNITED SERVICES CLUB, London, UK, 1826–28
- CARLTON HOUSE TERRACE, London, UK, 1827–33

NERVI, PIER LUIGI 1891–32
- STADIUM, Florence, Italy, 1930–32
- EXHIBITION HALL, Turin, Italy, 1948
- (WITH BREUER) UNESCO BUILDING, Paris, France, 1953–56
- (WITH PONTI) PIRELLI SKYSCRAPER, Milan, Italy, 1955–58
- (WITH PIACENTINI) PALAZZETTO DELLO SPORT, Rome, Italy, 1960

NEUMANN, JOHANN BALTHASAR 1687–1753
- RESIDENZ, Würzberg, Germany, begun 1719
- STAIRCASE, Schlöss Augustusburg, Brühl, Germany, 1740–48
- PILGRIMAGE CHURCH, Gössweinstein, Germany, 1729–39
- COLLEGIATE CHURCH OF ST PAULINIUS, Trier, Germany, 1734–54
- PILGRIMAGE CHURCH, Vierzehnheiligen, Germany, 1742–53
- BENEDICTINE ABBEY CHURCH, Neresheim, Germany, 1745–92
- MARIENKIRCHE, Limbach, Germany, 1747–52

NEUTRA, RICHARD JOSEF 1892–1970
- DR LOVELL HEALTH HOUSE, Los Angeles, California, USA, 1929
- KAUFMANN HOUSE, Palm Springs, California, USA, 1947

NIEMEYER, OSCAR, B.1907
- BRAZILIAN PAVILION, New York World Fair, NY., USA, 1939
- CASINO, CLUB, and SÃO FRANCISCO CHAPEL, Pamtulhe, Brazil, 1942–43
- PRESIDENT'S PALACE, SUPREME COURT, CATHEDRAL, GOVERNMENT BUILDINGS, Brazilia, Brazil, 1958–70
- APARTMENTS FOR INTERBAU EXHIBITION, Berlin, Germany, 1957
- MONDADORI BUILDING, Milan, Italy, 1968–76

NOUVEL, JEAN, B.1945
- ARAB WORLD INSTITUTE, Paris, France, 1981–1987
- COMPLEX OF MIXED USE BUILDINGS, Euralille, Lille, France, 1991–1994
- CULTURE AND CONVENTION CENTER, Lucerne, Switzerland 1993–2000
- TORRE AGBAR, Barcelona, Spain 1994–2004
- SAMSUNG MUSEUM OF ART, Seoul, South Korea, 2002–2004
- DANISH RADIO CONCERT HOUSE, Copenhagen, Denmark 2003–2009
- DOHA TOWER, Doha, Qatar, 2004–2011
- PARIS PHILHARMONIC HALL, Paris, France 2007–2015

PALLADIO SEE FEATURED ARTICLE

PAXTON, SIR JOSEPH 1803–65
- EDENSOR VILLAGE, Derbyshire, UK, 1838–48
- CRYSTAL PALACE, London, UK, 1850–51
- MENTMORE TOWERS, Buckinghamshire, UK, 1851–54

PEI, IEOH MING, B.1917
- MILE HIGH CENTER, Denver, Colorado, USA, 1952–56
- (WITH AFFLECK) PLACE VILLE MARIE, Montreal, Canada, 1956–65
- EAST WING, National Gallery of Art, Washington, DC, USA, 1971–78
- MERTON H MYERSON SYMPHONY CENTER, Dallas, Texas, USA, 1981–89
- BANK OF CHINA, Hong Kong, China, 1982–89
- LOUVRE EXTENSION, Paris, France, 1983–93

PERRAULT, CLAUDE 1613–88
- (WITH LA VAU AND LEBRUN) EAST FRONT OF LOUVRE, Paris, France, begun 1665–74
- OBSERVATOIRE, Paris, France, 1667

PIANO, RENZO, B.1937
- CENTRE POMPIDOU, Paris, France, 1971–1977

- **KANSAI INTERNATIONAL AIRPORT,** Osaka, Japan, 1988-1994
- **AURORA PLACE,** Sydney, Australia, 1996-2000
- **JEAN-MARIE TJIBAOU CULTURAL CENTRE,** Noumea, New Caledonia 1991-1998
- **POTSDAMER PLATZ,** Berlin, Germany, 1992-2000
- **ZENTRUM PAUL KLEE,** Bern, Switzerland, 1999-2005
- **CALIFORNIA ACADEMY OF SCIENCES,** San Francisco, USA, 2000-2008
- **THE SHARD,** London, UK, 2010
- **STAVROS NIARCHOS FOUNDATION CULTURAL CENTRE,** Athens, Greece, 2008-2016

PORTA, GIACOMO DELLA c. 1533–1602
- (TO DESIGN OF MICHELANGELO) PALAZZO DEI SENATORI, Rome, Italy, 1573-1602
- FAÇADE OF IL GESÙ, Rome, Italy, 1571-84
- NORTH AND SOUTH FOUNTAINS, Piazza Navona, Rome, Italy, 1574-78
- WESTERN ARM AND MINOR DOMES, St Peter's, Rome, Italy, 1586-92
- (WITH FONTANA) MAIN DOME, St Peter's, Rome, Italy, 1588-90
- PALAZZO DELLA SAPIENZA, Rome, Italy, completed 1575
- SANTA MARIA AI MONTI, Rome, Italy, begun 1580
- PALAZZO MARESCOTTI, Rome, Italy, completed 1590
- VILLA ALDOBRANDINI, Frascati, Italy, 1594-1603

PUGIN, AUGUSTUS WELBY NORTHMORE 1812–52
- (WITH BARRY) PALACE OF WESTMINSTER, London, UK, 1840-70
- ST GILES, Cheadle, Staffordshire, UK, 1841-46
- ST BARNABAS'S CATHEDRAL, Nottingham, UK, 1841-44
- ST AUGUSTINE, Ramsgate, UK, 1843-52

RAPHAEL, RAFAELLO SANZIO 1483–1520
- SANT'EGLIO DEGLI OREFICI, Rome, Italy, begun 1511
- PALAZZO PANDOLFINI, Florence, Italy, 1517
- PALAZZO BRESCIANO, Rome, Italy, completed 1515
- PALAZZO BRANCONI DELL'AQUILA, Rome, Italy, 1513
- CHIGI CHAPEL IN SANTA MARIA DEL POPOLO, Rome, Italy, begun 1512

RASTRELLI, BARTOLOMEO FRANCESCO 1700–71
- BIRON PALACE, Rundale, Latvia, 1736-40

- ST ANDREAS CHURCH, Kiev, Ukraine, 1747-67
- VORONTSOV AND STROGANOV PALACES, St Petersburg, Russia, 1750s
- SMOLNY CATHEDRAL AND CONVENT, St Petersburg, Russia, 1748-57
- GRAND PALACE, Tsarskoe Selo, Russia, 1749-59
- WINTER PALACE, St Petersburg, Russia, 1754-62

RICHARDSON, HENRY HOBSON 1838–86
- BRATTLE SQUARE CHURCH, Boston, Mass., USA, 1871-73
- TRINITY CHURCH, Boston, Mass., USA, 1873-77
- MEMORIAL LIBRARY, Woburn, Mass., USA, 1876-79
- WATTS SHERMAN HOUSE, Newport, Rhode Island, USA, 1874-75
- MARSHALL FIELD WAREHOUSE, Chicago, Ill., USA, 1885-87
- GLESSNER HOUSE, Chicago, Ill., USA, 1885-87
- SEVER HOUSE, Cambridge, Mass., USA, 1882-83

ROGERS, LORD RICHARD, B.1937
- CENTRE POMPIDOU, Paris, France, 1971-77
- FLEETGUARD FACTORY, Quimper, France, 1979
- LLOYD'S BUILDING, London, UK, 1978-86

SAARINEN, EERO 1910–61
- GENERAL MOTORS TECHNICAL CENTER, Warren, Michigan, USA, 1947-56
- KRESGE AUDITORIUM AND MEMORIAL CHAPEL, MIT, Cambridge, Mass., USA, 1952-56
- DAVID S INGALLS ICE HOCKEY RINK, Yale University, New Haven, Conn., USA, 1953-59
- TWA TERMINAL, Kennedy Airport, New York, NY., USA, 1956-62
- EZRA STILES & MORSE COLLEGES, Yale University, New Haven, Conn., USA, 1958-62
- DULLES INTERNATIONAL AIRPORT, Washington, DC, USA, 1958-63
- US EMBASSY, London, UK, 1955-60

SANSOVINO, JACOPO D'ANTONIO TATTI 1486–1570
- PALAZZO GADDI, Rome, Italy, 1518
- ZECCA (MINT), Venice, Italy, 1535-45
- BIBLIOTECA MARCIANA, Venice, Italy, begun 1537
- LOGIETTA, Venice, Italy, 1537-42

- PALAZZO CORNER DELLA CA'GRANDE, Venice, Italy, begun 1537
- SAN FRANCESCO DELLA VIGNA, Venice, Italy, 1534
- FAÇADE OF SAN GIULIANO, Venice, Italy, 1553-55
- VILLA GARZONI, Pontecasale, Italy, 1535-45

SCHINKEL, KARL FRIEDRICH 1781–1841
- NEUE WACHE, Berlin, Germany, 1816-18
- SCHAUSPIELHAUS, Berlin, Germany, 1818-21
- ALTES MUSEUM, Berlin, Germany, 1824-30
- FREIDRICHWERDERSCHKIRCHE, Berlin, Germany, 1824-27
- NIKOLAIKIRCHE, Potsdam, Germany, 1830-37
- BAUAKADEMIE, Berlin, Germany, 1831-36

SCOTT BROWN, DENISE B. 1931 (VENTURI SCOTT BROWN ASSOCIATES)
- VANNA VENTURI HOUSE, Philadelphia, USA, 1959-64
- TRUBEK - WISLOCKI HOUSES, Nantucket Island, Massachusetts, USA, 1971
- BRANT HOUSE, Greenwich, Connecticut, USA, 1972
- TUCKER HOUSE, Katonah, New York, USA, 1975
- ALLEN ART MUSEUM ADDITION, Oberlin, Ohio, USA, 1976
- HOUSE IN TUCKERS TOWN, Bermuda, 1976 GORDON WU HALL, Princeton, New Jersey, USA, 1983
- SEATTLE ART MUSEUM, Seattle, USA, 1991 SAINSBURY WING, National Gallery, London, UK, 1991
- CHILDREN'S MUSEUM OF HOUSTON, 1992
- PROVINCIAL CAPITOL BUILDING, Toulouse, France, 1999
- CHAPEL, EPISCOPAL ACADEMY, Newtown Square, Pa, 2008

SCOTT, SIR GEORGE GILBERT 1811–78
- CHAPEL OF EXETER COLLEGE, Oxford University, UK, 1856
- ST JOHN'S COLLEGE, Cambridge University, UK, 1863-69
- PARISH CHURCH KENSINGTON, London, UK, 1869-72
- KELHAM HALL, Nottinghamshire, UK, begun 1857
- ST PANCRAS STATION HOTEL, London, UK, 1868-74
- ALBERT MEMORIAL, London, UK, 1863-72
- GLASGOW UNIVERSITY BUILDINGS, Glasgow, Scotland, begun 1868
- WAR AND FOREIGN OFFICE, London, UK, 1862-73

SHAW, RICHARD NORMAN 1831–1912
- HOLY TRINITY, Bingley, Yorkshire, UK, 1864-68
- LEYS WOOD, Sussex, UK, 1868
- GRIM'S DYKE, Harrow Weald, UK, 1870-72
- NEW ZEALAND CHAMBERS, London, UK, 1871-73
- LOWTHER LODGE, London, UK, 1873
- NEW SCOTLAND YARD, London, UK, 1887-90
- PICCADILLY HOTEL, London, UK, 1905

SHU, WANG, B. 1963
- NINGBO MUSEUM OF ART, Ningbo, China, 2005
- SAHNE HOUSE, Jinhua, China, 2006
- TILED GARDEN, Venice Biennale, Venice, Italy, 2006
- NINGBO MUSEUM, Ningbo, China, 2008
- XIANGSHAN CAMPUS, CHINA ACADEMY OF ART, Hangzhou, China, 2007
- NINGBO TENGTOU PAVILION, Shanghai, China, 2010

SHUKHOV, VLADIMIR, 1853-1939
- ROTUNDA AND RECTANGULAR PAVILION, Nizhny Novgorod, Russia, 1896
- ADZIOGOL LIGHTHOUSE, Kherson, Ukraine, 1910-1911
- TOWERS ON THE OKA RIVER, Nizhny Novgorod, Russia, 1896
- POLIBINO, Lipetsk Oblast, Russia, 1909 1896
- PUSHKIN MUSEUM OF FINE ARTS, Moscow, Russia, 1912
- SHABOLOVKA TOWER (SHUKHOV TOWER), Moscow, Russia, 1922

SINAN SEE FEATURED ARTICLE

SKIDMORE, OWINGS & MERRILL, LOUIS SKIDMORE (1897–1962); NATHANIEL OWINGS (1903–84); JOHN OGDEN MERRILL (1896–1975)
- LEVER HOUSE, New York, NY., USA, 1952
- CHASE MANHATTAN BANK, New York, NY., USA, 1952-54
- US AIR FORCE ACADEMY, Colorado Springs, Colorado, USA, begun 1955
- INLAND STEEL BUILDING, Chicago, Ill., USA, 1958
- PEPSI COLA BUILDING, New York, NY., USA, 1960
- JOHN HANCOCK CENTER, Chicago, Ill., USA, 1970
- NINE WEST 57TH STREET, New York, NY., USA, 1972
- SEARS TOWER, Chicago, Ill., 1974

- **NATIONAL COMMERCIAL BANK,** Jeddah, Saudi Arabia,1982
- **CANARY WHARF,** London, UK, 1990

SMITH, D. ADRIAN, B.1944, (SKIDMORE, OWINGS & MERRILL LLP)
- **JIN MAO TOWER,** Shanghai, China, 1994-1998
- **TRUMP INTERNATIONAL HOTEL AND TOWER,** Chicago, USA, 2005-2009
- **ZIFENG TOWER, NANJING,** China, 2005-2010
- **BURJ KHALIFA,** Dubai, UAE, 2004-2010
- **JEDDAH TOWER,** Jeddah, Saudi Arabia, 2013 (under construction)

SMYTHSON, ROBERT C. 1535–1614
- **LONGLEAT HOUSE,** Wiltshire, UK, 1550-80
- **WOLLATON HALL,** Nottinghamshire, UK, 1568-72
- **MONTACUTE HOUSE,** Somerset, UK, 1588-1601
- **HARDWICK HALL,** Derbyshire, UK, 1590-97

SOUFFLOT, JACQUES–GERMAIN 1713–80
- **HÔTEL–DIEU,** Lyons, France, 1739-48
- **THÉÂTRE,** Lyons, France, 1753-56
- **PANTHÉON,** Paris, France, begun 1757
- **ECÔLE DE DROIT,** Paris, France, begun 1771

SULLIVAN, LOUIS HENRY 1856–1924
- (WITH ADLER) **AUDITORIUM BUILDING,** Chicago, Ill., USA, 1886-90
- **CARSON PIRIE SCOTT & CO,** Chicago, Ill., USA, 1899-1904
- (WITH ADLER) **ANSHE MAARIV SYNAGOGUE,** Chicago, Ill., USA, 1890
- **GARRICK THEATER,** Chicago, Ill., USA, 1892
- (WITH ADLER) **STOCK EXCHANGE,** Chicago, Ill., USA, 1893-94
- (WITH ADLER) **GUARANTY BUILDING,** Buffalo, New York, NY., USA, 1894-95
- (WITH ADLER) **WAINWRIGHT BUILDING,** St Louis, Missouri, USA, 1894
- **BAYARD (CONDICT) BUILDING,** New York, NY., USA, 1898
- **NATIONAL FARMER'S BANK,** Owatonna, Minnesota, USA, 1907-08

VANBRUGH, SIR JOHN 1664–1726
- (WITH NICHOLAS HAWKSMOOR) **CASTLE HOWARD,** Yorkshire, UK, 1699-1712
- (WITH NICHOLAS HAWKSMOOR) **BLENHEIM PALACE,** Oxfordshire, UK, 1705-24
- **KIMBOLTON CASTLE,** Huntingdonshire, UK, 1707-10
- **KING'S WESTON,** Gloucestershire, UK, 1710-19

- **SEATON DELAVAL,** Northumberland, UK, 1720-28

VASARI, GIORGIO 1511–74
- **UFFIZZI,** Florence, Italy, begun 1560
- **SANTA FIORA E SANTA LUCILLA,** Arezzo, Italy, begun 1566
- **LOGGIA,** Piazza Grande, Venice, Italy, 1570-96

VAUBAN, SÉBASTIEN LE PRESTRE DE 1633–1707
- **FORTIFICATIONS,** Lille, Italy, 1668-74
- **FORTIFICATIONS,** Maubeuge, Italy, 1683-85
- **FORTIFICATIONS,** Neuf-Brisach, Italy, 1697-1708

VENTURI, ROBERT, B.1925
SEE DENISE SCOTT BROWN

VIGNOLA, GIACOMO BAROZZI DA 1507–73
- **VILLA GIULIA,** Rome, Italy, 1551-55
- **PALAZZO FARNESE,** Caprarola, Italy, 1559
- **SANTA ANNA DEI PALAFRENIERI,** Rome, Italy, 1565
- **IL GESÙ,** Rome, Italy, 1568
- **PALAZZO FARNESE,** Piacenza, Italy, 1558
- **ARCHITECT TO ST PETER'S,** Rome, Italy, 1567-73

VIOLLET–LE–DUC, EUGÈNE–EMMANUEL 1814–79
- **RESTORATION,** Sainte Chapelle, Paris, France, begun 1840
- **RESTORATION,** Notre Dame, Paris, France, 1844-64
- **RESTORATION,** Carcassonne, France, begun 1844
- **RESTORATION,** Château de Pierrefonds, France, 1858-70

WATERHOUSE, ALFRED 1830–1905
- **TOWN HALL,** Manchester, UK, 1869-77
- **NATURAL HISTORY MUSEUM,** London, UK, 1873-81
- **ST PAUL'S SCHOOL,** London, UK, 1881-84
- **NATIONAL LIBERAL CLUB,** London, UK, 1885-87

WREN *SEE FEATURED ARTICLE*

WRIGHT *SEE FEATURED ARTICLE*

FILIPPO BRUNELLESCHI
1377–1446

"Of Filippo it may be said that he was given by Heaven to invest architecture with new forms ..."

Brunelleschi was born in Florence in 1377. He trained as a sculptor and goldsmith, becoming a master of his guild in 1404. He entered the famous design competition for the bronze doors of the Florence Baptistery, but lost to his rival Ghiberti. Turning his attention to architecture, he found himself in competition with Ghiberti again, for the job of building the dome of Florence Cathedral (Santa Maria del Fiore). This time he won. Brunelleschi's solutions to the engineering challenge of building so vast a dome were groundbreaking and are still viewed as the first work of post-medieval architecture.

The innovations he used on the dome of Florence Cathedral (1417–34) were both technical and artistic. Brunelleschi pulled off a technical feat by building it without using timber centering. His secret weapon was a dome inside the dome: the inner supporting the outer during the process of construction. The ribs that strengthened the outer dome became design elements, along with circular windows, architectural reliefs, and an elegant cupola.

In later works, like the unfinished Church of Santa Maria degli Angeli (1434–37), the Basilica of Santo Spirito (1434–82), and the Pazzi Chapel (1429–61), Brunelleschi applied the same mathematical rigor he had used on his dome to the geometry of smaller projects. The Santa Maria design was highly significant as the first central-plan church of the Renaissance.

Brunelleschi was a pioneer in a milieu that was ripe for a break with the past. His genius was to take classical forms and create a whole new architectural idiom: one that quickly defined Renaissance style, and one that continues to influence architecture to this day.

The Duomo of the cathedral at Florence, by Filippo Brunelleschi, 1420–36.

The Sulemaniye Mosque complex at Istanbul, Turkey, built by Sinan in the 16th century.

MIMAR SINAN
1489–1588

Sinan was born a Greek Christian in Anatolia, Turkey, in 1489. In 1512 he was drafted into the Ottoman army, converted to Islam, and trained to fight for the Sultan. He was taught the trade of carpentry, and quickly advanced to the rank of construction officer, which had him building fortifications, ships, and bridges. His gifts led to his appointment as chief architect to Sultan Suleiman ('the Magnificent') in 1538. For the next 50 years, until his death at the age of at least 90, he designed and built 133 mosques, 55 schools, 34 palaces, 33 public baths, 22 mausoleums, 3 hospitals, 16 alms houses, 7 madrassas (Islamic schools), 8 bridges, and 12 caravansaries or commercial buildings.

Mosques were Sinan's crowning achievements, and three of them illustrate the three distinctive stages of his career. Sinan himself called the Shezade Mosque (1542) an 'apprenticeship' work; the Suleimaniye Mosque (1557) a 'journeyman' work; and the Selimiye Mosque in Edirne (1574) his 'master' work. Shezade uses four half domes to link the central dome with the rest of the complex. Suleimaniye moves in the same direction on a much larger scale. Modeled after the great Byzantine Hagia Sofia in Istanbul (6th century), it includes not only a central mosque, but also a medical college, two mausoleums, numerous baths, a hospital, and four madrassas. Although exquisite and monumental, it does not yet achieve its creator's aim of an absolute unified internal space. That comes with the Selimiye Mosque in Edirne, Turkey. Here, Sinan executed his perfect centralized plan with a towering dome supported by eight interior columns and buttresses. Minarets at each corner frame the entire structure. Dazzling color, decorative components, and the choice of site contribute to Selimiye's standing as a groundbreaking masterpiece of harmonious design.

While Sinan's contemporaries in Renaissance Italy were working their own magic with domed structures, none of them built on a scale remotely approaching his one hundred-plus domed buildings. Sinan was the very face of Classical Ottoman architecture. His influence extended centuries beyond his death in 1588, and his works—testaments to the strength and sophistication of Ottoman culture—remain great emblems of Turkish pride.

217

ANDREA PALLADIO
1508–1580

"Guided by a natural inclination, I gave myself up in my most early years to the study of architecture."
Palladio

Palladio was born Andrea di Pietro della Gondola in 1508 in Padua. At age 13, he left an apprenticeship with a Paduan stonecutter to flee to Vicenza, near Venice, where he honed his craft of stonemasonry. As a young man he went to Rome to study the ancient monuments and the leading theorists of the Renaissance, as well as Vitruvius.

Much of Palladio's architecture consists of country villas and urban palaces such as the Villa Barbaro at Maser (c. 1554). The Villa Capra (Rotonda) (Vicenza, 1550–59) is one of the finest examples of his particular brand of Classicism. It consists of a square block surmounted by a dome, with porches on each side in the shape of Roman temple pediments. While the classicist Alberti had described a plan like this as ideal for a church, it was highly unusual to use such a design for a house. The Villa Rotonda was significant as a new type: not a functional everyday house, but an elegant retreat for the wealthy to escape their daily lives.

Commissions to design in Venice itself finally came to Palladio in the 1560s. His work there culminated in three splendid churches: San Giorgio Maggiore (1560–80); San Francesco della Vigna (1562–70); and Il Redentore (1576–91). At San Giorgio Maggiore, he faced head-on the problem of placing a Classical temple-front on a basilican church. His solution was novel: a high, narrow temple-front is placed at the end of the nave, with wider, lower temple-fronts set behind, outlining the aisles. Inside, the church is a paean to the Renaissance ideals of clarity, proportion, and light,

with a gray and white color scheme, reminiscent of Brunelleschi's Pazzi Chapel.

Palladio also favored Venice and its environs with civic buildings such as the Teatro Olimpico (Vicenza, 1580)—the first permanent theater since antiquity, and the Basilica of Vicenza, where he wrapped a perfect two-story classical loggia around an existing Gothic structure.

It was the publication in 1570 of *The Four Books of Architecture* that secured Palladio's place forever in architectural history. The writings articulated not only Palladio's philosophy of design, but also laid out practical advice for building.

Palladio has had many followers and Palladianism many revivals. Some of his most celebrated followers, great architects and thinkers in their own right, were Inigo Jones, in the early 17th century; Lord Burlington, in the early 18th century; and Thomas Jefferson in the mid-18th century in America. Jefferson's Virginia residence, Monticello, is probably the most famous Palladian building in America, although Palladian style was popular almost from the country's birth. Palladian-influenced buildings can be found all across America and the world.

Villa Capra, Vicenza.

SIR CHRISTOPHER WREN
1632–1723

Wren's path to architecture was not a predictable one. He was born in 1632 in East Knoyle, Wiltshire, the son of the rector. He was consumed with science and maths as a boy, and by the time he entered Oxford, aged 17, he had already invented an instrument that wrote in the dark, a pneumatic engine, and a new language for the deaf. He was made Professor of Astronomy at Gresham College, London, at age 25, and Professor of Astronomy at Oxford at age 29.

Nepotism is what got Wren his first architectural commission. His uncle, the Bishop of Ely, got him the job of designing Pembroke College Chapel at Cambridge University (1663). He followed that with the Sheldonian Theater in Oxford (1664–69), and started to make his reputation as an architect. The Great Fire of London (1666) was a watershed event in Wren's architectural career, as it prompted his master plan for the rebuilding of the city. His bold scheme of replacing London's narrow streets and snaking alleys with wide boulevards was not adopted. But Wren was appointed one of the architectural commissioners for the rebuilding project, with special responsibility for the rebuilding of London's churches.

St Paul's Cathedral in London (1675–1710) is Wren's undisputed masterpiece. The great dome towering over the church is an architectural and engineering wonder—grand, elegant, perfectly-formed solid. Wren had to alter his original central Greek cross plan for the church when the clergy deemed it too Roman Catholic. They insisted on a traditional medieval plan, cruciform-shaped, and Wren obliged—but not without eventually sneaking in elements from his original plan.

Wren's other notable London churches include St Stephen's, Walbrook; St Martin, Ludgate; St Bride, Fleet Street; St James's, Piccadilly; and St Mary Le Bow, Cheapside, among many others. St Mary Le Bow was the first to boast Wren's great Classical steeple, which came to be an architectural fingerprint

The dome of St Paul's Cathedral in London.

of sorts. His secular public works include the library of Trinity College, Cambridge; the library of Queens College, Oxford; the Royal Hospital, Chelsea; the Royal Hospital, Greenwich; and the garden façade of Hampton Court Palace. His contributions to English architecture were so enormous—and so admired—that he was knighted in 1675. He died at the age of 90 and was buried in his own masterpiece—St Paul's Cathedral.

JOHN NASH

1752–1835

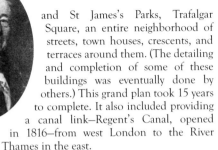

The son of a Welsh millwright who took up architecture as his profession, John Nash defined the style of an era. He is best remembered for his transformation of London into an elegant and magnificent city.

He began his training and career in London with Sir Robert Taylor, but, on inheriting a vast family fortune, abandoned it in favor of pursuing business interests. He soon went bankrupt and moved to Wales, to practice architecture. A working partnership with the landscape garden designer Humphry Repton resulted in several successful country houses, pioneering the so-called Picturesque Movement. In 1792, he returned to London.

However, it was in 1811, at the relatively advanced age of 60, that his career took an upswing. He came to the notice of the Prince Regent (later King George IV), who commissioned him to develop an area then known as Marylebone Park. The master plan for the area included Regent Street, Regent's and St James's Parks, Trafalgar Square, an entire neighborhood of streets, town houses, crescents, and terraces around them. (The detailing and completion of some of these buildings was eventually done by others.) This grand plan took 15 years to complete. It also included providing a canal link–Regent's Canal, opened in 1816–from west London to the River Thames in the east.

The remodeling of Buckingham House to create Buckingham Palace followed (1825–35), in which Nash hoped to emulate Paris' splendid Palais Royal. However, as he was unable to complete the palace, this came to be regarded as "the most notorious architectural failure of its time." The failure cost him a baronetcy. Yet, the scheme gave rise to two significant landmarks: Marble Arch (originally designed as a triumphal entrance arch to the Palace, but moved to its current location in 1851), and the Royal Mews. An unrealized but ambitious plan of his was to create a garden city, composed of 26 villas in the Palladian style, with porticoes, pediments, and statues, in the Regent's Park area. A legacy of this is 5 Cumberland Terrace, acknowledged as "a breathtaking architectural panorama."

The remodeled Brighton Pavilion, a strange, incongruously exotic mansion in the seaside town of Brighton, is another of his famous works. Originally a house, it was to be converted to a palace for the Prince Regent. Nash accomplished this as an opulent, eclectic confection of the then fashionable Indian palatial style, coupled with Chinese design elements.

Nash also designed the Haymarket Theater (1820) and All Soul's Church in Langham Place (1822–25). Unorthodox and ebullient, he was at times erratic, tearing down large sections of his buildings to redo them. He is most remembered for the Regency style made famous through buildings that are a magnificent part of London's precious architectural legacy. He died at the Isle of Wight, where he is buried in St James's Church.

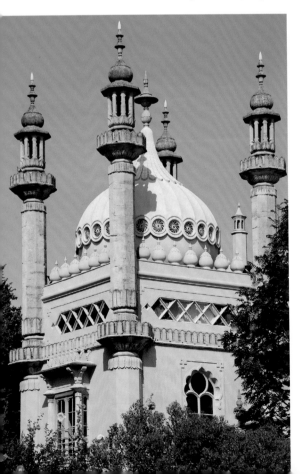

The cupolas and domes of the Royal Pavilion at Brighton, built in an oriental style.

ANTONI GAUDÍ
1852–1926

"The straight line belongs to man, the curve to God." Gaudí

Antoni Gaudí y Cornet was born in 1852 in Reus, Spain, the son of a coppersmith. He began his training at the University of Barcelona in 1869, and designed his first major commission for the Casa Vicens (1878–85) in Barcelona. While the structure is fairly conventional, Gaudí put his stamp on it with brilliant multicolored tiling, elaborate ironwork, and striking Neo-Moorish decoration.

Gaudí's sheer inventiveness began to assert itself with the Palau Guell (1885–89). This extraordinary building features a highly unusual entrance of two parabolic gateways and a rooftop of tile-encrusted chimneys and ventilators. Inside, the main room has the feel of a cavern—dark, spacious, and capped by a blue-tiled dome. In this period, Gaudí's embrace of eastern forms met with another marked trend in his work: a devotion to natural forms. This is perhaps the most remarked-upon aspect of Gaudí's work. The Parc Guell (1900–14) is a no-holds-barred expression of Gaudí's love of naturalism. It was conceived as a 'garden city,' where snaking paths lead up to a forest of distorted Doric columns, marking an area intended as a marketplace. Terrace benches are covered with dazzling, broken mosaic work, as is the ceramic-clad roof of a porter's house. The complex is built from native stone, and the terrain's original contours were left unchanged.

The Casa Batlló (1904–06) and Casa Milá (1906–11] are high examples of Gaudí's naturalist bent, but known so much more for their uniqueness and, to many, downright bizarreness. Casa Batlló has been called the House of Bones, because its balconies appear to be made of the bones of mythical creatures, while its façades are like the skin of a reptile. Casa Milá (La Pedrera) appears utterly organic. Its rounded façade seems to undulate like waves; and its roof is topped by mysterious sculptural forms. The interior is emphatically curvilinear—there is not a right-angled room in the complex.

Gaudí's masterwork, by his own reckoning, is the design of the Expiatory Church of the Sagrada Familia (1883–), which even today is not even close to completion. He devoted 16 years of his life to its construction, taking up residence on the site and living there like a hermit. To say there is no more unconventional church in Europe is an understatement. What started as a Gothic structure gave way to a more free-flowing composition, and a test of new structural possibilities. The Nativity façade, apse, and crypt (where Gaudí is buried), were the only portions completed in Gaudí's lifetime.

Gaudí died when he was run over by a street car on Barcelona's Gran Via. Initially, nobody recognized the old man, and he was taken to a public ward in a local hospital. When his identity was discovered, Barcelona gave him something akin to a state funeral. Efforts are underway by some Catholic clergy to go one better than that: they want to canonize him.

Casa Batló in Barcelona, Spain, is one of the distinctive examples of Gaudi's work.

FRANK LLOYD WRIGHT
1867–1959

Beginning with only a brief period of study at the University of Wisconsin and apprenticeship with the famous Chicago architect Louis Sullivan, Wright set up his own practice in 1893. His work for the next 15 years was a model of success combined with principle, as he developed the Prairie House, characterized by its spreading eaves, solid chimney mass, leaded-glass windows, and specially designed furniture. This initial body of work was a stunning interpretation of traditional architectural elements.

Frustration with work and family led him to flee to Europe with a client's wife. On his return he built his home and studio—Taliesin (a name from his mother's Welsh heritage)—in 1911 at Spring Green, Wisconsin. Taliesin shows a greater freedom from axial design and a deeper sympathy for the site—an exploration of freedom and order.

For the next 20 years he experimented with various materials and geometries as he worked in Japan and California. In 1938 Wright built Taliesin West, a brilliant adaptation to its Arizona desert landscape.

In his sixties Wright took his spatial and structural principles to new heights with his Usonian houses; 'Fallingwater'; the Johnson Wax headquarters; and the Guggenheim Museum, New York. A comparison of the Guggenheim (Wright's design dates from 1943) with the Unity Temple, Oak Park (1905) illustrates the similarities and disparities. Both are made of concrete, both have two masses with a central entry, both have balconies overlooking a central space lighted from above. Unity Temple, however, is rectilinear and assembled from blocks; the Guggenheim is circular, with a thin ribbon serving as structure and volume at once. The latter represents 'continuity' and 'plasticity'— what he thought architecture should be.

Interior of Unity Temple, Oak Park, USA.

From the classic symmetry of his first house, the Winslow house of 1893–94, to the incredible explosion of ornament in Midway Gardens of 1914, the Imperial Hotel, Japan, of 1922–28, the drama of 'Fallingwater', to the planning proposal for Broadacre City, Frank Lloyd Wright's powerful imagination, his 'honest arrogance', and his complete dedication to his art place him in the very highest rank of the architectural pantheon. One can be moved or agitated by his work (as well as his personality) but he remains the most intriguing and masterful American architect, whose range is unmatched.

LUDWIG MIES VAN DER ROHE
1886–1969

In 1953 some of Mies's students asked him why he had never written a book. Mies looked astonished. "Why should I write a book?" he said, "If people want to know what I have to say, they should look at my buildings."

Farnsworth House, Plano, Illinois, USA.

Born in Aachen, Germany, the son of a stonemason, Ludwig Mies van der Rohe attended the cathedral school and a technical high school, and that was as far as his formal education went.

Between 1919 and 1923 a series of five unbuilt projects, including two visionary, all-glass skyscrapers firmly established Mies as one of the leaders of the rising Modern movement in German architecture.

By the end of 1928 he was at work on two projects destined for immortality: the German Pavilion at the International Exposition in Barcelona, and the Tugenhadt House in Brno, Czech Republic. The Barcelona Pavilion was constructed in the spring of 1929, dismantled at the end of the Exposition in 1930, fully rebuilt in 1986, when it established itself as a pole-star of 20th-century architecture. Space in the pavilion is fluid, defined by vertical planes rather than enclosed by walls, which here, are mere abstractions. Interior and exterior seamlessly inter-react. Chromium-plated steel columns are seen against, and independent of, the space-defining planes, asserting the structural grid. The other materials used in the Barcelona Pavilion were Roman travertine, Tinian marble, onyx, and gray glass.

The same spatial approach and similarly rich palette of materials were used in the Tugendhat House, all adapted to serve the needs of family living and accommodation of the site. Some criticism has been made of Mies's so-called indifference to the site of his buildings. Nothing could be further from the truth. From the beginning to the end of his career he adopted a system of photographic collaging to superimpose drawings or photographs of his intended building on photographs of the site. As a small but significant example illustrates, the giant maple tree that was on the site of the Farnsworth House (begun 1945) was included in all of Mies's plans and carefully incorporated into the final execution.

In 1930 Mies was invited to become the director of the Bauhaus (the foremost modern design institution of its day, but then on the point of collapse after two years of disastrous leadership by Hannes Meyer). He took on the task and completely revitalized the Bauhaus which, however, could not escape the Nazi hatred of Modernism, and was forced to close in 1933.

Driven from Germany, Mies emigrated to America in 1938 and became head of the School of Architecture at the Illinois Institute of Technology, Chicago, where he put in place an entirely new curriculum and undertook the design of a new campus. Mies's ITT campus designs (begun 1940) were soon followed by the twin glass-and-steel towers at 860–880 Lake Shore Drive, Chicago, a building type that he was to re-study, repeat, and refine until it culminated in the Seagram Building, New York, in 1956 (which a leading critic has hailed as "the building of the millennium").

It was the pursuit of the essentially one-room, clear span building, such as the Farnsworth House (1945-49), Crown Hall (1952-54), the unbuilt Chicago Convention Hall, and others, which led Mies to his final and crowning masterpiece, the New National Gallery, Berlin, completed in 1968.

Mies's buildings are meant to teach a lesson; reflecting with brilliant clarity the principles on which his architecture was founded. They may captivate us with their elegant proportions, impeccably crafted details, or masterful adaptation to site, but their main goal was to contribute to the creation of a new language for architecture: an everyday language that could be spoken by everyone.

In the past, western architecture had produced two vocabularies: the Gothic and the Classical. The Gothic used groined vaults, pointed arches, and flying buttresses to give a clear and forceful expression of structure, with emphasis on each constituent element in the overall composition. The Classical had its Orders, domes, arcades, and plinths to convey the spirit of unity, serenity, and repose. The usefulness of these vocabularies ended with the eclecticism of the 19th century. The modern architecture that began to emerge at the beginning of the 20th century was chaotic in its variety, and it was this void that Mies sought to fill with logic, clarity, and order. The National Gallery, Berlin, Mies's last work, is a perfect example in which the structure is strongly and clearly revealed and forcefully articulated but which conveys a profound serenity and order.

Some critics have accused Mies of creating merely generalized buildings, 'universal spaces', which did not express the nature of the building or the functions they were to house. Mies, however, realized that modern society—especially in the USA—was based on continuous change and that buildings would have to be designed to adapt to different functions. His genius was to create the possibility of change in a context of serene rationality.

Barcelona Pavilion.

LE CORBUSIER
1887–1965

Le Corbusier was the name adopted by Charles-Edouard Jeanneret to distinguish his architectural career from his early work as a painter. Jeanneret was born in 1887 in La Chaux-de-Fonds, Switzerland. He attended art school where he studied to be a watch engraver, like his father. As a young man he designed a series of houses for family and friends, exhibiting a clear talent for architecture. After traveling throughout Europe and the Middle East, Jeanneret worked in Paris for the famous architect Auguste Perret, a pioneer in the architectural use of reinforced concrete. He also apprenticed in Germany in the office of Peter Behrens, a noted architect and industrial designer.

In 1917 he settled in Paris and soon became part of the intellectual and artistic community. Influenced by the work of Picasso and Braque, Jeanneret espoused a theory of art called Purism, which rejected perspective space. An important early commission for Le Corbusier was the house and studio he designed for his friend, the painter Ozenfant in Paris. Built at the same time as the publication of his first book *Vers une architecture* (1923), translated as 'Toward a New Architecture', the building and the book set forth the principles that were the beginnings of the so-called International Style of modern architecture. The images which illustrated Le Corbusier's book were photographs of machines—cars, airplanes, and oceanliners. His memorable dictum, "the house is a machine for living" was embodied in the ship-like imagery of important early works. These include the Ozenfant Studio (1922); the house in Garches (a suburb of Paris) built for Gertrude Stein's brother (1927); and the extraordinary house built for Doctor Savoie at Poissy just outside Paris (1931).

Le Corbusier also worked as a theoretical city planner. It is possible to argue that many of his built works were based on the components of his utopian city plans. In his book *Urbanisme* (1925) translated into English as 'The City of Tomorrow', Le Corbusier argued that it was the new city, clean, efficient, and built in a continuous park-like setting that would bring Europe into the 20th century and provide the 'good life' for its inhabitants. His continuing preoccupation with urbanism led to his design for the Radiant City, described in a book of the same name (*La Ville Radieuse*, 1933). His city plan, more like a zoning diagram than a formal plan, contained a catalogue of building types which were to dominate Le Corbusier's architectural production for the rest of his life. Most important among them was his Unité d'Habitation in Marseilles (1946–52) a prototype housing block, raised off the ground on columns, containing an interior shopping street, a roof terrace, and balconies for each apartment. In the Unité each apartment was conceived as a duplex townhouse inserted into the unifying framework of the building's structural grid.

Le Corbusier's post-World War II architecture was markedly different from the machine aesthetic and painterly flatness of his early work. It was far more sculptural, primitive, and tactile in its use of exposed concrete. Le Corbusier's new exposed concrete buildings had an enormous impact on a younger generation of architects in England, America, and Japan, creating a style of architecture called the 'New Brutalism.' Le Corbusier's most important works from this period were his pilgrimage chapel at Ronchamp, France (1953), and the city of Chandigarh in India (1950–65).

The chapel at Ronchamp was the most poetic, intensely personal, and in some ways most enigmatic of Le Corbusier's later works. Sited on a hill top that Le Corbusier compared to the Greek Acropolis, Ronchamp's ground plan is a transformation

of a Latin cross-church plan, while its roof shell, its dominant architectural element, relates to Le Corbusier's fascination with tent structures and pavilions.

As an architectural innovator, Le Corbusier was a genius. He was an architect who painted, created furniture, wrote books, and designed cities. While the development of his work embodied changing aesthetic ideas, it always reflected a singular world view, his belief that the built environment had the power to effect social change.

Above: Engraving of a man in the wall of the Corbusier building in Marseilles. Left: Villa Savoie, Poissy, France.

LOUIS KAHN
1901–1974

Known for his poetic sensibilities, Louis Kahn, one of the most influential architects of the 20th century, was called a "philosopher among architects." Born in a poor Estonian Jewish family, who migrated to America in 1906, the gifted Louis received his early education in Philadelphia and lived there the rest of his life. He won a scholarship to study architecture at the University of Pennsylvania under the Frenchman Paul Philippe Cret (1876-1945), trained in the Beaux Arts tradition. His first job in 1924 was as senior draftsman in the office of City Architect John Militor.

A visit to Europe in 1928 exposed him to the first seminal buildings of the Modern Movement, and to masters like Le Corbusier. On his return he joined Cret's office, and soon became involved in the populist social agenda, working on various public housing development schemes. He started his own firm in 1935. In 1947, despite an offer from Harvard University, Kahn started teaching at Yale as it was closer to Philadelphia, and after eight years returned to the University of Pennsylvania as professor.

Another trip to Europe in the 1950s, where he visited the ancient ruins of Italy and Greece, as well as Egypt, inspired him to

The Indian
Institute of
Management
at Ahmedabad,
India.

develop a distinctive style of his own, which discarded the 'tinny' quality of Modernism for monumentalism, imbued with spiritualism, yet with respect for human scale. His first major commission was an extension to the Yale Art Gallery in 1951. This was followed by the Trenton Boathouse in New Jersey (1954-59) and the Richards Medical Towers in Philadelphia (1957-62). He worked with simple materials such as brick and concrete. However, his sensitive handling of space and light created a sensory experience of continually transforming spaces. This became a distinctive hallmark of his architecture, culminating in one of his most acclaimed projects, the Salk Institute in La Jolla, California (1959-67).

The relationship of architecture to landscape was another concern that Kahn had masterfully articulated at the Salk Institute, and which was expressed time and again in buildings that followed, such as the campus at Bryn Mawr College, Pennsylvania (1960-65); Exeter Library, New Hampshire (1967-72); Yale Center for British Art (1968-74); and finally, the impressive Kimbell Art Museum, Fort Worth (1967-72).

A shy temperament and reluctance to compromise with clients on time and budget constraints cost him several major commissions, which went to less gifted architects. It was finally in the Indian subcontinent that Kahn was able to realize two of the most outstanding projects of his career: the Indian Institute of

Management, Ahmedabad, (1962–74), and the magical Capitol complex, Dhaka, Bangladesh. (The latter, begun in 1962, was completed after his death.) Working closely with engineers and contractors on his buildings, he was able to achieve unusual technical standards with a high degree of refinement. Kahn inspired a whole generation of architects that followed, some of whom apprenticed with him: Renzo Piano, Moshe Safdie, Robert Venturi, and Norman Foster.

He was returning from a work visit to India in 1974 when he died of a heart attack, alone, and unidentified for three days at New York's Penn Station. In his briefcase were renderings of the Franklin D Roosevelt Memorial, Four Freedoms Park, his last completed plan, a project that may yet be built.

Dulles International Airport, Washington, Virginia, USA.

EERO SAARINEN
1913–1961

First recognized for his design of a chair, together with Charles Eames, for the Organic Design section in the Home Furnishings competition in 1940, Eero Saarinen's reputation rests as much on his architectural œuvre as on his brilliance in furniture design.

Saarinen was born in Helsinki. His father, Eliel Saarinen, a celebrated Finnish architect, migrated to America when Eero was 13 years old. Although he initially studied sculpture in Paris (1929), he switched to architecture at Yale University, from where he graduated in 1934. On his return from Europe on a traveling scholarship, he taught at the Cranbrook

Academy of Art (1934–35), where his father had been the first president. His association with Charles and Ray Eames began in 1937, and culminated in several prize-winning designs and a long lasting collaboration with furniture designers Knoll International. He became a naturalized citizen of America in 1940.

Until 1944, Saarinen worked for the Office of Strategic Services, primarily making illustrations for bomb disassembly manuals. He established his own office, Eero Saarinen and Associates, in 1950. The Jefferson National Expansion Memorial, St Louis, Missouri, for which he won first prize in a competition in 1948, was an early major project. The Gateway Arch (built 1963–67), later became an integral part of the scheme and an icon of the city, framing the Old Courthouse.

Mies van der Rohe was a significant influence on Saarinen's style, as can be

discerned in his first major work, General Motors Technical Center in Michigan, done in steel and glass, along with his father. This led to more corporate projects, such as those for IBM and CBS, as also campus buildings in Ivy League institutions such as Yale, Vassar, and MIT.

Saarinen became internationally well known for his design of the TWA terminal (1962), now Terminal 5, at John F Kennedy Airport, New York. Still considered one of the most arresting works of architecture today, it ushered in a sculptural, symbolic quality, hitherto unknown in airport design—in this case, an abstract symbol of flight. It was also a testimony to his genius in making thin-shell concrete structures, as apparent in some of his earlier campus designs, such as the Kresge Auditorium (MIT) and Ingalls Rink (Yale).

His furniture designs, which have received iconic status, are whimsically named: the *Grasshopper* lounge chair and ottoman (1946); the *Womb* chair and ottoman; the *Womb* settee; and the famous *Tulip* or *Pedestal* group of side and arm chairs, dining, coffee and side tables and stool. The latter are still in production today.

Saarinen died young, at the age of 51, during an operation for a brain tumor. Ten of his unfinished projects, including the St Louis Arch, were completed by his partners Kevin Roche and John Dinkeloo, who subsequently donated their Saarinen archives to Yale University. They also changed the name of the firm to Kevin Roche John Dinkeloo and Associates. Though strongly criticized in his time for having no definitive style of his own, Saarinen is nevertheless considered one of the masters of 20th-century architecture in America.

IEOH MING PEI
1917–

Born in Guangzhou, China, Ieoh Ming Pei was the son of a prominent banker who rose to become the governor of the Central Bank of China. The family then moved to Shanghai. At the age of 17 Pei went to the United States to study architecture. He graduated from MIT in 1940 with several awards: the Alpha Rho Chi Medal, the MIT Traveling Fellowship, and the AIA Gold Medal.

Further studies took him to the Harvard Graduate School of Design in 1942, where he studied under Walter Gropius. He received a Masters degree in architecture in 1946, while simultaneously teaching on the faculty of Harvard. In 1951, Pei was recipient of the Harvard Traveling Fellowship, and in 1954 he became a citizen of the USA.

In 1948, Pei joined the firm of Webb & Knapp, real estate developers, as Director of Architecture, a post specially created for him. His own firm of IM Pei & Associates, later known as IM Pei & Partners, was formed in 1955. In 1989 the name changed to Pei Cobb Freed and Partners. The firm received the prestigious Architectural Firm Award of the American Institute of Architects in 1968.

IM Pei's vast experience and body of work lies in a variety of architectural types: institutional, cultural, corporate, and mixed-use buildings. They are recognized by their crisp, geometric and sculptural quality, and sensuous use of rigid materials such as glass, concrete, and marble. His first important project was the National Center for Atmospheric Research in the Rocky Mountains, designed in the 1960s.

He received national recognition when he was commissioned by Jacqueline Kennedy in 1964 to design the John F Kennedy Library in Boston. The projects that followed included the East Building of the National Gallery of Art in Washington (1979, voted one of America's 'Ten Best Buildings' by the American Institute of Architects); the glass Pyramid, in the Louvre, now a landmark in Paris, but highly controversial when it was completed (1989); the Morton H Meyerson Symphony Center in Dallas (1989); and the Rock and Roll Hall of Fame and Museum in Cleveland, Ohio (1995). His 70-story Bank of China Tower in Hong Kong (1989) is one of the landmarks of high-rise architecture in the world.

Pei has been honored with innumerable awards and honorary memberships to the world's most prestigious academic and design institutes, both in America and outside. He was the first architect to become Chancellor of the American Academy and Institute of Arts and Letters (1978). In 1979 he received the Gold Medal of the American Institute of Architects, the highest architectural honor in America. The celebrated Pritzker Architecture Prize was awarded to him in 1983, which he used to establish a scholarship fund for Chinese architects to study in America, with the condition that they return to China to practice. President Mitterand of France appointed him Chevalier in the Legion d'Honneur in 1993 (he is now an Officier), and the Royal Academy of Arts in London elected him Honorary Academician, also in 1993.

Though he retired from active management of his firm in 1990, Pei continues to work on major projects associated with it.

The revolutionary and breathtaking design for the Pyramid at the Louvre museum, Paris, France.

NORMAN ROBERT FOSTER
1935–

The most prolific British architect of his generation, Foster is famous for his high-tech architecture.

Through his childhood in Manchester, which Foster calls "one of the workshops of the world", and the work of his father in an electrical engineering company, he developed an interest in design and engineering; a lifelong interest in airplanes and trains started in his young years, and later Foster even joined the Royal Air Force.

In 1956 he got admission at the University of Manchester School of Architecture and City Planning, and graduated in 1961. Foster met his future business partner Richard Rogers at the Yale School of Architecture where he won the Henry Fellowship. After returning to UK in 1963 he set up Team 4, an architectural practice with Rogers, Sue Brumwell and Wendy Cheesman. Team 4 became known for its modern, industrial and high-tech style of design. The firm ran its course and was followed, in 1967, by Foster Associates (which later became Foster and partners), founded by Foster and Cheesman. A fruitful collaboration—one of the products of which was the Samuel Beckett Theatre—with the architect Richard Buckminster Fuller lasted for about 15 years until the latter's death in 1983.

A watershed point in Foster's career came with the new, socially sensitive design for the headquarters of the insurance company Willis Faber & Dumas in Ipswich. The office had an open plan, the managers and workers were not separated anymore, and the building included a swimming pool and gymnasium for employees. The Sainsbury Centre for Visual Arts (1974–78) and the HSBC headquarters building in Hong Kong (1979–86), with its stepped profile of three individual towers and a peripheralised service core established him as a premier high-tech designer. Projects such as the terminal building at London Stansted Airport (1981–91), which won the European Union's Mies van der Rohe Award, and

HSBC headquarters building, Hong Kong.

Commerzbank Tower, Frankfurt (1991–97), illustrate his approach of accommodating maximum natural light into futuristic public and business spaces. With the redevelopment of the Great Court of the British Museum, London (1994–2000), and the Reichstag, Berlin (1992–99), he applied his ideas to existing buildings of distinction. Foster's creative imprint can be found across the globe. Some of his more recent international projects are The Aleph, Buenos Aires, Argentina (2006–12), Nazarbayev Centre, Kazakhstan (2011–14), Hankook Tyre Research & Development Facility, Daejeon, South Korea (2013), Marseille Vieux Port, Marseille, France (2011–13) and Apple Store Westlake, Hangzhou, China (2013–15).

Through his career, Foster has stayed true to his high-tech industrial style of design. He was knighted in 1990, and later raised to the peerage rank of baron.

ZAHA HADID
1950–2016

Born in Iraq in a wealthy upper-class family, Zaha had the opportunity to be educated at the world's best schools and universities. She studied mathematics at the American University of Beirut, then in 1972 moved to London to study at the Architectural Association School of Architecture. Hadid's brilliance was evident from very early days. As a student she was known for her own spectacular vision which she didn't waver from through her professional career. Famous for the curved-line forms in her work—and thus dubbed 'queen of the curve'—she is regarded as the liberator of architectural geometry. Her style of design has been given many names like neo-futurism and parametricism, but in essence it stayed dramatic, big and different—as was her personality.

Following her graduation in 1977, Hadid went to work for her former professors, Rem Koolhaas and Elia Zenghelis, at their firm Office for Metropolitan Architecture, in the Netherlands, and went on to become a partner. Soon after, she became a naturalized citizen of the United Kingdom and opened her own architectural firm in London in 1979.

Hadid grew in stature with lecturing and teaching architecture at some of the top institutions of learning like Harvard, Cambridge and the Hochschule fur Bildende Kunste in Hamburg. After many conceptual projects, the first one was built in Weil am Rhein, Germany: a fire station for the furniture company Vitra (1990-93). Though the fire station was to finally serve as an exhibition space, its 'alert' form of clashing diagonals composed in raw concrete and glass fired up her professional career. Many projects followed all over the world and they stayed easily recognizable as Zaha's. Amongst her many acclaimed works are the two bridges: one across the Ebro in Zaragoza, Spain (2005-08), and the other spanning the Maqtah channel in Abu Dhabi (1997-2010). Like many of Hadid's projects both take inspiration from their natural contexts: the former, a covered construction, from gladioli and the flow of water, and the latter from the rippling sand of the desert. Baku's sinuously soft and swirly Heydar Aliyev Center, winner of the 2014 London Design Museum's Design of the Year, was famously described by a jury member as "pure and sexy as Marilyn's blown skirt". The quality of poised motion that many of Hadid's works evoke is very palpable on a grand wrap-around scale at the Galaxy Soho building in central Beijing (2009-12), and as a totally different vision with the shifting, tilting effect of the Jockey Club Innovation Tower of Hong Kong's Polytechnic University (2007-14). Though the queen of curve passed on due to a heart attack, some of her best could be yet to come as several incomplete projects are still taking shape.

Meanwhile, Zaha continues to remain, probably, the most influential woman in the man-dominated world of architecture.

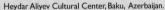

Heydar Aliyev Cultural Center, Baku, Azerbaijan.

(chi) = Chinese   (isl) = Islamic
(jap) = Japanese   (hin) = Hindu
(cla) = Classical

Abacus A slab forming the top member of a capital, usually square or curved-sided, made of either stone or marble.

Ablaq (isl) Decorative system, that alternates dark and light layers, or white and black, in stones or arch stones.

Abutment Solid masonry that resists the lateral pressure or thrust of an arch.

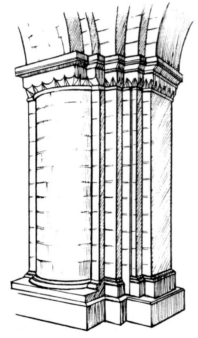

Abutment. Bartholomew the Great, London, c. 1123.

Acanthus (cla) A leaf form used in Classical ornament.

Acropolis Means "High city". Many Ancient Greek cities were built on hills; the citadel at the top usually contained the principal temples and treasure-houses, and the term implies some form of fortification.

Acroteria (cla) Blocks resting on the vertex and lower extremities of a pediment to support statuary or ornaments.

Adobe Brick dried in the sun, often used behind a facing of stone bricks as the core of a wall.

Adyton or adytum The most sacred room of a Greek temple. Usually approached from the *naos* by a doorway.

Aedicule A small temple-like arrangement that became an oft-used motif in the Classical system: columns or pilasters carry a pedimented entablature and enframe a niche or window. The term 'tabernacle' is sometimes used to express a similar meaning.

Agora The Greek equivalent of the Roman forum, an open assembly, generally a market.

Aisles Lateral divisions parallel with the nave in a basilica or church.

San Lorenzo, Rome, built 434 and 578 CE.

Alabaster A fine-grained, white, translucent gypseous mineral. Alabaster can be treated to simulate marble, a practice that evolved in Italy many centuries ago.

Alae Small side alcoves, extensions, or recesses opening from the atrium of a Roman house.

Alcazar A Spanish term for a castle or fortress.

Alicatado Uniformly sized glazed tiles used to cover a wall; common in Spain and Latin America.

Alcove A large niche or recess set off from a room. Often arched, it is usually large enough to accommodate a bed or desk.

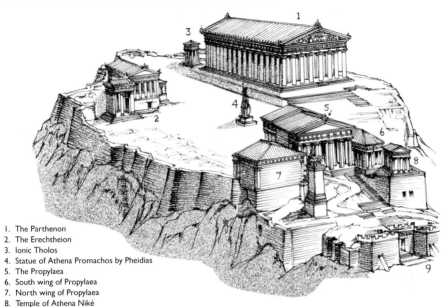

1. The Parthenon
2. The Erechtheion
3. Ionic Tholos
4. Statue of Athena Promachos by Pheidias
5. The Propylaea
6. South wing of Propylaea
7. North wing of Propylaea
8. Temple of Athena Niké
9. Main entrance to Acropolis

The Acropolis, Athens, Greece.

Alfiz (isl) Rectangular frame, slightly in relief, surrounding a horseshoe arch in an Islamic building.

Alveole A part of the 'honeycomb' structures forming stalactites. They were derived from the subdivision of pendentives into spherical triangles, corbeled one above the other. Alveoles gradually lost their structural character to become purely decorative.

Amalaka (hin) Horizontal disk with lateral ribs set at the top of a temple tower in northern India.

Ambulatory An aisle or covered passage that gives access, behind the altar and the apse of the church.

Andalus, al- (isl) Derived from 'vandalusie' or the country of the Vandals. This Arabic name was applied to all of Muslim Spain, after the barbarian invaders who had occupied the country.

American Order The replacement of the acanthus-leaf decoration at the top of a Corinthian capital with traditional American motifs like corn-cobs, ears of corn, and tobacco leaves. First popularized by Benjamin Latrobe on the Capitol building, Washington, DC (1793).

Amphitheater A bowl-like walled space used for theatrical events and, during Roman times, gladiatorial games. The most notable example is the Colosseum, Rome (c. 70 CE).

Amphitheater, the Colosseum, Rome, 70–82 CE.

Amsterdam School The building style originally employed for municipal, low-cost housing for the working class in Amsterdam in the first half of the 20th century. A subset of the Expressionist movement, it is characterized by varying brickwork façades, rounded forms like towers and ornamental spires, use of glass and wrought iron, all as an integrated expression.

Anta A pilaster finishing the side wall of a Greek or Egyptian temple, with base and capital differing from those of adjacent columns.

Antechamber A small room preceding a larger room, often used as a waiting area.

Antefixae Carved blocks, fixed vertically at regular intervals along the lower edges of a roof in Classical architecture.

Anthemion Based on the honeysuckle flower, this Classical ornament is seen in Greek and Roman architecture.

Anthemion

Apsara (hin) Celestial nymph often found among the carvings decorating a temple.

Apse Semi-circular or multangular termination of a church sanctuary. Most commonly found on the eastern or transeptal elevations. The apse is a continental feature that contrasts with the square termination of English Gothic churches.

Aqueduct A bridge-like structure with channels running the length of the top span to carry

Apse, San Apollinare in Classe, Ravenna, Italy, 534–49 CE.

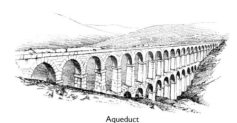

Aqueduct

water over a valley, river bed, or road. The Pont du Gard (*c.* 14 CE) in southern France is one of the greatest examples of Roman aqueducts.

Arabesque A light and flowing surface decoration. Often in flower and leaf design, it was used a lot by Arabic as well as Renaissance artists.

Arcade A series of arches supported on piers or columns.

Arch A structure of wedge-shaped blocks over an opening. Designed to be held up when supported only from the sides.

Arch of Titus, Rome, 81 CE.

Architrave The lowest division of the entablature. The word is also applied to the molded frame around a door or window.

Arcuated construction Whereby the structure is supported on arches.

Ardha-mandapa (hin) A form of vestibule to the main temple usually in the form of a small pillared hall. The northern temple style is known as *antarala*.

Arris The vertical sharp edges formed by the meeting of two surfaces.

Art Deco A style of European and American design that flourished in the 1920s and 1930s. Named after the Exposition Internationale des Arts Décoratifs in Paris, 1924–25. Much influenced by Egyptian style as well as Modernist preoccupations with speed, polished steel, and angularity. The Chrysler Building (1928–30) in New York is an outstanding example.

Art Nouveau (France: Style Moderne; Germany: Jugenstil; Italy: Floreale; Netherlands: Nieuwe Kunst) A primarily decorative style of architecture launched in Belgium in the 1890s that lasted about 20 years, and morphed into similar styles in other European countries. It was called Jugendstil in Germany, Stile Liberty in Italy, Sezession in Austria, for example. It was characterized by the stylized use of organic motifs, with sinuous, flowing lines.

Articulation The designing, defining, and dividing up of a façade into vertical and horizontal architectural members.

Arts and Crafts Movement Late 19th-century English movement influenced by William Morris, among others. It sought to revive the skills and dedication of medieval craftsmen in a world increasingly dominated by mindless automation and standardization. It had particular influence in the USA.

Ashlar Hewn and squared masonry used as a building material.

Astragal A small semi-circular molding at the top of the column, or between panes of glass in window.

Atrium In early Christian and Byzantine architecture the term denoted an open square or courtyard. More commonly known as the entrance court or hall in Roman houses. Also describes courtyard in front of churches.

☆ The Residence Apartments ☆

WALDORF·ASTORIA

Art Deco. An advert for the Waldorf-Astoria hotel, New York City.

Atrium of San Amrosio, Milan, Italy, c. 1140.

Attic A term applied in the Renaissance period to the upper story of a building above the main cornice.

Aula regia Audience chamber or throne room.

Avatar (hin) The incarnation of a deity. In Hinduism, Krishna is regarded as an *avatar* of Vishnu.

Axis The line that divides two symmetrical elements.

Balcony A railed platform cantilevered out from a wall and usually supported by brackets, columns, or corbels. Access to the balcony is by window or door, often glazed.

Baldacchino A canopy supported on pillars, generally set over an altar or throne.

Baluster A pillar or column supporting a handrail or coping.

Baptistery A building that contains the font

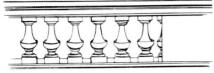

Baluster

for the baptismal rite.

Barbican Exterior defense to a city or castle. Generally a double tower over a bridge or gate.

Baroque A classical form of architecture prevalent in 17th-and early 18th-century Europe, originating in Italy. The words may derive from the Portuguese *barocco*, meaning a misshapen pearl. The style is characterized by curved forms and a bold massing of large-scale shapes. The term was at first used in a derogatory sense, referring to curving, bizarre, and bulbous shapes. The style is exuberant and theatrical, employing swirls, sweeps, curves, and scrolls. There is sometimes exaggerated modeling in the service of religious zeal, especially in Italy and Spain. Only in France

and England was it less hysterical and tempered by Classicism.

Barrel-vault An arch-like roof like a barrel cut in half down its length.

Basilica Originally used in Roman architecture as a hall for the administration of justice. It was later adapted by the early Christians for their church designs. It was usually a rectangular building with an apse at one end. Inside, it was divided into nave and aisles by columns supporting a timber roof.

Battlement A parapet having a series of indentations or embrasures, between which are raised portions known as merlons.

Bauhaus Literally 'house of building'. A school of design founded by Walter Gropius in Germany in 1919. Mies van der Rohe became its director in 1930 and served until the Nazis closed the school down in 1933. The Bauhaus was probably the most radical and influential school of design in the 20th century, not only in the field of architecture but throughout many related disciplines.

Bay Compartments into which the nave or roof of a building is divided, it contrasts with the nave, which is longitudinal. The term can also be used to describe projecting windows.

Baptistery (upper building) of Pisa Cathedral.
Baptistery 1153–1278.

Baroque. Façade of the Cartuja Church at Jerez de la Frontera, begun 1715.

most strongly in France and America during the second half of the 19th century. The Opera House, Paris, by Garnier, is a good example of Beaux-Arts opulence and self-confidence.

Bema In ancient Athens the term referred to a raised platform in a place of public assembly. It was later adapted by the early Christians and used in their church design. It was generally at the apsidal end of a basilica for use by the clergy.

Belfry The upper room of a tower in which the bells are hung. The term often applies to the tower itself.

Belvedere Usually located at the roof-top of a dwelling, it is a roofed but open-sided structure affording an extensive view. The term can also refer to an independent building in a landscape or a formal garden.

Bogha-mandapa, Bogha-mandira (hin) Hall in a hindu temple which offerings were made.

Boss The term refers to an ornament that projects at the intersection of the ribs of ceilings, whether vaulted or flat.

Brownstone A popular building material in the 19th century in New York, this brown sandstone was found principally in New Jersey, Pennsylvania, and Connecticut. Brownstone is also a term used to describe nineteenth-century terraced houses built of this material.

Bead A cylindrical molding often carved to resemble a string of beads.

Beaux-Arts Originally a French late 18th-century school of architecture based at the Ecole Nationale Supérieure des Beaux-Arts in Paris. However, the Beaux-Arts style flourished

Beaux-Arts. Opera House, Paris, 1858–64.

Buttress A mass of masonry that is built against a wall to resist the pressure of an arch or a vault. The term 'flying buttress' refers to an arch starting from a detached pier and abutting against a wall to take the thrust of the vaulting (see overleaf).

Angle buttress

Flying butttresses, Reims Cathedral, France, 1210.

Buyids (isl) Dynasty of Shiite emirs, who occupied Baghdad in the 10th and 11th centuries.

Byzantine architecture In 330 CE the Roman emperor Constantine transferred the imperial seat of government to Constantinople (modern Istanbul), originally a Greek city founded in 666 BCE. Byzantine architecture draws on this Greek foundation as well as Persia, Syria, and Armenia. Brick was a prime building material; carved decoration was replaced by mosaic and marble cladding. The style reached its full flowering in the sixth century and influenced building styles in Italy, Russia, Greece, and throughout the Balkans.One of the greatest buildings of Byzantine architecture is Hagia Sophia (532–37 CE), Istanbul, and in western Europe, St Mark's (begun 1042), Venice.

Caisson Sunk panels, caissons, or *lacunaria* sunk into a ceiling, dome, or vault, often ornamented.

Caldarium A hot room in a Roman Bath.

Caliph (isl) The caliph was the commander of the believers. He was the head of the Islamic community in the line of the Prophet's successors.

Campanile The Italian word refers to a bell tower, generally detached from the main building.

Candrashala (hin) Northern Indian term that refers to an arch which is a barrel-vault seen in section. The symbolic role of the *candrashala* signifies the residence of the gods.

Campanile, Pisa, 1174–1350.

240

Cantilever A specially shaped beam that is supported securely at one end, and unsupported at the other end. It carries a load distributed uniformly along the beam. The cantilever principle is frequently used in designs of large bridges, e.g., the Forth Railway Bridge, near Edinburgh, Scotland.

Capital The crowning feature of a column or pilaster (see overleaf).

Caravanserai (isl) A large enclosed courtyard or inn for travelers.

Carrara marble From the Carrara district in Tuscany, Italy. This snow-white marble was the favored medium of Michelangelo. The Romans knew it as Luna.

Cartouche Ornament in the form of elaborate scrolls framing tablets and coats of arms.

Cartouche

Byzantine. The façade of St Mark's, Venice, 13th century.

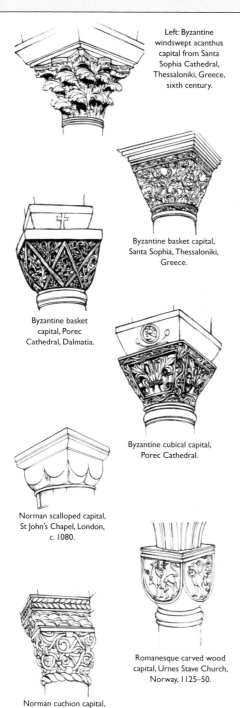

Left: Byzantine windswept acanthus capital from Santa Sophia Cathedral, Thessaloniki, Greece, sixth century.

Byzantine basket capital, Santa Sophia, Thessaloniki, Greece.

Byzantine basket capital, Porec Cathedral, Dalmatia.

Byzantine cubical capital, Porec Cathedral.

Norman scalloped capital, St John's Chapel, London, c. 1080.

Romanesque carved wood capital, Urnes Stave Church, Norway, 1125–50.

Norman cuchion capital, Leominster Priory, England.

Caryatid In Classical architecture, a female figure used as a support of an entablature. The term traditionally derived from the destruction of the city of Carya by the Greeks, who then enslaved the women. The caryatid symbolizes the enslavement by depicting a woman who is condemned to hold up a building.

Caryatid

Casement A strongly fortified chamber built into the thickness of a fortress wall. Today, the term applies to other forms of armored enclosure, eg., gun turret.

Casement window Opens on a hinge, like a door.

Casino An ornamental garden or summer-house.

Cast-iron Used largely in late 18th-century building works, particularly bridges. Cast-iron was shaped by pouring the molten metal into molds.

Cathedra The chair or throne of a bishop in his cathedral church, originally placed in the apse behind the high altar.

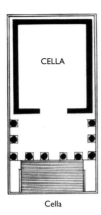
Cella

Ceiling cove Curved part of the ceiling where it meets the wall.

Cella The enclosed, central part of an ancient temple.

Cement From the Latin *caementum*, 'rough stones'. In early times it referred to a mixture of broken stones held together by lime, clay, gypsum, and sand.

Centering A structure set up to support a vault, ceiling, or dome during construction. Usually made of wood.

Chahar bagh (charbagh) (isl) A Persian term describing a garden surrounded by walls and divided by four waterways that represented the four rivers of Paradise.

Chaitya Buddhist prayer hall, with apsidal ending; the barrel-vault forms the *chaitya* arch.

Chancel Often referred to as the choir, this is the space for clergy and choir that is separated by a screen from the body of a church.

Chantry A small chapel, generally attached to a church. It was often endowed with lands for the maintenance of priests who said, or originally sang, mass for the dead. The word derives from the Old French *chanterie* and the medieval Latin *cantaria*, meaning 'to chant'.

Chapel From the Italian *cappella* meaning 'little cloak' in reference to the cloak of St Martin, which was preserved by the Frankish kings as a saintly relic over which oaths could be sworn. In time the term came to be applied to a sanctuary in which holy relics were preserved. Early chapels were also known as oratories (places in which prayers could be said).

Chapter house The chapter of a monastery or cathedral church is its governing and administrative body. This is where the members of the chapter met to discuss their ecclesiastical business.

Chashitsu (jap) A room within a house, or a small garden pavilion that was designed specifically for the tea ceremony.

Chevet Term given to circular or polygonal apse when surrounded by an ambulatory from which radiate chapels.

Chevron Romanesque decoration in zig-zag form.

Chigi (jap) The continuation of cross gable-end boards forming V-shape projections above the ridge of a Shinto shrine.

Choir Area within a Christian church where the choir sings, usually at the eastern end near the altar.

Chumon (jap) The middle gate located between the outer south gate and the actual shrine or temple buildings.

Ciborium Roman. A small building in the form of a canopy supported by columns.

Cimborio The Spanish word for lantern or fenestrated cupola.

Clapboard Sometimes called weatherboard. An exterior timber cladding usually of overlapping boards to provide insulation and weatherproofing.

Classical The Latin word *classis* referred to the classes of Roman citizens and *classicus* denoted those who belonged to the highest class. During the Renaissance 'Classical' came to refer to the highest accomplishments of Ancient Greece and Rome in art, architecture,

Cloister. Le Puy Cathedral, France, 12th century.

and literature.

Claustram Molded or finely-carved panel made of brick or wood openwork. It lets light in while filling an architectural space.

Clerestory The upper story of a church, generally pierced by a row of windows.

Cloister Covered passage round an open space, that connects the church to the chapter house, refectory, and other parts of the monastery. They were usually west of the transept and south of the nave, probably to secure sunlight.

Coffer Sunken panels in a ceiling, vault, or dome, also known as caissons or lacunae (literally 'holes'). In Classical architecture they may be square, hexagonal, octagonal, or

Coffered ceiling, the Pantheon, Rome, 120 CE.

diamond-shaped.

Colonnade A row of columns supporting an entablature or arches.

Column A vertical support, generally consisting of base, circular shaft, and spreading capital. Pairs of columns are described as coupled. An engaged, applied, or attached column is one where part of the column's surface makes contact with the wall (a half or demi column).

Conch The domed ceiling of a semi-circular apse.

Concrete From the Latin *concretus*, 'grown or run together'. One of the oldest building materials, it is composed of sand, cement, stone, and water. The first two ingredients are inert but the cement and water form a chemical bond, turning the whole into a rock-hard conglomerate. The earliest examples date from 5600 BCE and concrete was certainly used by the Ancient Egyptians. The Romans used it extensively, using volcanic earth from the region of Pozzuoli near Vesuvius. They also experimented with concrete reinforced with bronze strips. They built massive walls and vaults with pozzolana concrete, the Colosseum in Rome being a famous example. Reinforced concrete is concrete strengthened by the incorporation of reinforcement bars or fibers.

Constructivism A form of modern architecture in the Soviet Union in the 1920s and early 1930s, combining advanced technology and engineering with a Communist social purpose.

Coping The protective capping or covering to a wall designed to shed water.

Corbel A block of stone projecting from a wall, supporting the beams of a roof, floor vault, or other feature, it is often elaborately carved or molded.

Corbeling Courses built out beyond one another generally to support roofs, vaults, and domes. Creating a pyramidal roof.

Corbel table A projecting section of wall supported by a range of corbels and forming a parapet crowned by a coping.

Corbel

Corinthian The Corinthian Order has a fluted shaft and a bell-shaped capital, from which eight acanthus stalks (*caulicoli*) emerge to support the moderate volutes.

Cornice A molded projection which crowns a wall, building, or arch. In Classical architecture it represents the top member of the entablature.

Cortile The Italian name for the internal court which is surrounded by an arcade.

Cour d'honneur The finest court of a great house or château, where visitors were formally received.

Crenellation An opening in the upper part of the parapet of a castle furnished with indentations or 'crenelles'.

Crocket A projecting block of stone carved with foliage to decorate the raking lines formed by angles of Gothic spires and canopies.

Crossing Central area of nave, chancel, and transepts in a cathedral. Above this lofty space is generally set a tower or a cupola.

Cruciform A church plan based on the form of a cross.

Crypt A space in churches, generally beneath the chancel, and used for burial in early times.

Cul-de-four Roof in the form of a semidome at the corners of a cupola resting on pendentives or above a niche.

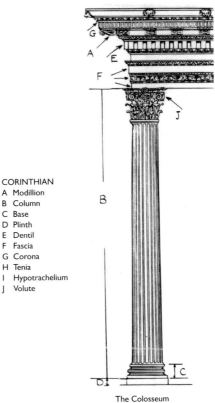

CORINTHIAN
A Modillion
B Column
C Base
D Plinth
E Dentil
F Fascia
G Corona
H Tenia
I Hypotrachelium
J Volute

The Colosseum

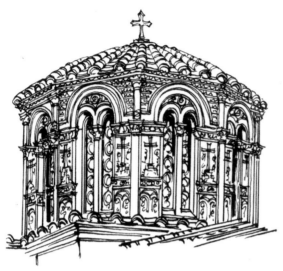

Cupola. Romanesque Church of the Virgin, Stiris, Greece.

Cupola A spherical roof, placed like an inverted cup over a square, circular, or multiangular apartment.

Curtain wall In modern architecture this term describes external walls that serve no load-bearing purpose but are suspended on the face of a building like a curtain. Generally composed of repeated modular elements such as glass in metal framing.

Cusp Point forming the foliations in Gothic tracery.

Cyclopean Masonry walling composed of immense blocks of masonry, named after the Cyclops. Examples can be seen in the buildings at Mycenae, Crete.

Cyma Used in Classical architecture especially, the term refers to a molding in a section of two contrasting curves—either *cyma recta* or *cyma reversa*.

Deconstructivism A Post Modern movement, where, visually, architectural creations are made to appear as an aggregation of apparently unrelated, disharmonious, and abstract elements.

Decorated Prevalent during the 14th century, the term refers to the style of English Gothic architecture.

Dentil Classical form of ornament 'like teeth' in Ionic and Corinthian cornices.

Deul (hin) Used especially in northern India, the name refers to the tower of a temple or the whole layout.

Divan (isl) Persian term that designated the sovereign's council of state. A distinction was made between the chamber for public audiences with the prince, and the private audience room used during courtly ceremonies. The formula of the two courtyards developed further under the Romans and Sassanids, evolving into many forms of Arab courtyards.

Diwan-i-Am (isl) The hall for public audiences in an Indian Moghul palace.

Diwan-i-Khas (isl) Hall for private audiences in an Indian Moghul palace.

Dome A convex covering, usually hemispherical or semi-elliptical, over a circular or polygonal space.

Domus Roman private house.

Donjon The inner great tower, or keep, of a castle.

Doric The Doric order of Greek architecture is unique in having no base to the column. The shaft is fluted with the capital plain (see facing page and overleaf).

Dormer A window in a sloping roof, usually that of a sleeping apartment.

Dosseret A deep block sometimes placed above the Byzantine capital to support the wide *voussoirs* of the arch above.

Dravidian (hin) The architectural style of southern India, named after the group of languages spoken in southern and central India.

Donjon (central tower)

Dressings Worked and finished stones used in architectural features such as doorways and window openings.

Drum The circular or poly-sided vertical walling supporting a dome, in which windows might be placed to light the central area of a building.

Dvarapala (hin) Symbolic guardian of the gates of a Buddhist, Jain, or Hindu temple.

Early English The style, prevalent during the 13th century, of English Gothic architecture.

Eaves The lower part of a roof that projects beyond the face of the wall.

Echinus A curved or projected molding supporting the abacus of the Doric order. The curve resembles the shell of a sea-urchin and the name is derived from the Greek for sea-urchin.

Egyptian Revival A style originated in late 18th-century France reflecting the revived interest in things Egyptian, following Napoleon's Egyptian campaigns and the growth of Egyptian archaeology. The clarity of line and austerity of form played an important part in Neo-Classicism.

Elizabethan The building style of the reign of Elizabeth I of England (1558–1603). It was a time of extensive building, particularly for the aristocracy and merchant class, and a stylistic transition between late Gothic and the

Doric Order. Temple of Zeus, Olympia, Greece, c. 460 BCE.

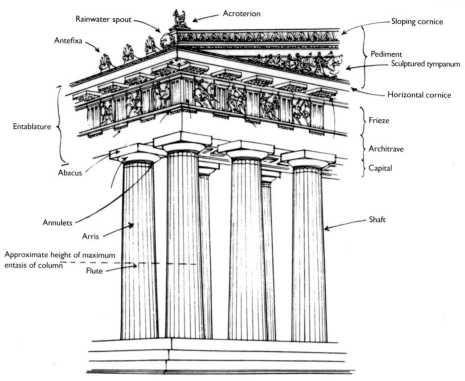

Doric Order. From the Parthenon, Athens, 447–432 BCE.

Renaissance.

Engaged column In Classical architecture, a column which is attached to the wall so that only a half to three-quarters of its circumference is visible.

Entablature Horizontal, lintel-like slab

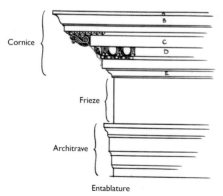

supported by columns in a Classical building.

Entasis A swelling or curving outwards along the line of a column shaft. Designed to counteract the optical illusion which gives a shaft bounded by straight lines the appearance of curving inwards. It is derived from the Greek word 'distension'.

Expressionism Architecturally, northern Europe's dominant trend in the period 1905-25. Regarded as a continuation of Art Nouveau, it emphasized that design should go beyond functionality into the realm of conveying emotion through abstract sculpture.

Façade The face or elevation of a building.

Fan Vault Vaulting in which all the ribs have the same curve and resemble the framework of a fan. This vaulting was characteristic of the Perpendicular Gothic period in England.

Fillet A flat, narrow band that separates column

flutes and divides moldings from one another.

Finial Ornament Finishing off the upper portion of a gable, roof, bench-end, or other architectural feature.

Finial

Flamboyant A phase of French Gothic (late 13th–mid-16th centuries). The word derives from the French *flammes* (flames), which describes the style of tracery.

Flèche From the French word meaning 'shaft' or 'arrow'. A slender wooden or metal spire generally found over the crossing on a Gothic church. It was widely used in French churches because it caused fewer problems of stress and

Flèche. Central spire of Notre Dame Cathedral, Paris, 1180–1330.

thrust than a tower. A classic example is that of Notre Dame, Paris.

Flute Vertical channeling in the shaft of a column.

Folly A purely decorative building set in a picturesque landscape garden or park. Often a faux-medieval ruin or a Chinese pagoda. Particularly popular in France, England, and the USA during the 18–19th centuries.

Font A dish-like vessel in the nave of a Christian church, usually of stone, that contains consecrated water for baptism. Some examples have elaborate carved wooden covers.

Forum The public space used for markets, courts of justice, and business in every Roman town.

Fret ornament Classical decoration consisting of an assemblage of straight lines intersecting at right angles, and of various patterns.

Frieze The central division of the Classical entablature.

Frigidarium The large, cold water swimming bath of a Roman Bath.

Frontispiece The two- or-three stage entrance feature applied to the main façade of a building or court.

Fusuma (jap) Interior partitions that are made of a latticework wood frame and are covered with heavy opaque paper.

Gable The triangular upper part of the end wall of a building which rises to the slopes of a pitched roof. The entire wall is known as a gable end.

Gallery (*a*) A long narrow chamber or passage constructed above the aisle of a church. In many churches there is a gallery at the west end to contain an organ loft; (*b*) In medieval halls a minstrel's gallery was built at the opposite end to the dais at which the lord and lady sat; (*c*) an apartment for the display of painting and sculpture; (*d*) the upper tier of seats in a theater.

Garbha griha (hin) The shrine or sanctum of the temple.

Gargoyle A decorative stone water spout originally on medieval buildings, particularly cathedrals. It was often carved into grotesque animal or human forms.

Gatehouse A protective entrance gateway on medieval castles, grand houses, abbeys, and fortified towns.

Gazebo A pavilion or summer house usually set on rising ground within the gardens of a grand house.

Geodesic dome A portion of a sphere constructed by interlocking hexagons. An invention by Buckminster Fuller.

Georgian English and American architecture

of mainly Classical design built during the reigns of the four King Georges of England, a period covering 1714–1830.

Ghanta kalasha (hin) Emblematic bell-shaped vase set on the roof of a Hindu temple

Giant order Also known as colossal order in Classical architecture, it consists of columns and pilasters extending through two or more stories of a façade.

Gopuram (hin) Access to a Dravidian temple precinct in the form of a monumental gateway.

Gothic The style of building current in Europe between the later 12th century and the middle of the 16th century. Gothic architecture is characterized by the pointed arch, the ribbed vault, flying buttresses, traceried windows, slender piers, and lofty steeples. Although some of these features were used in different parts of the world at an earlier date it is the fusion of all of them into delicate yet strong structures that creates a Gothic building. The emphasis is on height, in contrast to Classical Greece and Rome with their emphasis on the horizontal entablature. The term 'Gothic' was first used by Giorgio Vasari, the Renaissance Italian artist and historian, who used it to denote something crude and barbaric—made by the Goths.

Gothic. Norwich Cathedral, England, 1096–1120. Spire c. 1464–72.

Gothic Revival A romantic and nostalgic architectural movement that had started in the late 18th century but became an important trend from about 1840. One of the most outstanding examples is the Palace of Westminster, London, built between 1836 and 1865 by Sir Charles Barry and AWN Pugin.

Greek cross plan A cruciform plan where the four arms of the cross are of equal length.

Greek Revival Inspired by archaeological finds in Greece and Italy as well as the romanticism generated by the Greek War of Independence. Widely adopted in USA, England, Prussia, and Bavaria. A good example is Schinkel's Altes Museum (1824–28), Berlin.

Guilloche Classical ornament in the form of an intertwined plait, frequently used to ornament the 'torus' molding.

Gumpha (gufa) (hin) Word meaning 'cave', used particularly in association with the caves of Orissa, India.

Gymnasium A place for physical exercise and training in Ancient Greece.

Half-timber building A building, usually a house, of timber posts, struts, and rails. The interspaces are filled with brick or are sometimes plastered. Western Europe, particularly Britain, 15–17th centuries, and 17th- and early 18th-century colonial America.

Hall Church A rectangular church, generally of Gothic design, in which the nave and aisles are of equal height. Most commonly found in Scandinavia and Germany.

Hamam (isl) Following the model of Roman baths, these are public or private baths in the Islamic world.

Haniwa (jap) Minature clay models of houses and figures found in ancient tombs and imperial burial mounds.

Haram (isl) Usually a prayer hall, it is a consecrated space in a mosque where rituals

Gothic Revival. St Pancras station and hotel, London, 1863–75.

and prayers take place. The term can also be applied to an entire sacred area such as the Haram-e-sharif in Jerusalem.

Herm Statue composed of a human bust joined to a tapering quadrangular pedestal. Found in Ancient Greece and Rome, it was revived in the Renaissance and 18th century and used extensively as a garden ornament.

Hippodrome A course for horse or chariot racing, in Ancient Greece, it was the equivalent to the Roman circus.

Hisashi (jap) Covered verandas or corridors that are attached to the main rooms of a dwelling.

Honden (jap) The main sanctuary building of a Shinto shrine which holds the representation of the deity.

Horseshoe arch (isl) An upper stilted arch with the stonework between the imports and the springing line resembling stilts.

Hôtel-particulier Grand French townhouse usually consisting of an arched gateway leading to a courtyard. The main house was often flanked by wings.

Hoysala (hin) Describes the highly ornamental architecture typical of the southern Deccan Hoyasala dynasty in India.

Hypocaust An underfloor chamber of brick or stone in ancient Roman buildings for heating. Hot air from the basement furnace passed through wall flues to heat all the rooms. The term is derived from the two Greek words meaning 'the place heated from below'.

Half-timbering. The Guildhall, Lavenham, England, c. 1529.

Hypostyle A pillared hall in which the roof rests on columns; also applied to the many columned halls of Egyptian temples.

Impost The slightly protruding block of stone which supports the springer of one arch in an arcade.

Insula A Roman multi-storied tenement block.

Intercolumniation The space between two columns.

International Style A very widely used but misleading term to describe a modern architecture that is functional, flat-roofed, unornamented, and crisply geometrical.

Intersecting vault Where two vaults intersect at right angles. Most often seen in the crossing of a church where the transepts cross nave and choir.

Intrados The curved inner surface of a vault or an arch.

Ionic A Classical order of architecture. Light and elegant with slim columns that are generally fluted. It is distinguished principally by the volutes of its capital.

Italian Rationalism The Rationalist theory propagates that reason, rather than religion, is the guiding principle for sureness of knowledge. Architecturally, it is used for a group of Italian architects whose work was influenced by the growth of Fascism in Italy during the period between the two World Wars.

Iwan (isl) Originating in Iran, the vaulted architectural space usually has an open façade. The *iwan* is characteristic of Islamic art influenced by Persia.

Jacobean English architecture during the reign of James I (1603–25). A continuation of Elizabethan, the style blended Italian Renaissance and Flemish influences.

Jagamohan (hin) The name of the assembly or dance hall in Hindu temples of Orissa, India.

Jali (isl) Created by piercing a slab of stone in imitation of lattice work that allows some light to filter into the building while blocking a bay.

Jodan (jap) A raised area in a room on which tokonama, tana, and shoin are usually placed, designating the most important area of the room.

Kaaba (isl) Sacred centre of Islam in Mecca. The Koran decrees that every Muslim makes the journey to Mecca at least once in their lifetime.

Kalasha (hin) Emblematic water vessel that

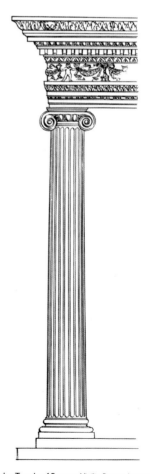

Ionic Order. Temple of Fortuna Virilis, Rome, 1st century BCE.

crowns the tower of a temple.

Kasr (isl) A fortified palace or castle in the desert.

Katsuogi (jap) Tapered wood cylinders along the ridges of a Shinto shrine building.

Keep The inner great *donjon* or tower of a castle.

Keystone The central stone of a semicircular arch.

Kiosk A light, open pavilion.

Kokoshniki Russian term for series in arches set in rows that is often seen in Byzantine constructions.

Kondo (jap) The 'Golden Hall' within a Buddhist temple that houses the most sacred images.

Kuan (chi) Watch tower.

Kudu (hin) Referring to the residence of the gods, this is a term for the *chaitya* arch and is often highly decorated with a bust-length figure in it.

Lady-chapel A subsidiary chapel within a large church, devoted to the Virgin Mary.

Lakhmids (isl) Dynasty of pre-Islamic Arab princes in Iraq, fourth century CE.

Lantern A small circular or polygonal structure mounted on top of a dome or hall roof, allowing light into the main structure.

Leitmotif A recurrent decorative theme.

Lych (or lich) gate A sheltered gateway to a churchyard. Used as a resting place for a coffin during the funeral service.

Linga (hin) The symbolic phallus of Shiva, often found in the sanctum of a Shaivite temple.

Lintel A horizontal slab of stone or wood spanning an opening such as a doorway, and supporting the wall above it.

Loggia Open-sided gallery or colonnade.

Lunette A semicircular window let into the base of a concave dome or vault.

Machiolation A defensive feature in some castles and fortified houses where a parapet, supported on corbels, projected from the wall with an opening in the floor, allowing the defenders to pour boiling oil or drop stones on to the attackers below.

Madrassa (isl) Koranic shool whose architectural form follows the tradition of mosques, with Persian-style courtyards containing *iwans*. It was extensively developed during the era of the Seljuks.

Mahadeva (hin) The Great God, epithet of Shiva, is also applied to Vishnu.

Mahal Palace.

Maha-mandapa (hin) Vestibule in southern Indian temple style.

Mandala (hin) The circle as a symbolic diagram consisting of circles and rectangles representing the world in its cosmic development.

Mandapa (hin) Columned hypostyle hall in a Hindu temple, where the ritual dances take place.

Mandira (hin) The north Indian term for the *mandapa*.

Mannerism Architectural style in Europe dating from the period of Michelangelo (1475–1564) to the end of the 16th century. It used Classical elements in a deliberately 'abnormal' way and often in opposition to their original

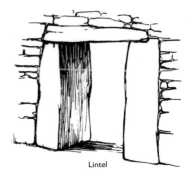

Lintel

context.

Manueline Named after the Portuguese king Dom Manuel I, a decorative architectural style in the 16th century.

Mansard roof A roof with a flatter upper portion and a steep lower slope, also known as a 'gambrel' roof.

Maqsura (isl) Enclosed area around the most sacred part of the mosque where the sovereign attended prayers.

Martyrium Christian sanctuary dedicated to a martyr.

Masjid (isl) Mosque.

Mastaba Used to cover a burial chamber, this Ancient Egyptian word describes a rectangular, flat-topped funerary mound.

Mausoleum A monumental building to house a tomb or tombs usually of dignitaries. Named after the Mausoleum of Harlicarnassos (modern Bodrum, Turkey), which was built by King Mausolus for his wife Artemisia who died in 353 BCE.

Maydan (isl) Large open spaces often used for army parades and victory marches.

Metabolism A Japanese architectural movement of the 1960s advocating self-contained megastructures which could grow and be modified organically.

Metope The space between Doric triglyphs. Commonly decorated with sculptured groups or carved ornaments.

Mezzanine An intermediate floor built within a lofty story.

Mihrab (isl) Niche in the *qibla* wall that indicates the direction of Mecca. The mosque's holy of holies, it forms a small internal space preceded by an arch.

Minaret A slender tower above a mosque, from which the muezzin calls the faithful to prayer.

Minbar (isl) Raised seat or pulpit in a mosque, from which the cleric addresses the congregation.

Minimalism An artistic movement that took shape in the 1950s, characterized by "a rediscovery of the value of empty space." In content and form the emphasis is on simplicity and avoidance of personal expression.

Misericord Literally a 'mercy seat'. A hinged seat, designed to support a standing person, often a member of the choir, who was obliged by the liturgy to stand for long periods of time. The underside is often carved with grotesques.

Mithuna (hin) Depiction of amorous couple, often found sculpted in temple decoration.

Modernism With its beginnings in the early 20th century, the Modernist doctrine stresses that the design of a building should emphasize its functional identity. There is a disregard for traditional vocabulary, ornamentation is very limited, and form displays a 'machine-made' appearance.

Modillion A small bracket that supports a cornice or corbel in Classical architecture.

Module A unit of measurement by which the parts of a Classical order or building are regulated. Generally taken from the half diameter of a column at its junction with the base.

Moghul (Mughal) Indian Islamic architecture of the 16–18th centuries. The Taj Mahal (1631–53) is probably the best-known example.

Monolithic column A column whose shaft is made from one piece of stone or marble as opposed to one made up in hollow drums.

Moorish Term used to describe Islamic architecture of north Africa and the Iberian peninsula during the time of the Arab occupation (711–1492 CE). The Alhambra, Granada, Spain, is a famous example.

Mosaic Small cubes made from marble, stone, or glass. Used to make up decorative surfaces.

Motte The earthen conical mound of a castle. Motte-and-bailey castles were a common form before c. 1100. The bailey was an area of land surrounding the motte, itself protected by a wall or palisade.

Moldings The contours given to projecting

members.

Moya (jap) The central interior space of a *shinden*.

Mudejar A style of Spanish architecture, particularly of Castile and Aragon, that blends Christian and Muslim characteristics. It was mainly seen between the 12th–16th centuries but survived into the 17th century.

Mullions The vertical divisions in windows that separate them into different number of lights.

Muqarnas (isl) Characteristic of Islamic architecture, these decorative stalactites adorn the cupolas or corbels of a building.

Mushrabeyeh (isl) The wooden lattice-work in the upper windows of Islamic houses.

Mutule (cla) Blocks attached under Doric cornices from which the guttae depend.

Nagara (hin) Refers to the architectural style of north India.

Nageshi (jap) Resembling a beam between posts, this horizontal wooden plank is usually near the top of the room.

Nandi (hin) A bull, the vehicle of Shiva.

Naos The inner sanctum of a Greek temple that contained the cult statue. In Byzantine churches it refers to the sanctuary.

Nata-mandir (hin) The dance hall of a northern Indian-style temple.

Narthex A rectangular entrance hall between the porch and the nave of a church. Also a portico at the west end of a basilica or a church.

Nave Longitudinal areas in a covered building, the most common views is in a church.

Necking The space between the astragal of a column shaft and the actual capital.

Necropolis A burial ground.

Neo-Classicism Late 18th century, early 19th century in Germany, France, Britain, and the USA. The severe Classicism of Ancient Greece and Rome was an inspiration and an antidote to the high decoration of the Baroque and Rococo. The 18th century saw the foundation of modern archaeology and this was also a

Neo-Classicism. Neue Wache, Berlin, 1816.

powerful stimulus.

Neo Futurism An architectural aesthetic, which emerged in the late 20th and early 21st century, that wouldn't have been possible without cutting-edge computer technology and new materials.

New Urbanism An approach to urban planning that emerged in the USA in the 1980s. The objective was to provide sustainable, self-sufficient neighborhoods, incorporating features like variety in dwelling design, walkable distances, schools, shopping and recreation centers, etc.

Niche A recess in a wall, often used to place a statue or an ornament.

Nave. Abbey church of Fontevrault, France, 1104–50.

Obelisk A tall, square section of pillar that tapers upwards and ends in a pyramid.

Odeion A building designed for musical contests, resembling a Greek theater.

Oeillet From the French *oeil*, eye. The slit in the walls of medieval castles through which arrows could be fired.

Orchestra The space in a Greek theater where the chorus sang and danced.

Order In Classical architecture, an order comprises a column with a shaft, capital, and

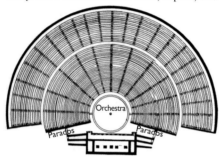

Orchestra. Epidauros, Greece, c. 350 BCE.

usually a base.

Organic architecture A term coined by Frank Lloyd Wright for his own design philosophy which, as opposed to the 'form follows function' approach, regarded form and function as a unified whole. Wright held that the environmental context of a building should determine its architecture.

Pada (hin) The base of a building, typical of eastern Indian temples.

Paga (hin) Vertical projection on a temple tower.

P'ai-lou (chi) Commemorative or decorative arch, often with 1–3 or five openings.

Panchayatana (hin) Hindu word describes a group of five temples. One central temple surrounded by four smaller shrines.

Paneling The practice of lining the interior walls with wooden boards became widespread

in western Europe during the 13th century but reached its most decorative level in the 16th and 17th centuries.

Parametricism An avant-garde style of architecture, rooted in digital animation, claimed to be the next great style after Modernism.

Parapet Seen in platforms, bridges, and balconies, the portion of wall above the roof-gutter that is sometimes battlemented.

Patio A Spanish arcaded or colonnaded courtyard.

Pavilion A projecting part of a façade of a building, usually at the ends or center. The term is also applied to a small ornamental building in a garden.

Pedestal Usually made up of a base, die, cornice, or cap-mould, and used as a support for a statue, column, or vase.

Pediment A triangular piece of wall above the entablature, enclosed by raking cornices, seen in Classical architecture.

Pendentive The term applied to the spherical triangles formed by the intersecting of the dome by two pairs of opposite arches, themselves supported over a square or polygonal compartment.

Peribolus Consecrated area, defined by a wall or enclosure that surrounds a church or temple.

Peristyle A row of columns that surrounds a cloister, temple, or court. It also describes the area that is enclosed.

Piano nobile In Classical building it is the first

Peristyle: Pompeii, house of the Vettii.

Pier

and principal floor of the house.

Piazza Describes an open, public space surrounded by buildings.

Pidas (hin) Series of superimposed corbels, typical of the step-roofs of mandapas.

Pier A mass of masonry from which an arch springs in a bridge or an arcade.

Pilaster A rectangular feature in the shape of a pillar, often engaged in the wall.

Pilaster strip Low relief vertical strips with the appearance of pilasters. They have solely decorative purposes.

Pilotis Derived from the French word for pile or stake. A term used in modern architecture to describe buildings that stand supported on columns and piers (see overleaf).

Piscina A stone water basin usually set into a niche near the altar of a Christian church. They were used for washing the vessels used in the Mass or Communion.

Pishtaq (isl) A large rectangular screen that frames an Islamic *iwan*, also the gateway to a mosque or mausoleum.

Pita deul (hin) The meeting or dance pavilion.

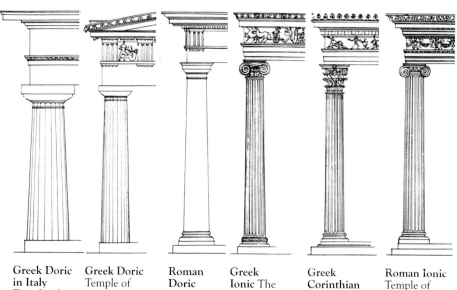

| **Greek Doric in Italy** Temple of Athena, Paestum, 510 BCE | **Greek Doric** Temple of Hephaistos (the Thesion), Athens, *c.* 449 BCE | **Roman Doric** Theater of Marcellus, Rome, 23–13 BCE | **Greek Ionic** The Erechtheion, Athens, *c.* 421 BCE | **Greek Corinthian** Monument of Lysicrates, Athens, *c.* 334 BCE | **Roman Ionic** Temple of Fortuna Virilis, Rome, second century BCE |

Comparative Orders

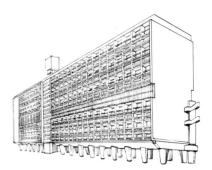

Pilotis. Unité d'Habitation, Marseilles, France, 1946–52.

Portico. The Pantheon, Rome, 120 CE.

Plateresque A term used to describe an intricate style named after its likeness to silverwork. This phase of Spanish architecture took place between the 15th and 16th centuries.

Plinth The projected or molded base of any building, it is also the lowest square member of the base of a column.

Podium (cla) A continuous projecting base or pedestal. It also describes the enclosing platform of the arena of the amphitheater.

Porphyry A red or purple rock used as a building stone or sculpture, particularly by the Greeks, Egyptians, and Romans.

Portcullis A heavy latticed wooden or iron gate in the portal of a defended building that could be raised and lowered.

Portico A colonnaded space that forms a vestibule or entrance, with a roof supported on at least one side by columns.

Porte-cochère Usually applied to a canopy projecting beyond the main entrance of a grand house of the 19th century. The canopy was large enough to shelter a carriage from rain.

Post Modernism A group of mainly American architects like Philip Johnson, Michael Graves, Robert Stern, and Robert Venturi, who rejected the rationality of Bauhaus Modernism in favor of an eclectic architectural vocabulary, sometimes playful, sometimes kitschy. Where Mies van der Rohe, the quintessential Modernist, had proclaimed "less is more", Robert Venturi countered with "less is a bore."

Pradakshinapatha (hin) The passageway around a shrine that the devotee walked as part of the ritual of worship.

Presbytery The area of a Christian church containing the high altar. Also refers to a priest's house.

Pronaos The vestibule of a Greek or Roman temple.

Propylaeum In Greek architecture this referred to an important gateway or entrance. A famous example is the propylaeum on the Acropolis hill in Athens leading to the temple area.

Putto From the Italian word meaning 'child'; describes the baby and cherub sculptures on Baroque architecture.

Pylon Describes the mass of masonry with a central opening forming a monumental entrance to Egyptian temples.

Qasr (isl) A palace, castle, or mansion.

Qibla (isl) The wall of a mosque which is oriented towards Mecca. During prayer the faithful prostrate themselves towards the *qibla*.

Quoin From the French *coin*, 'corner' or 'angle'. Quoins or quoin-stones are the dressed stones forming the angle of two joining exterior walls.

Qubba (isl) Originally referred to a domed building, it has come to mean an Islamic mausoleum or tomb.

258

Ramma (jap) Decoratively carved panels above sliding *fusuma* doors.

Rampart An earthen bank that surrounds a fortress, castle, or fortified city, used as a defense.

Ratha (hin) The word has two meanings: the first refers to a chariot in the form of a movable temple that was used to transport images of the gods during festivals; the second is a generic term for the projections on temple towers.

Refectory The dining hall of a convent, monastery, or college.

Rekha (hin) In Orissa, India, the word means the tower of a temple.

Relieving arch A slab or relieving arch is constructed to stop the weight of masonry above from crushing the lintel stone below.

Renaissance From the Italian *rinascimento* and the French *renaître*, both meaning 're-born'. What the rebirth refers to is the rediscovery of the glories of Ancient Greece and Rome by Italian scholars, artists, and architects in the 15th century. The impact of these discoveries had a profound effect on European and American architecture for 400 years.

Retablo A Spanish word that is used to describe a framing or altarpiece that encloses painted panels above a church altar.

Rib A projecting

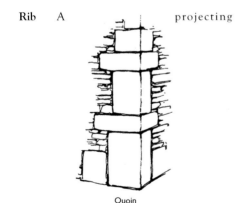

Quoin

band on a ceiling or vault.

Ribat (isl) A fortified monastery, often found on the frontiers of the Islamic empire.

Richardsonian Romanesque This free revival style, named after the American architect Henry Hobson Richardson, incorporates 11th- and 12th-century southern French, Spanish, and Italian Romanesque characteristics. It is marked with rough stone and cylindrical towers. Described as a 'massive and masculine' individualization of Romanesque.

Rococo A highly romantic style, elegant, playful and light, that originated in France and Italy in the 18th century but was also adopted brilliantly in southern Germany.

Romanesque An architectural style flourishing between the seventh and 12th centuries CE of Europe. Characterized by basilica or circular-form churches, rounded arches with strongly carved decoration, sturdy cylindrical piers, thick walls, and simple barrel-vaulted ceilings. A classic example is the nave of Durham Cathedral, England, begun 1093 (see overleaf).

Rotunda A building with a circular ground plan and often topped by a dome.

Rustication Stones used in a building's façade (often on the lower stories of Renaissance and Mannerist buildings) where the face of the stone protrudes and has been roughened to contrast with the smooth surface of the rest of the façade.

Second National Architecture Movement A trend in Turkey during 1930–50, the fundamental thread of which was a distancing from foreign architectural influences, while looking at traditional forms for inspiration. The political backdrop of the movement was the rise of totalitarian regimes in parts of Europe. The building style focused on monumental, symmetrical, cut-stone-clad buildings.

Set-off A horizontal member that connects the lower and thicker part of a wall with the receding upper part.

Sgraffito A form of decoration where the

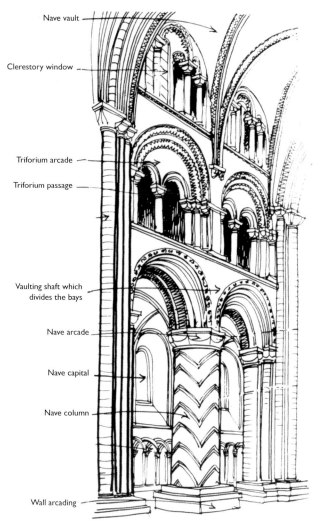

Nave vault

Clerestory window

Triforium arcade

Triforium passage

Vaulting shaft which
divides the bays

Nave arcade

Nave capital

Nave column

Wall arcading

Romanesque. Durham Cathedral, England, 1093.

upper coat of white stucco is partly cut away to show a dark undercoat so forming a design.

Shaft The portion of column between the base and the capital.

Shala (hin) The name of the small arches that decorate the rooftops of Dravidian temples.

Shikhara (hin) The tower of a temple.

Shinden (jap) The chief building of a Heian period mansion-estate.

Shingle style An American early 20th-century style. External walls that are clad in shingles (wooden tiles) over a timber frame.

Shitomido (jap) Paper-covered wood lattice 'doors', they can be swung up horizontally and hooked open. They form the front of Shinden buildings.

Shoin (jap) A desk alcove that projects out onto the veranda, with a *shoji* window above it.

Shoji (jap) Outer partition doors that are made of a latticework wood frame and covered with translucent white paper.

Shrine A place of worship or sanctuary dedicated to a person or an object, usually in a holy building.

Shthapaka (hin) The Hindu word for the architect who designs the temples according to ritual requirements.

Shthapati (hin) The architect who carries out the plan of the *shthapaka*.

Soffit The underside or ceiling of any architectural member.

Span The distance between the supports of a roof, beam, or arch.

Spandrel

Spandrel Triangular space enclosed by the curve of an arch and the rectangle of outer moldings as in a doorway.

Spire The tapering end of a tower prevalent in the Gothic style.

Squinch A small bracket, arch, or similar device that is placed across the internal angles of a tower to convert the square from an octagonal base for a dome or spire.

Stave church The medieval wooden churches of Scandanavia.

Steeple A tower topped by a spire.

Stilted arch An arch that has its springing arch higher than the line of the impost moldings. It is then connected by vertical pieces of walling or stilts.

Stoa A portico or detached colonnade found in Ancient Greek architecture.

Strapwork A type of relief ornament that resembles leather straps, intertwined and forming panels. Especially used in early Mannerist type renaissance work in Britain and the Low Countries.

String course A molding or projecting course running along the elevation of a building.

Stucco A plaster covering applied to masonry or brickwork that is sometimes molded to imitate architectural features like cornices. It was used by ancient Roman and Islamic builders but reached its most sophisticated form during the Renaissance, and in the Baroque and Rococo styles.

Stupa (hin) A funeral mound that symbolises the presence and law of Buddha.

Stupi (hin) A rounded finial section of a Dravidian temple.

Stylobate The upper step forming a platform on which a colonnade is placed, seen in Greek temple design.

Sudare (jap) Horizontal roll-up bamboo blinds made of thin bamboo strips.

Sukiya (jap) A *chashitsu* or inner room for the elaborate tea ceremony.

T'a Chinese term (perhaps derived from the Indian stupa) for a pagoda.

Tainoya (jap) Pavilions that are located on either side of a central house and contain subsidary living quarters.

Tantra (hin) Religious writings that deal with

Stoa of Attalos, Athens, c. 150 BCE.

ritual and symbolism.

Tatami (jap) A rectangular floor mat made of rush, measuring approximately 6 × 3 ft (1.8 × 0.9 m) and about 2 inches thick, the edges are bound by cloth strips.

Tateana (jap) Prehistoric thatch-roofed pit dwellings.

Temenos Greek word for a sacred space or an urban area consecrated to a deity.

Tempietto The term is usually reserved for Renaissance and later buildings of an ornamental character. Temple-like structures, they were often erected in parks and gardens of country houses.

Tepidarium Room in Roman baths that is of moderate heat.

Terracotta The baked and glazed earthenware used in the decoration of exterior and interior walls, as well as floors.

Tesserae Cubes made from glass, marble, or semi-precious material that are used to create a mosaic.

Tholos Greek word for a circular building with a domed or conical roof. Remains of *tholoi* survive at Olympia, Epidauros, Delphi, and Athens.

Tie-beam Generally the lowest member of a roof truss, it extends from wall plate to wall plate and is intended to prevent the walls from spreading.

Tien (chi) Hall.

Tie Rod A metal or wooden strut that connects the imposts of an arcade to brace an architectural structure and to ensure stability.

Tokonoma (jap) A recessed alcove in a room that is used for displaying paintings, ceramics, or flower arrangements.

Torana (hin) A portal with a monolithic or linteled arch that is set before a Buddhist or Hindu arch.

Torii (jap) The entrance gate to a Shinto shrine.

Trabeated construction A structure that is composed of horizontal lintels and vertical posts.

Tracery The 'veins' or ribs of stonework that sub-divide windows, screens, panels, or ceilings of Gothic buildings.

Tracery

Transept Set at right angles to the nave and choir, transepts are the arms of a cruciform church.

Travertine A porous Italian stone with a yellowish appearance.

Trefoil arch A triple arch having three concave sections.

Triconch or triple apse Seen largely in late Roman Empire architecture, a space with a trefoiled arch with three lobes, one axial, and the other two to right and left.

Triforium A shallow passage above the nave arcade and the choir in a medieval church. The triforium is usually arcaded.

Triglyph Blocks with vertical channels which are set at regular intervals in the frieze of the Doric Order.

Trimurti (hin) An image showing the deities, Brahma, Vishnu, and Shiva which symbolize creation, preservation, and destruction.

Trikutashala (hin) A three-celled temple or a triple shrine.

Triratha (hin) The tower of a temple with three projecting *rathas*.

Trumeau Describes the pier between two openings or, in Gothic architecture, the pier dividing a large portal in two parts.

Truss A framework of members used to support roofs, floors, bridges, etc.

Tsuridono (jap) A small open pavilion set over a garden pond in a *shinden* style estate and used as a place for aesthetic diversion.

Tudor Describes English late Gothic architecture between 1485–1558.

Tufa Building stone that originates from a volcano or other source and is rough or cellular in texture.

Tumulus (isl) The marking of a tomb with artificial earth or stone.

Turrets Especially seen in medieaval

Turrets

architecture, a small tower that often contains stairs.

Tuscan Order (cla) Very similar to the Doric Order except for its very plain entablature. The shaft is properly unfluted.

Tympanum The triangular space bounded by the sloping and horizontal cornices of a Classical pediment.

Undercroft In medieval architecture, a chamber partly or completely underground. In a house or castle it would have been used for storage, while in a church it was the crypt.

Usonian An adjective proposed by Frank Lloyd Wright to describe the nature of the American landscape as distinct and unfettered by existing architectural axioms.

Vault Essentially an arched ceiling (which may or may not support a floor above) constructed of stones that when stressed against each other create stability.

Vaulting bay A square or rectangular area that is bounded by piers or columns and covered by a ribbed or groined vault.

Vaulting boss An ornamental feature set at intervals in a ribbed vault to hide the junctions between one rib and another.

Vault springing The point at which the vault ribs spring upwards from the capital, corbel, or arch impost.

Vedika (hin) A low wall or a post-and-rail type stone balustrade that surrounds a temple.

Vernacular 'Ordinary' architecture without pretensions to grandness. Using local materials in traditional ways, vernacular 'architecture' includes farm buildings, factories, cottages, and other simple houses. Sometimes described as "architecture without architects."

Vesara (hin) Architectural style between Dravidian and Nagara styles.

Vihara (hin) Word for Buddhist monastery.

Volute A scroll or spiral occurring in Ionic, Corinthian, and composite capitals.

Voussoir The wedge-shaped stones that make up an arch.

Watadono (jap) The corridors connecting the *shinden* and *tainoya* in *shinden*-style architecture.

Ziggurat An important element in ancient Mesopotamian temple complexes, these high pyramidical staged towers had angles oriented to the cardinal points.

Ziyada (isl) The outer courtyard that surrounds a mosque and separates it from the outside world.

Drawings of unbuilt structures and destroyed buildings known only from drawings have played an important role in the history of architecture. When Frank Lloyd Wright prepared the first major publication of his work issued in 1910, it is significant that he chose not to include any photographs. Each project, built or unbuilt, was represented by specially prepared, extraordinarily beautiful drawings. Wright understood the impact the drawings would have, giving equal weight to his built and unbuilt projects.

Before photography and easy travel, published volumes of drawings were the method by which architectural knowledge was transmitted. In the Middle Ages this knowledge was carefully guarded by the guilds. The Renaissance revived Classical architecture and reprinted the oldest surviving text on the subject, the *Ten Books on Architecture* written by Marcus Vitruvius Pollio (first century BCE) making knowledge of architecture available to a larger audience. Various editions of Vitruvius over the years have each had contemporary illustrations added to the text. The most famous of these is probably the edition illustrated by Andrea Palladio (1556). Palladio, whose Villa Capra near Vicenza is perhaps the most copied house ever built, issued his own theoretical treatise on architecture, his *Four Books of Architecture* (1570). This he illustrated with woodcuts of ancient buildings as well as both built and unbuilt buildings of his own design.

Architecture that has been considered visionary goes beyond what exists and often beyond what is buildable in its time. The first visionary architectural projects were the designs for ideal cities produced during the Renaissance. These design proposals predate the first appearance of utopias in literature (Sir Thomas Moore, *Utopia*, 1516), by nearly 100 years. These cities equated the *good life* with the perfection of geometric form. In his plan for the ideal city of Sforzinda (1460), the Italian architect, Filarete, designed not only the city but also its principal buildings. Designing the city as well as its buildings began a tradition that has continued

Cita Nuova

into the 20th century with Tony Garnier's *Cité Industrielle* (1917), Le Corbusier's *Ville Contemporaine* (1922) and *Ville Radiuse* (1933), and Frank Lloyd Wright's design for Broadacre City (1934), a visionary proposal that prefigured the contemporary American suburb. In the 1960s the English group Archigram proposed futurist images of buildings and great mechanized cities that could walk across the landscape, float on water, and hover above the earth. Among the most arresting unbuilt images of the modern city and its buildings were those created by the Italian Futurist architect Antonio Sant'Elia (1888–1916) and the American architect and illustrator Hugh Ferris, in his book *The Metropolis of Tomorrow*, 1929. On film, memorable images of the city of the future abound: Fritz Lang's *Metropolis* (1926), Ridley Scott's *Blade Runner* (1982), and architect Anton Furst's Gotham city designed for Tim Burton's *Batman* (1989).

The term *visionary architecture* was probably first used to describe the unbuilt work of the French architects, Boullée (1728–99), Ledoux (1736–1806), and LeQueu (1757–1825). Boullée's project for a cenotaph for Sir

Isaac Newton and his unbuilt design for the expansion of the Bibliothèque Nationale in Paris (1790), are among the most powerful architectural images ever produced. In the library project the tiers of books form a visual foundation for a colonnaded Forum, with groups of people in the central space discussing the great ideas of the world. Like the work of Boullée, Piranesi's fanciful etchings of Carceri (Prisons, 1750s) and the set designs of Giuseppe Bibiena (1740s) draw their power from their manipulation of scale and the suggestion of infinitely deep perspective space. In the 20th century, visionary architecture has been largely the province of the Futurists and Expressionists such as Hermann Finsterlin, Hans Poelzig, Bruno Taut, Erich Mendelsohn, and Frederick Kiesler.

Although more common in Europe than America, the tradition of awarding commissions for public buildings by architectural competition, has produced important and influential unbuilt architectural projects for more than two centuries. Friedrich Gilly's unbuilt design (1797) for a monument to Frederick the Great had an enormous influence not only on Schinkel and 19th-century German architecture, but on the development of European Neo-Classicism. Significant 20th- century design competitions included the 1922 *Chicago Tribune* newspaper's competition for the design of a new skyscraper office tower for their headquarters. The unbuilt entries by Eliel Saarinen and Walter Gropius along with Mies van der Rohe's contemporaneous designs for a glass skyscraper for Friedrichstrasse, Berlin (1919), and for a concrete office building (1922) influenced the design of skyscrapers and commercial structures for the next 50 years. Le Corbusier's unbuilt

Saarinen's Tribune Tower

entries to the League of Nations (1927–28) and Palace of the Soviets (1931) competitions had an equally important influence on the development of 20th-century Modernism.

Like the one that got away, many architects' most significant works have often remained unbuilt or were intended as purely visionary statements of what could be. It is a curiosity that in a field as concrete as architecture, conceptual and theoretical works have often taken on, as ideas, greater importance than realized works. Perhaps it is only in a theoretical project that an uncompromised distillation of an architectural idea can be explored.

Stuart Cohen FAIA
Professor Emeritus, University of Illinois, Chicago.

Boulee cenotaph

265

c. 2778 BCE Step pyramid of Zoser, Egypt.

c. 221 BCE Great Wall of China, China.

c. 1304 BCE The temple of Abu Simbel, Egypt.

70 CE Colosseum, Rome, Italy.

569 CE Temple of the Magician, Uxmal, Mexico.

c. 447 BCE The Parthenon, Athens, Greece.

c. 1040 St Mark's, Venice.

1362 Alhambra, Spain.

1631 Taj Mahal, Agra, India.

1669 Palace of Versailles, France.

1769 Monticello, USA.

1889 Eiffel Tower, Paris, France.

1929 Empire State Building,
New York, USA.

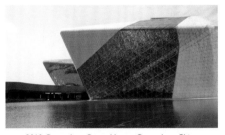

2002 The Culture and Entertainment Complex
and Monument, Kazan, Russia.

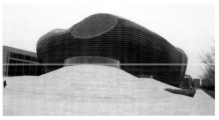

2010 Guangzhou Opera House, Guangzhou, China.

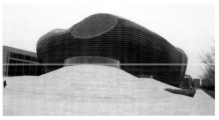

2011 Ordos Museum, Ordos, Mongolia.

INDEX

INDEX

INDEX

INDEX

Doreen Yarwood (*with permission of BT Batsford Ltd*): 11 Mesolithic hut; 19 Etruscan tumulus; 22 Pantheon; 29 San Vitale, Hagia Sophia; 30 Church of San Martin de Frómista; 31 Brixworth Church, Gallarus Oratory; 37 Santa Maria de Naranco, Little Metropole Cathedral; 39 Trier Cathedral; 40 Cologne Cathedral; 41 Tournai Cathedral, St-Etienne, St Mark's; 44 Doge's Palace, Burgos Cathedral; 49 Abbey of Maria Laach, Palazzo Loredan; 50 Santa Maria la Blanca; 51 San Zeno, Borgund Stave Church; 55 San Millan; 57 Siena Cathedral, Toledo Cathedral; 59 Palazzo Pubblico Siena, Halles Bruges; 61 Sør Fron; 65 Ospidale degli Innocenti; 69 Iroquois Longhouse; 75 Cathedral of the Annunciation; 77 Cour Carrée (Louvre); 79 Alcalà de Henares, Longleat; 83 Little Moreton Hall; 84 Santa Maria Novella, Palazzo Rucellai, Il Tempietto; 86 St Peter's; 87 Butchers' Guild Hall; 88 Cour des Adieux; 91 Mauritshuis; 93 Fredricksborg, Val-de-Grâce; 94 Seville Town Hall; 99 Melk Abbey, Castle Howard; 101 Blenheim; 102 Vaux-le-Vicomte; 103 Bom Jesus do Monte, Santiago de Compostella, Royal Palace (Madrid); 104 St Paul's Cathedral; 106 Zwinger; 113 Park Crescent; 114 Bibliothèque Nationale; 117 Altes Museum, Vittorio Veneto; 119 Crystal Palace, Museum of Natural History; 123 New Scotland Yard; 135 Fagus Factory; 137 Schröder House; 145 Unité d'Habitation; 151 Palazzetto dello Sport; 172 Porte San André; 183 Alcantara; 184 Segovia. Glossary: all illustrations.

Sue Rose: 11 Idlib house, *Ma'dan*; 13 Ziggurat of Ur; 19 Ishtar Gate; 23 Yurt, House of the Vetii, Celtic hut; 25 *Fale tele*; 27 Ruma Gorga, Petra; 29 Sung Yüeh, 31 Elephanta, Temple of the Magician; 33 Temple of the Sun, Shore Temple, Wild Goose Pagoda; 35 Temple II, Kailasa; 37 Kairouan, Susah; 39 Lingaraja; 41 Enemy Observation Pagoda; 45 Rajarani, Masjid-i-Jami; 51 Kutubiyya; 55 San Giminiano, Cliff Palace; 61 Ibn Tulun; Mansura; 63 Little Hall (Lavenham); 65 Dogon house; 75 *Gopurums*; 77 Château de Chambord, P'ai lou; 85 Raja Birbal's House, Villa Aldobrandini; 89 Queen's House; 95 Rinshunkaku; 97 Groot Constantia; 99 Annamese houses; 111 Mount Vernon; 113 Petrovsky Palace, Turkanoan Clan House; 147 Ronchamp; 157 Hong Kong & Shanghai Bank.

Mike Rose: 13 Ziggurat of Ur; 174 Krak des Chevaliers.

Automobile Association Library (UK): 8 Durham Cathedral; 13 Newgrange; 15 Karnak; 16Palace of Minos; 19 Sanctuary of Asklepios; 25 Pont du Gard; 29 Santa Maria Maggiore; 33 Dome of the Rock; 53 La Giralda; 55 Bourges Cathedral; 57 Burgos Cathedral; 69 Frauenkirche; 79 Villa Capra; 83 Escorial; 91 Santa Maria della Salute; 93 Red Fort; 101 Belvedere; 119 Opera House; 121 Sagrada Familia; 127 Casa Milá; 157 Louvre Pyramid; 176 Harlech; 177 Carnarvon, Conway; 187 Ironbridge; 188 Forth Bridge; 202 World Trade Center.

Balthazar Korab. 82 Pazzi Chapel; 120 National Gallery (Berlin); 122 Salk Institute; 139 Swiss Student Center; 143 Johnson & Son HQ; 145 UN Secretariat; 147 Crown Hall; 151 Dulles Airport, Guggenheim Museum; 153 National Gallery (Berlin), John Deere HQ; 155 East Wing, Washington Gallery of Art, Kimbell Art Gallery.

Jeffrey Howe. 107 King's Chapel; 111 Monticello; 125 Monadnock; 137 Bauhaus; 143 Gropius House; 174 Gravensteen; 170 Pierrefonds; 175 Carcassonne; 198 Woolworth Building; 199 Tribune Tower; 203 Sears Tower.

Chicago Historical Society/Hedrich Blessing. 127 Unity Temple, Robie House; 139 Tugendhat House; 145 Farnsworth House; 224 Barcelona Pavilion.

Library of Congress. 118 Bayard Building; 121 Auditorium Building; 125 Carson Pirie Scott Store.

Sidney Robinson. 145 Jacobs House.

Louis I. Rocah. 137 PSFS Building; 139 Rusakov Workers' Club.

©Dennis Finnin/AMNH. 157 Rose Center.

Roy Flam/Peter Dodge. 153 Cary House.

Michael Stephenson. 119 Law Courts; 139 Empire State; 155 Lloyds Building; 188 Brooklyn Bridge; 190 Tower Bridge; 197 Flatiron; 200 Empire State; 201 Seagram Building.

Cadmium. 12 Pyramids; 13 Cheops Pyramid, Stonehenge; 18 Parthenon; 19 Parthenon; 24 Colosseum; 25 Colosseum; 27 Pantheon; 35 Yaxchilán; 36 Notre Dame; 37 Borobudur; 39 Chichén Itzá, Mont-St-Michel; 49 Angkor Wat; 53 Notre Dame, Chartres, Campanile (Pisa); 57 Salisbury Cathedral; 63 Winchester Cathedral, Milan Cathedral; 65 Tulum, Forbidden City; 71 Great Wall of China; 75 Machu Picchu, St Peter's; 83 St Basil's; Mexico City Cathedral; 85 San Giorgio Maggiore; 87 Shwe Dagon; 89 Zuiderkirke, Delft Town Hall; 97 Grand Place Brussels; 99 Schönbrunn; 100 Piazza Navona; 101 Cathedral of Sts Peter and Paul; 107 Radcliffe Camera, Peterhof; 111 Winter Palace, Panthéon;

PICTURE CREDITS

113 Capitol (Washington DC); 123 GUM; 125 Métro; 130 Abu Simbel; 153 Sydney Opera House; 155 Centre Pompidou; 175 Eileen Donan, Rhodes; 178 Bodiam, Amsterdamsche Poort; 179 Neuschwanstein; 186 Ponte Vecchio; 191 Golden Gate Bridge; 196 Eiffel Tower.

Abraham Ahn. 78 Nijo Castle.

April Clark. 64 Red Fort.

I stock. 30 Bourges Cathedral, *Daoud Beghoura*; 42 Cologne Cathedral, *Marco Richter*; 66 Forbidden City, *Liang Zhang*; 80 Vatican, *Sumbul*; 92 Antwerp town hall, *Franky de Meyer*; 96 Palais de Versailles, *Anzeletti*; 108 Madeleine church, *Kermarrec Aurelien*; 109 Panthéon, *Marek Slusarczyk*; 133 Medina at Marrakesh, *Giorgio Fochesato*; 130 Humayun's Tomb, *Asli Orter*; 131 Windsor Castle, *Trevor Hunt*; 159 Modern Art Museum (Fort Worth), *Sterling Stevens*; 161 Scottish Parliament building, *Francisco*; 161 Taipei; 194 Petronas Towers *Serge Leguevacques*.

Dreamstime. 6 Guggenheim Museum, *Serban Enache*; 14 Karnak, *Davidgarry*; 15 Palace of Minos, *Mirek Hejnicki*; Abu Simbel, *Ashwin Kharidehal Abhirama*; 20 Acropolis, *Pavlos Rekas*; 23 Great Wall of China, *Kiankhoon*; 27 Hadrian's Villa, *Valeria Cantone*; 28 Alexander Nevsky Cathedral, *Evgeny Dontsov*; 38 Canterbury Cathedral, *Ben Green*; 45 White Tower, *Alamar*; 46 Dome of the Rock, *Dejan Gileski*; 48 Great Mosque at Kairouan, *Shariff Che' Lah*; 52 Cairo Citadel, *Holger Mette*; 58 Kailashnatha Temple, *Rene Drouyer*; 63 Alhambra, *Woyski*; 66 Forbidden City, *Anzhela Buch*; 69 The Duomo, *John Loader*; 72 Matsumoto Castle, *Bogdan Lazar*; 88 Villa Capra, *Drimi*; 91 Taj Mahal, *Xdrew*; 92 Town Hall (Delft), *Ina Van Hateren*; 95 Les Invalides, *Partick Hermans*; 98 Baldacchino (St Peter's), *Ginasanders*; 105 St Paul's, *Jaroslaw Grudzinski*; 106 Passau Cathedral, *Madmannix*; 112 Mount Vernon, *Sandra Henderson*; 116 Houses of Parliament, *Kmiragaya*; 123 Eiffel Tower, *Frances Chau*; 124 Bukhara, *Galyna Andrushko*; 126 Hermitage Museum, *Charles Outcalt*; 133 Venice, *Alberto Dubini*; Konarak, *Prasanta*; Kremlin, *Pavel Losevsky*; Uxmal, *Dongfan Wang*; 130 White House, *Timehacker*; Statue of Liberty, *Gary718*; 135 Woolworth Building, *Philip Lange*; 134 Hadrian's Villa, *Valeria Cantone*; 138 Kinkakuji Temple, *Odeon16*; 141 Versailles, *David Máška*; 140 Stourhead Gardens, *Patrick Wang*; 142 Central Park, *Aleksandr Stikhin*; 146 Pueblo Bonito Great House, *David Lloyd*; 149 Geodesic domes, *Henryk Sadura*; 150 Eco-apartments (Adelaide), *Matthew Weinel*; 152 Green office, *Jeff Whyte*; Tulum housing, *Catcha*; 154 Council housing, *Douglas Freer*; 157 Burj Dubai, *Haider Yousef*; 159 Jewish Museum, *Ali Ashe*; Al Faisaliyah Center, *Swisshippo*; 160 Mexico condominiums, *Robert Nystrom*; 161 Crown fountain, *Jayne McCarthy*; 162 Guangzhou housing, *Hua Zhuang*; 163 Hauptbahnof Berlin, *Philip Lange*; Beijing National Stadium, *Miao*; 171 Babylon, *Martina Meyer*; 173 Tower of London, *Agencyby*; 183 Pont du Gard, *Daniel Haller*; 192 Gateshead Millennium Bridge, *Redeyed*; 200 Chrysler building, *Luis Estallo*; 203 Bank of China, *Warren Gibb*; 205 Shanghai World Financial Center, *Moosetracks*; 217 Sulemaniye Mosque, *Cosmopol*; 218 Villa Capra, *Tom Ricciardi*; 220 Royal Pavilion, *Bradley Steenkamp*; 221 Casa Batló, *Gringos4*; 225 Engraving on wall, *Dan Talson*; 230 Louvre Pyramid, *Bruce Robbins*.

Contributed by authors: 134 Moghul Gardens at Pinjore *courtesy Mohan Rao*; 149 Bamboo structure and 150 Torre Agbar *courtesy Sanjay Prakash*.

Nigel Young / Foster + Partners 159 Berlin Reichstag; 163 Beijing Airport.

Wikimedia Commons: 8 Hagia Sophia, *Omar David Sandoval Sida*; 127 House with Chimaeras, *Dmytro Sergiyenko*; 131 Heijo Palace, *Kenpei*; Elbe Philharmonic Hall, *Specialpaul*; 132 Alte Pinakothek, *Andreas Praefcke*, Castelvecchio Museum, *Hans-Juergen Breuning*; Rijksmuseum, *Vincent Steenberg*; 133 Palmyra, *Bernard Gagnon*; Mountains Abbey, *Alastair Moore*; Chiquitos, *Geoffrey Groesbeck*; Riga, *Diego Delso*; 147 Brasilia, *Government of Brazil*; 149 California Academy, *WolfmanSF*; 151 Beijing Railway Station, *Mike Stenhouse*; 162 Astillero, *Enrique Arruti*; 163 Acropolis Museum, *Jean Housen*; 164 Rinkeby, *Holger Ellgaard*; 165 Kanagawa Institute, *Epiq*; Seed Cathedral, *Littleyiye*; Metropol Parasol, *José Luiz Bernardes Ribeiro*; The Shard, *Colin*; 166 Mountain Dwellings, *Seir+Seir*, CCTV Center, *poeloq*; 167 CIAC, *Petegal-half*; 168 Ningbo Museum, *Siyuwi*; 169 Palm Jumeirah, *Richard Schneider*; Museum of Tomorrow, *Caio Costa Ribeiro*; Freedom Tower, *Ariarmstrong*; Poly Grand Theater, *Bruno Corpet*; 204 Burj Khalifa, *Donaldytong*; 232 Norman Foster, *bigbug21*; HSBC Building, *WiNG*; 233 Zaha Hadid, *Forgemind ArchiMedia*; 267 Kazan Pyramid, *Gradmir*; 267 Guangzhou Opera House, *Mr a*; Ordos Museum, *Popolos*.

Flickr: 90 Château de Blois, *Dennis Jarvis*; 129 Masarykovo School, *Sludge G*; Majestic Theater, *Jocelyn Kinghorn*; Edicule, *Jlascar*; 167 Louvre-Lens, *Yann Caradec*; Fogo Island Inn, *Wyatt Clough*; Queen Alia Terminal, *Andrew Moore*; 168 Floating School, *Forgemind ArchiMedia*; 193 Helix Bridge, *aotaro*.